Documents and Debates in American History and Government

VOL. 2, 1865–2009

Documents and Debates in American History and Government

~ VOL. 2, 1865–2009 ~

Selected and Introduced by

David Tucker

ASHBROOK PRESS

Copyright © 2019 Ashbrook Center, Ashland University

Library of Congress Cataloging-in-Publication Data
Documents and Debates in American History and Government: Vol. 2, 1865–2009;
Selected and Introduced by David Tucker
    p.   cm.
Includes Index
1. United States—Politics and government.
ISBN 978-1-878802-43-9 (pbk.)

Cover images, above the title, left to right:
Franklin D. Roosevelt portrait [ca. 1941]. Library of Congress, LC-USW33-042784-ZC.
Col. Ely S. Parker, photographed by Mathew Brady. National Archives, ID 528267.
Congresswoman Shirley Chisholm announcing her candidacy for presidential
    nomination, photographed by Thomas J. O'Halloran. Library of Congress,
    LC-U9-25383-33.
Frederick Douglass, photographed by George Francis Schreiber on April 26, 1870.
    Library of Congress, LC-USZ62-15887.
President Ronald Reagan interviewing with journalists at the Williamsburg Economic
    Summit on May 31, 1983. Ronald Reagan Presidential Library, C15025-24.

Cover image, below the title:
"The Wealth of the Nation" by Seymour Fogel

Interior design/composition: Brad Walrod/Kenoza Type, Inc.

Ashbrook Center at Ashland University
401 College Avenue
Ashland, Ohio 44805
www.ashbrook.org

Contents

Introduction

This collection of documents presents American history from 1865 to 2009 as a series of 14 topics. For each of these, a selection of documents recreates a debate over a particular issue critical to understanding the topic and the corresponding period in American history. Taken together, the debates highlight enduring issues and themes in American life, such as the effort to balance freedom and equality as well as liberty and order; the struggle for inclusion and full participation of African Americans, women, and working people; the conflict over how America should organize its economy and what role government should have in American economic life; and the argument over how America should use its power in the world.

Each chapter has an introduction that provides necessary context and three sets of study questions. The first set (A) covers the documents in the chapter; the second (B), other documents in the volume; and the third (C)), documents in the companion volume. Each of the documents is annotated with footnotes that provide biographical information on document authors and identify obscure words, events or individuals.

This volume and its companion, which covers American history to 1865, are part of an ongoing series of document volumes produced by the Ashbrook Center at Ashland University. When the series is complete, it will be comprehensive, and also authoritative, because it will present America's story in the words of those who wrote it—America's presidents, labor leaders, farmers, philosophers, industrialists, politicians, workers, explorers, religious leaders, judges, soldiers; its slaveholders and abolitionists; its expansionists and isolationists; its reformers and stand-patters; its strict and broad constructionists; its hard-eyed realists and visionary utopians—all united in their commitment to equality and liberty, yet all also divided often by their different understandings of these most fundamental American ideas. The documents are about all this—the still unfinished American experiment with self-government.

David Tucker selected the documents for this volume with the help of Dennis Boman, Rob McDonald, John Moser, Lucas Morel, Sean Sculley, Sarah Morgan Smith, Jace Weaver, and Scott Yenor. Tucker excerpted the documents, annotated them, and wrote the introductions and study

questions A and B. Chapter 22 draws from *The Great Depression and the New
Deal: Core Documents*, edited by John Moser. Sarah Morgan Smith was the
volume's General Editor and wrote study questions C. Ellen Tucker did the
copyediting. Lisa Ormiston oversaw production. Ali Brosky provided all
sorts of help, including getting permissions and organizing the work of the
interns who supported the project. Ashbrook interns who assisted with tran-
scription and research include: Madeleine Emholtz, Martha Sorah, Dennis
Cerney, McKenzie Jones, Caroline Toth, Sabrina Maristela, Brennan Kun-
kel, Nick Thielman, Kailyn Clarke and Frances Boggs.

Documents and Debates in American History and Government

VOL. 2, 1865–2009

CHAPTER 16

Reconstructing the South

A. President Abraham Lincoln to Nathaniel Banks, August 5, 1863

B. President Abraham Lincoln, Second Inaugural Address,
    March 4, 1865

C. Representative Thaddeus Stevens, "Reconstruction,"
    September 6, 1865

D. Frederick Douglass, "Reconstruction," December, 1866

E. Jubilee Singers, "Many Thousand Gone," 1872

F. Senator Benjamin R. Tillman, Speech in the Senate, March 23, 1900

A s the Civil War progressed and Union forces gained control of territory in states that had seceded, the question arose as to how that territory and its people—slave and free—should be dealt with (Document A). This issue became more pressing as the war ended. President Lincoln encouraged reconciliation (Document B), and a respect for the constitutional limits of the authority of the President, the Congress and the states (Document A). Other Republicans believed that the South had to be reconstructed in a fundamental way (Documents C and D). They, too, considered constitutional limits (especially Document C), and concluded that, for the ultimate good of the Union and all its people, the seceding states had to be treated as conquered territories. Meanwhile, the freed men and women sought to construct new lives in extraordinarily difficult circumstances (Document E). The long-term effects of Reconstruction—or its failure—are evident in Senator Tillman's speech from 1900 (Document F). He defended the system of segregation developed in the South after Reconstruction (including lynching); segregation was not challenged until the 1950s and 1960s (see Chapter 26).

Study Questions

A. What explains President Lincoln's attitude toward Louisiana in his letter to General Banks? Does his Second Inaugural Address explain his attitude? How do Lincoln, Douglass, and Stevens' attitudes toward the South differ? Is Stevens' constitutional argument about the basis of Reconstruction sound? If so, was that sufficient to make his approach to the seceded states sound?

Do Stevens' remarks about Jews, the Irish and others undermine his claim to be a champion of the principles of the Declaration of Independence? Was the response of Southerners as described and defended by Tillman inevitable, or could some version of restoration or reconstruction have prevented it?

B. Do the views expressed in the Documents in Chapter 26 differ from those expressed in the documents below? For example, compare the views of Senators Tillman and Thurmond, both Democrats from South Carolina. Did the constitutional arguments change between the 1860s and the 1960s?

C. How true does President Abraham Lincoln's remark in Document B that both Northerners and Southerners prayed to the same God and read the same Bible appear in light of the very different interpretations of said Bible on the question of slavery, as evidenced in Volume 1, Chapter 12?

A. President Abraham Lincoln to Nathaniel Banks, August 5, 1863[1]

My dear General Banks,[2]

... Governor Boutwell read me to-day that part of your letter to him, which relates to Louisiana affairs. While I very well know what I would be glad for Louisiana to do, it is quite a different thing for me to assume direction of the matter. I would be glad for her to make a new Constitution recognizing the emancipation proclamation, and adopting emancipation in those parts of the state to which the proclamation does not apply.[3] And while she is at it, I think it would not be objectionable for her to adopt some practical system by which the two races could gradually live themselves out of their old relation to each other, and both come out better prepared for the new. Education for young blacks should be included in the plan. After all, the power, or element,

---

[1] Abraham Lincoln, *Abraham Lincoln Papers: Series 1. General Correspondence. 1833–1916*: Abraham Lincoln to Nathaniel P. Banks, Wednesday, August 5, 1863. Manuscript/Mixed Material. Retrieved from the Library of Congress, https://goo.gl/J8K8G4

[2] Nathaniel Banks (1816-1894) was a Democratic politician who was appointed military commander for the Gulf District, which included Louisiana.

[3] New Orleans had fallen into Union hands at the end of April 1862. Hence, when the Emancipation Proclamation was issued in January 1863, those slaves living in the New Orleans area had not been freed, since the proclamation applied only to slaves in areas still in rebel hands.

of "contract" may be sufficient for this probationary period; and, by its simplicity, and flexibility, may be the better.

As an anti-slavery man I have a motive to desire emancipation, which pro-slavery men do not have; but even they have strong enough reason to thus place themselves again under the shield of the Union; and to thus perpetually hedge against the recurrence of the scenes through which we are now passing.

Gov. Shepley has informed me that Mr. Durant is now taking a registry, with a view to the election of a Constitutional convention in Louisiana. This, to me, appears proper. If such convention were to ask my views, I could present little else than what I now say to you. I think the thing should be pushed forward, so that if possible, its mature work may reach here by the meeting of Congress.

For my own part I think I shall not, in any event, retract the emancipation proclamation; nor, as executive, ever return to slavery any person who is free by the terms of that proclamation, or by any of the acts of Congress.

If Louisiana shall send members to Congress, their admission to seats will depend, as you know, upon the respective Houses, and not upon the President.

If these views can be of any advantage in giving shape, and impetus, to action there, I shall be glad for you to use them prudently for that object. Of course you will confer with intelligent and trusty citizens of the State, among whom I would suggest Messrs. Flanders, Hahn, and Durant; and to each of whom I now think I may send copies of this letter. Still, it is perhaps better to not make the letter generally public. Yours very truly,

A. Lincoln

B. President Abraham Lincoln, Second Inaugural Address, March 4, 1865[4]

Fellow Countrymen:

At this second appearing to take the oath of the presidential office, there is less occasion for an extended address than there was at the first. Then a

---

[4] Abraham Lincoln, *Abraham Lincoln papers: Series 3. General Correspondence. 1837–1897*: Abraham Lincoln, March 4, 1865 (Second Inaugural Address; endorsed by Lincoln, April 10, 1865). Manuscript/Mixed Material. Retrieved from the Library of Congress, https://goo.gl/TtrLMh.

statement, somewhat in detail, of a course to be pursued, seemed fitting and proper. Now, at the expiration of four years, during which public declarations have been constantly called forth on every point and phase of the great contest which still absorbs the attention, and engrosses the energies of the nation, little that is new could be presented. The progress of our arms, upon which all else chiefly depends, is as well known to the public as to myself; and it is, I trust, reasonably satisfactory and encouraging to all. With high hope for the future, no prediction in regard to it is ventured.

On the occasion corresponding to this four years ago, all thoughts were anxiously directed to an impending civil war. All dreaded it, all sought to avert it. While the inaugural address was being delivered from this place, devoted altogether to saving the Union without war, insurgent agents were in the city seeking to destroy it without war—seeking to dissolve the Union, and divide effects, by negotiation. Both parties deprecated war; but one of them would make war rather than let the nation survive; and the other would accept war rather than let it perish. And the war came.

One eighth of the whole population were colored slaves, not distributed generally over the Union, but localized in the Southern part of it. These slaves constituted a peculiar and powerful interest. All knew that this interest was, somehow, the cause of the war. To strengthen, perpetuate, and extend this interest was the object for which the insurgents would rend the Union, even by war; while the government claimed no right to do more than to restrict the territorial enlargement of it. Neither party expected for the war, the magnitude, or the duration, which it has already attained. Neither anticipated that the cause of the conflict might cease with, or even before, the conflict itself should cease. Each looked for an easier triumph, and a result less fundamental and astounding. Both read the same Bible, and pray to the same God; and each invokes His aid against the other. It may seem strange that any men should dare to ask a just God's assistance in wringing their bread from the sweat of other men's faces; but let us judge not that we be not judged.[5] The prayers of both could not be answered; that of neither has been answered fully. The Almighty has His own purposes. "Woe unto the world because of offences! for it must needs be that offences come; but woe to that man by whom the offence cometh!"[6] If we shall suppose that American Slavery is one of those offences which, in the providence of God, must needs come, but which, having continued through His appointed time, He now wills to

---

[5] Matthew 7:1
[6] Matthew 18:7

remove, and that He gives to both North and South, this terrible war, as the woe due to those by whom the offence came, shall we discern therein any departure from those divine attributes which the believers in a Living God always ascribe to Him? Fondly do we hope, fervently do we pray, that this mighty scourge of war may speedily pass away. Yet, if God wills that it continue, until all the wealth piled by the bond-man's two hundred and fifty years of unrequited toil shall be sunk, and until every drop of blood drawn with the lash, shall be paid by another drawn with the sword, as was said three thousand years ago, so still it must be said "the judgments of the Lord, are true and righteous altogether."[7]

With malice toward none; with charity for all; with firmness in the right, as God gives us to see the right, let us strive on to finish the work we are in; to bind up the nation's wounds; to care for him who shall have borne the battle, and for his widow, and his orphan—to do all which may achieve and cherish a just and a lasting peace, among ourselves, and with all nations.

C. Representative Thaddeus Stevens, "Reconstruction," September 6, 1865[8]

FELLOW-CITIZENS: In compliance with your request, I have come to give my views of the present condition of the rebel States—of the proper mode of reorganizing the government, and the future prospects of the republic. During the whole progress of the war, I never for a moment felt doubt or despondency. I knew that the loyal North would conquer the rebel despots who sought to destroy freedom. But since that traitorous confederation has been subdued, and we have entered upon the work of "reconstruction" or "restoration," I cannot deny that my heart has become sad at the gloomy prospects before us.

Four years of bloody and expensive war, waged against the United States by eleven States, under a government called the "Confederate States of America," to which they acknowledged allegiance, have overthrown all

---

[7] Psalm 19:9

[8] "Reconstruction," Hon. Thaddeus Stevens on the Great Topic of the Hour. An Address Delivered to the Citizens of Lancaster, Sept. 6, 1865, *The Lancaster Daily Evening Express*, September 10, 1865. Also published as a pamphlet, "Reconstruction, Speech of the Hon. Thaddeus Stevens, delivered to the City of Lancaster, September 7, 1865" (Lancaster, Pa.: Examiner and Herald Print, 1865). Stevens (1792–1868) was a member of the U.S. House of Representatives from 1849 to 1868, and a leading Radical Republican.

governments within those States which could be acknowledged as legitimate
by the Union. The armies of the Confederate States having been conquered
and subdued, and their territory possessed by the United States, it becomes
necessary to establish governments therein which shall be republican in
form and principles and form a "more perfect Union" with the parent government. It is desirable that such a course should be pursued as to exclude
from those governments every vestige of human bondage, and render the
same forever impossible in this nation; and to take care that no principles
of self-destruction shall be incorporated therein. In effecting this, it is to be
hoped that no provision of the Constitution will be infringed, and no principle of the law of nations disregarded. Especially must we take care that in
rebuking this unjust and treasonable war, the authorities of the Union shall
indulge in no acts of usurpation which may tend to impair the stability and
permanency of the nation. Within these limitations, we hold it to be the duty
of the government to inflict condign punishment on the rebel belligerents,
and so weaken their hands that they can never again endanger the Union;
and so reform their municipal institutions as to make them republican in
spirit as well as in name.

We especially insist that the property of the chief rebels should be seized
and appropriated to the payment of the National debt, caused by the unjust
and wicked war which they instigated.

How can such punishments be inflicted and such forfeitures produced
without doing violence to established principles?

Two positions have been suggested.

First—To treat those States as never having been out of the Union because
the Constitution forbids secession, and therefore, a fact forbidden by law
could not exist.

Second—To accept the position to which they placed themselves as sev-
ered from the Union; an independent government de facto, and an alien
enemy to be dealt with according to the laws of war....

... To say that they were States under the protection of that Constitution
which they were rending, and within the Union which they were assaulting
with bloody defeats, simply because they became belligerents through crime,
is making theory overrule fact to an absurd degree. It will, I suppose, at least
be conceded that the United States, if not obliged so to do, have a right to
treat them as an alien enemy, now conquered, and subject to all the liabilities
of a vanquished foe.

If we are also at liberty to treat them as never having been out of the

Union, and that their declarations and acts were all void because they contravened the Constitution, and therefore they were never engaged in a public war, but were merely insurgents, let us inquire which position is best for the United States. If they have never been otherwise than States in the Union, and we desire to try certain of the leaders for treason, the Constitution requires that they should be indicted and tried "by an impartial jury of the State and district wherein the crime shall have been committed, which district shall have been previously ascertained by law.". . .

. . . Select an impartial jury from Virginia, and it is obvious that no conviction could ever be had. Possibly a jury might be packed to convict, but that would not be an "impartial" jury. . . . The same difficulties would exist in attempting forfeitures, which can only follow conviction in States protected by the Constitution; and then it is said only for the life of the malefactor. Congress can pass no "bill of attainder."

Nor, under that theory, has Congress, much less the Executive, any power to interfere in remodeling those States upon reconstruction. . . . The sovereign power of the nation is lodged in Congress. Yet where is the warrant in the Constitution for such sovereign power, much less in the Executive, to intermeddle with the domestic institutions of a State, mold its laws, and regulate the elective franchise? It would be rank, dangerous and deplorable usurpation. In reconstruction, therefore, no reform can be effected in the Southern States if they have never left the Union. But reformation must be effected; the foundation of their institutions, both political, municipal and social, must be broken up and re-laid, or all our blood and treasure have been spent in vain. This can only be done by treating and holding them as a conquered people. Then all things which we can desire to do, follow with logical and legitimate authority. As conquered territory, Congress would have full power to legislate for them; for the territories are not under the Constitution, except so far as the express power to govern them is given to Congress. They would be held in a territorial condition until they are fit to form State constitutions, republican in fact, not in form only, and ask admission into the Union as new States. If Congress approve of their constitutions, and think they have done works meet for repentance, they would be admitted as new States. If their constitutions are not approved of, they would be sent back, until they have become wise enough so to purge their old laws as to eradicate every despotic and revolutionary principle—until they shall have learned to venerate the Declaration of Independence. I do not touch on the question of negro suffrage. If in the Union, the States have long ago regulated that, and for the Central Government to interfere with it would be mischievous impertinence. If they are to be admitted as new States they must form their own constitution; and no enabling act could dictate its terms. Congress could prescribe the qualifications of voters while a Territory, or when proceeding to call a convention to form a State government. That is the extent of the power of Congress over the elective franchise, whether in a Territorial or State condition....

Upon the character of the belligerent, and the justice of the war, and the manner of conducting it, depends our right to take the lives, liberty and property of the belligerent. This war had its origin in treason without one spark of justice. It was prosecuted before notice of it, by robbing our forts and armories, and our navy-yards; by stealing our money from the mints and depositories, and by surrendering our forts and navies by perjurers who had sworn to support the Constitution. In its progress our prisoners, by the authority of the government, were slaughtered in cold blood. Ask Fort Pillow and Fort Wagner.[9] Sixty thousand of our prisoners have been deliberately starved to death because they would not enlist in the rebel armies. The graves at Andersonville[10] have each an accusing tongue. The purpose and avowed object of the enemy "to found an empire whose corner-stone should be slavery,"[11] rendered its perpetuity or revival dangerous to human liberty.

Surely, these things are sufficient to justify the exercise of the extreme rights of war—"to execute, to imprison, to confiscate." How many captive

---

[9] Confederate forces massacred black Union soldiers at Fort Pillow, April 1864. Stevens may be referring to the Second Battle of Fort Wagner, July 1863. Following the battle Union dead were buried by Confederates in a mass grave, but there was no massacre.

[10] Andersonville was a Confederate prisoner of war camp near Andersonville, Georgia, notorious for its terrible conditions. Nearly a third of the Union soldiers held there died.

[11] Paraphrase of a remark in a speech by Thomas Hedges Genin (1796–1868), October 1865. Genin was an Ohio Congressman. Genin was paraphrasing, as Stevens knew, the words of the Vice-President of the Confederacy, Alexander Stephens (1812–1883), who in a speech delivered on March 21, 1861, said that the Confederacy rests "its corner- stone..., upon the great truth that the negro is not equal to the white man; that slavery—subordination to the superior race—is his natural and normal condition." The Georgia legislature elected Stephens to the U.S. Senate in 1866, but the Senate refused to seat him. He served in the U.S. House of Representatives from 1873 to 1882.

enemies it would be proper to execute, as an example to nations, I leave others to judge. I am not fond of sanguinary punishments, but surely some victims must propitiate the manes[12] of our starved, murdered, slaughtered martyrs. A court-martial could do justice according to law.

But we propose to confiscate all the estate of every rebel belligerent whose estate was worth $10,000, or whose land exceeded two hundred acres in quantity. Policy, if not justice, would require that the poor, the ignorant, and the coerced should be forgiven. They followed the example and teachings of their wealthy and intelligent neighbors. . . .

What loyal man can object to this? Look around you, and everywhere behold your neighbors, some with an arm, some with a leg, some with an eye, carried away by rebel bullets. Others horribly mutilated in every form. And yet numerous others wearing the weeds which mark the death of those on whom they leaned for support. Contemplate these monuments of rebel perfidy, and of patriotic suffering, and then say if too much is asked for our valiant soldiers.

Look again, and see loyal men reduced to poverty by the con-fiscations by the Confederate States, and by the rebel States—see Union men robbed of their property, and their dwellings laid in ashes by rebel raiders, and say if too much is asked for them. But, above all, let us inquire whether imperative duty to the present generation and to posterity, does not command us to compel the wicked enemy to pay the expenses of this unjust war. In ordinary transactions, he who raises a false clamor, and prosecutes an unfounded suit, is adjudged to pay the costs on his defeat. We have seen that, by the law of nations, the vanquished in an unjust war must pay the expense. . . .

If "Restoration," as it is now properly christened, is to prevail over "Recon-struction," will some learned pundit of that school inform me in what condition slavery and the slave laws are? I assert that upon that theory [*restoration*] not a slave has been liberated, not a slave law has been abrogated, but on the "Restoration" the whole slave code is in legal force. Slavery was protected by our Constitution in every State in the Union where it existed. While they remained under that protection no power in the federal Government could abolish slavery. If, however, the Confederate States were admitted to be what they claimed, an independent belligerent de facto, then the war broke all treaties, compacts and ties between the parties, and slavery was left to its rights under the law of nations. These rights were none; for the law declares

---

[12] deceased, god-like spirits of ancestors

that "Man can hold no property in man." (Phillimore, page 316.)[13] Then the laws of war enabled us to declare every bondman free, so long as we held them in military possession. And the conqueror, through Congress, may declare them forever emancipated. But if the States are "States in the Union," then when war ceases they resume their positions with all their privileges untouched. There can be no "mutilated" restoration. That would be the work of Congress alone, and would be "Reconstruction."....

The whole fabric of Southern society must be changed, and never can it be done if this opportunity is lost. Without this, this government can never be, as it never has been, a true republic. Heretofore, it had more the features of aristocracy than of democracy. The Southern States have been despotisms, not governments of the people. It is impossible that any practical equality of rights can exist where a few thousand men monopolize the whole landed property. The larger the number of small proprietors the more safe and stable the government. As the landed interest must govern, the more it is subdivided and held by independent owners, the better. What would be the condition of the State of New York if it were not for her independent yeomanry? She would be overwhelmed and demoralized by the Jews, Milesians[14] and vagabonds of licentious cities. How can republican institutions, free schools, free churches, free social intercourse, exist in a mingled community of nabobs and serfs: of the owners of twenty thousand acre manors with lordly palaces, and the occupants of narrow huts inhabited by "low white trash?" If the South is ever to be made a safe republic, let her lands be cultivated by the toil of the owners, or the free labor of intelligent citizens. This must be done even though it drive her nobility into exile. It they go, all the better. It will be hard to persuade the owner of ten thousand acres of land, who drives a coach and four, that he is not degraded by sitting at the same table, or in the same pew, with the embrowned and hard-handed farmer who has himself cultivated his own thriving homestead of one hundred and fifty acres. This subdivision of the lands will yield ten bales of cotton to one that is made now, and he who produced it will own it and feel himself a man....

Let all who approve of these principles rally with us. Let all others go with

---

[13] a reference perhaps to Robert Phillimore (1810–1885), an English jurist who wrote a commentary on international law
[14] the Irish

Copperheads[15] and rebels. Those will be the opposing parties. Young men, this duty devolves on you. Would to God, if only for that, that I were still in the prime of life, that I might aid you to fight through this last and greatest battle of freedom!

D. Frederick Douglass, "Reconstruction," 1866[16]

The assembling of the Second Session of the Thirty-ninth Congress may very properly be made the occasion of a few earnest words on the already much-worn topic of reconstruction.

Seldom has any legislative body been the subject of a solicitude more intense, or of aspirations more sincere and ardent. There are the best of reasons for this profound interest. Questions of vast moment, left undecided by the last session of Congress, must be manfully grappled with by this. No political skirmishing will avail. The occasion demands statesmanship.

Whether the tremendous war so heroically fought and so victoriously ended shall pass into history a miserable failure, barren of permanent results,—a scandalous and shocking waste of blood and treasure . . . [and a futile] effort to bring under Federal authority States into which no loyal man from the North may safely enter, and to bring men into the national councils who deliberate with daggers and vote with revolvers, and who do not even conceal their deadly hate of the country that conquered them; or whether, on the other hand, we shall, as the rightful reward of victory over treason, have a solid nation, entirely delivered from all contradictions and social antagonisms, based upon loyalty, liberty, and equality, must be determined one way or the other by the present session of Congress. The last session really did nothing which can be considered final as to these questions. The Civil Rights Bill and the Freedmen's Bureau Bill and the proposed constitutional amendments, with the amendment already adopted and recognized as the law of the land,[17] do not reach the difficulty, and cannot, unless the

---

[15] Copperhead (after the poisonous snake of the same name) was a derisive term used by Republicans during the Civil War to describe Democratic politicians who wanted to negotiate a peace settlement with the South.

[16] *Atlantic Monthly* 18 (1866): 761–765. Douglass (1818–1895) was a former slave who became a leading abolitionist.

[17] Douglass refers to federal legislation and constitutional amendments passed in an effort to end slavery and deal with its aftermath: the Civil Rights Act of 1866; the Freemen's Bureau Bills of 1865 and 1866; the Thirteenth Amendment, which

whole structure of the government is changed from a government by States to something like a despotic central government, with power to control even the municipal regulations of States, and to make them conform to its own despotic will.

While there remains such an idea as the right of each State to control its own local affairs,—an idea, by the way, more deeply rooted in the minds of men of all sections of the country than perhaps any one other political idea,—no general assertion of human rights can be of any practical value. To change the character of the government at this point is neither possible nor desirable. All that is necessary to be done is to make the government consistent with itself, and render the rights of the States compatible with the sacred rights of human nature.

The arm of the Federal government is long, but it is far too short to protect the rights of individuals in the interior of distant States. They must have the power to protect themselves, or they will go unprotected, in spite of all the laws the Federal government can put upon the national statute-book.

Slavery, like all other great systems of wrong, founded in the depths of human selfishness, and existing for ages, has not neglected its own conservation. It has steadily exerted an influence upon all around it favorable to its own continuance. And to-day it is so strong that it could exist, not only without law, but even against law. Custom, manners, morals, religion, are all on its side everywhere in the South; and when you add the ignorance and servility of the ex-slave to the intelligence and accustomed authority of the master, you have the conditions, not out of which slavery will again grow, but under which it is impossible for the Federal government to wholly destroy it, unless the Federal government be armed with despotic power, to blot out State authority, and to station a Federal officer at every cross-road. This, of course, cannot be done, and ought not even if it could. The true way and the easiest way is to make our government entirely consistent with itself, and give to every loyal citizen the elective franchise,—a right and power which will be ever present, and will form a wall of fire for his protection.

One of the invaluable compensations of the late Rebellion is the highly instructive disclosure it made of the true source of danger to republican

---

abolished slavery, ratified in 1865; the Fourteenth Amendment, which defined citizenship, proposed in 1866, ratified in 1868; and the Fifteenth Amendment, proposed in 1869, ratified in 1870, which established that voting rights could not be denied "on account of race, color, or previous condition of servitude."

government. Whatever may be tolerated in monarchical and despotic governments, no republic is safe that tolerates a privileged class, or denies to any of its citizens equal rights and equal means to maintain them. What was theory before the war has been made fact by the war....

It is no disparagement to truth, that it can only prevail where reason prevails. War begins where reason ends. The thing worse than rebellion is the thing that causes rebellion. What that thing is, we have been taught to our cost. It remains now to be seen whether we have the needed courage to have that cause entirely removed from the Republic. At any rate, to this grand work of national regeneration and entire purification Congress must now address itself, with full purpose that the work shall this time be thoroughly done. The deadly upas,[18] root and branch, leaf and fiber, body and sap, must be utterly destroyed. The country is evidently not in a condition to listen patiently to pleas for postponement, however plausible, nor will it permit the responsibility to be shifted to other shoulders. Authority and power are here commensurate with the duty imposed. There are no cloud-flung shadows to obscure the way. Truth shines with brighter light and intenser heat at every moment, and a country torn and rent and bleeding implores relief from its distress and agony.

If time was at first needed, Congress has now had time. All the requisite materials from which to form an intelligent judgment are now before it. Whether its members look at the origin, the progress, the termination of the war, or at the mockery of a peace now existing, they will find only one unbroken chain of argument in favor of a radical policy of reconstruction. For the omissions of the last session, some excuses may be allowed. A treacherous President[19] stood in the way; ... Congress knows now that it must go on without his aid, and even against his machinations.[20] ... The members go to Washington fresh from the inspiring presence of the people.... Radicalism,

---

[18] a poisonous Asian tree

[19] Andrew Johnson, from Tennessee, was the only sitting Senator from a seceding state to remain loyal to the Union. A Southern Democrat who supported the Union War effort, he became Vice-President in 1864 as a symbol of national unity. He became President upon Lincoln's assassination, April 14, 1865. Those who thought that radical reconstruction was necessary viewed Johnson as too conciliatory to the South. Johnson vetoed reconstruction measures passed by Congress, and was eventually impeached, but by one vote acquitted by the Senate in 1868.

[20] Republicans increased their majorities in both the House and the Senate in the elections of 1866.

so far from being odious, is now the popular passport to power. The men most bitterly charged with it go to Congress with the largest majorities, while the timid and doubtful are sent by lean majorities, or else left at home. The strange controversy between the President and the Congress, at one time so threatening, is disposed of by the people. The high reconstructive powers which he so confidently, ostentatiously, and haughtily claimed, have been disallowed, denounced, and utterly repudiated; while those claimed by Congress have been confirmed....

Without attempting to settle here the metaphysical and somewhat theological question (about which so much has already been said and written), whether once in the Union means always in the Union,—agreeably to the formula, once in grace always in grace,—it is obvious to common sense that the rebellious States stand today, in point of law, precisely where they stood when, exhausted, beaten, conquered, they fell powerless at the feet of Federal authority. Their State governments were overthrown, and the lives and property of the leaders of the Rebellion were forfeited. In reconstructing the institutions of these shattered and overthrown States, Congress should begin with a clean slate, and make clean work of it. Let there be no hesitation. It would be a cowardly deference to a defeated and treacherous President, if any account were made of the illegitimate, one-sided, sham governments hurried into existence for a malign purpose in the absence of Congress.[21] These pretended governments, which were never submitted to the people, and from participation in which four millions of the loyal people were excluded by Presidential order, should now be treated according to their true character, as shams and impositions, and supplanted by true and legitimate governments, in the formation of which loyal men, black and white, shall participate.

It is not, however, within the scope of this paper to point out the precise steps to be taken, and the means to be employed. The people are less concerned about these than the grand end to be attained. They demand such a reconstruction as shall put an end to the present anarchical state of things in the late rebellious States,—where frightful murders and wholesale massacres are perpetrated in the very presence of Federal soldiers. This

---

[21] Douglass refers here to governments created in the South on the basis of Johnson's proclamations that left authority in the hands of those who had led secession, sent such men to Congress, and passed so-called "Black Codes" that restricted the activities of the former slaves.

horrible business they require shall cease. They want a reconstruction such as will protect loyal men, black and white, in their persons and property; such a one as will cause Northern industry, Northern capital, and Northern civilization to flow into the South, and make a man from New England as much at home in Carolina as elsewhere in the Republic. No Chinese wall[22] can now be tolerated. The South must be opened to the light of law and liberty, and this session of Congress is relied upon to accomplish this important work....

Men denounce the negro for his prominence in this discussion; but it is no fault of his that in peace as in war, that in conquering Rebel armies as in reconstructing the rebellious States, the right of the negro is the true solution of our national troubles. The stern logic of events, which goes directly to the point, disdaining all concern for the color or features of men, has determined the interests of the country as identical with and inseparable from those of the negro.

The policy that emancipated and armed the negro—now seen to have been wise and proper by the dullest—was not certainly more sternly demanded than is now the policy of enfranchisement. If with the negro was success in war, and without him failure, so in peace it will be found that the nation must fall or flourish with the negro.

Fortunately, the Constitution of the United States knows no distinction between citizens on account of color. Neither does it know any difference between a citizen of a State and a citizen of the United States. Citizenship evidently includes all the rights of citizens, whether State or national. If the Constitution knows none, it is clearly no part of the duty of a Republican Congress now to institute one. The mistake of the last session was the attempt to do this very thing, by a renunciation of its power to secure political rights to any class of citizens, with the obvious purpose to allow the rebellious States to disfranchise, if they should see fit, their colored citizens. This unfortunate blunder must now be retrieved, and the emasculated citizenship given to the negro supplanted by that contemplated in the Constitution of the United States, which declares that the citizens of each State shall enjoy all the rights and immunities of citizens of the several States,—so that a legal voter in any State shall be a legal voter in all the States.

---

[22] like the Great Wall of China, something to block the movement of people or information

E. Jubilee Singers, "Many Thousand Gone," 1872[23]

No more auction block for me
No more, no more
No more auction block for me
Many thousand gone

No more peck o' corn for me
No more, no more
No more peck o' corn for me
Many thousand gone

No more driver's lash for me
No more, no more
No more driver's lash for me
Many thousand gone

No more pint o' salt for me
No more, no more
No more pint o' salt for me
Many thousand gone

No more hundred lash for me
No more, no more
No more hundred lash for me
Many thousand gone.

No more mistress' call for me
No more, no more
No more mistress' call for me
Many thousand gone

---

[23] *Jubilee Songs, as Sung by the Jubilee Singers, of Fisk University* (New York: Biglow & Main, 1872) 27. Fisk University was incorporated in 1867 to provide a liberal arts education to all races, but its initial students were recently freed slaves. To raise money for the school, beginning in 1871, a musical group of its students, the Jubilee Singers, traveled in the Northern states and eventually in Europe to give concerts. Among the songs they sang were spirituals, including "Many Thousand Gone."

F. Senator Benjamin R. Tillman, Speech in the Senate, March 23, 1900[24]

Mr. President, I regret that I feel the necessity of bringing up again some parts of the speech of the Senator who has just taken his seat. However, he would not allow me to answer or interject an objection as he went along. It has reference to the race question in the South, the question which has been the cause of more sorrow, more misery, more loss of life, more expenditure of treasure than any and all questions which have confronted the American people from the foundation of the Government to the present day. Out of it grew the war, and after the war came the results of the war, and those results are with us now. The South has this question always with it. It cannot get rid of it. Is it there. It is like Banquo's ghost, and will not down.[25] I have felt called on to attack the Republican policy of this day and time and to accuse the Republicans in this Chamber with being hypocrites in regard to that issue; I have felt constrained to do so by reason of the facts and of the events of the past few years.

The Senator from Wisconsin[26]... gave us a picture of the condition of the slave during the war, and of the debt of gratitude which the Southern people owe to those slaves, who had charge of our wives and children and homes, and, to their everlasting credit, during those four long and bloody years not one solitary crime was reported against them of the kind that is now reported every week. I say that he cannot exceed me in appreciation of the fact that the Southern people did owe and do owe and will exceedingly owe a debt of gratitude to their slaves for their behavior.

But I would call the Senator's attention to the absolute and inevitable corollary, that if the slaves of the South, with the opportunities which were afforded them during those years when all the men were at the front, and when their wrongs, if they had any, would have prompted revenge, were

---

[24] *Congressional Record*, 56th Congress, 1st Session, 3223-3224. Tillman (1847–1918) was Governor of South Carolina (1890–1894) and U.S. Senator (1895–1918). He played an active role in anti-black violence in the 1870s and helped draft the state constitution that disenfranchised blacks.

[25] Lord Banquo, Thane of Lochaber, from the play *Macbeth*, by William Shakespeare. Macbeth murders Banquo in the first half of the play in an attempt to secure his claim on the throne; Banquo's ghost reappears at various points in the second half of the play to torment the king.

[26] John Coit Spooner (1843–1919) was a Republican Senator, 1885–1991, 1897–1907. He enlisted in the Union Army during the Civil War.

guilty of no crime against their mistresses and their children, it in thunder tones gives the lie to the charges as to the cruelty of the slave system in the South.

There were numerous instances, possibly too numerous, of cruelty and wrongdoing, and I shall not apologize for the system, for, thank God, it is gone—torn up by the roots at a great cost of life and sacrifice of property. I would not restore it if I could by the waving of a hand. But I say to him when he parades that as a reason why we ought to be grateful—and I acknowledge that we ought—he at once convicts himself and those of his fellows who went on that crusade of blood and destruction for the purpose of liberating those people of having been misled and of having given Harriet Beecher Stowe's *Uncle Tom's Cabin* undue weight in inaugurating that crusade. I have already given due credit on this floor to the North for patriotism and honesty of purpose and I realize that the love of the Union was a mighty factor in that great struggle. But it cannot be denied that the slaves of the South were a superior set of men and women to the freedmen of today, and that the poison in their minds—the race hatred of the whites—is the result of the teachings of Northern fanatics. Ravishing a woman, white or black, was never known to occur in the South till after the reconstruction era. So much for that phase of the subject.

As to the rights of the negros in the South, of which he now claims to be the champion—

Mr. Spooner. [*interrupting*] No.

Mr. Tillman. Well, I do not understand the Senator. I am very unfortunate in being unable to fathom his meaning. He speaks clearly, and I usually have the means of interpreting language that is plain and unmistakable; but he did say something about the rights of those people.

Mr. Spooner. I did.

Mr. Tillman. And he said we had taken their rights away from them. He asked me was it right to murder them in order to carry the elections. I never saw one murdered. I never saw one shot at an election. It was the riots before the election, precipitated by their own hotheadedness in attempting to hold the government, that brought on conflicts between the races and caused the shotgun to be used. That is what I meant by saying we used the shotgun.

I want to call attention to one fact. He said that the Republican Party gave the negroes the ballot in order to protect themselves against the indignities and wrongs that were attempted to be heaped upon them by the enactment of the black code.[27] I say that [*the negroes were given the ballot*] because the Republicans of that day, led by Thad Stevens, wanted to put white necks under black heels and to get revenge. There is a difference of opinion. You have your opinion about it, and I have mine, and we can never agree.

I want to ask the Senator this proposition in arithmetic: In my State, there were 135,000 negro voters, or negroes of voting age, and some 90,000 or 95,000 white voters. General Canby[28] set up a carpetbag government[29] there and turned our State over to this majority. Now, I want to ask you, with a free vote and a fair count, how are you going to beat 135,000 to 95,000? How are you going to do it? You had set us an impossible task. You had handcuffed us [*and*] thrown away the key, and you propped your carpet bag negro government with bayonets. Whenever it was necessary to sustain the government you held it up by the Army.

Mr. President, I have not the facts and figures here, but I want the country to get the full view of the Southern side of this question and the justification for anything we did. We were sorry we had the necessity forced upon us, but we could not help it, and as white men we are not sorry for it, and we do not propose to apologize for anything we have done in connection to it. We took the government away from them in 1876. We did take it. If no other Senator has come here previous to this time who would acknowledge it, more's the pity. We have had no fraud in our elections in South Carolina since 1884. There has been no organized Republican Party in the State.

We did not disfranchise the negroes until 1895. Then we had a constitutional convention convened which took the matter up calmly, deliberately, and avowedly with the purpose of disenfranchising as many of them as we could under the fourteenth and fifteenth amendments. We adopted the educational qualification as the only means left to us, and the negro is as contented and as prosperous and as well protected in South Carolina today as in any State of the Union south of the Potomac. He is not meddling with politics, for he found that the more he meddled with them, the worse off he got. As to his "rights"—I will not discuss them now. We of the South have

---

[27] Black codes were laws passed by Southern states at the end of Civil War to restrict the freedom of freedmen.

[28] Edward Canby (1817–1873) was Military Governor of the Second Military District (August 1867 to August 1868) that included North and South Carolina. Canby was assassinated by Modoc Indians during a negotiation.

[29] "Carpetbaggers" is a derogatory term for a Northerner who went to the South after the Civil War and held office, or otherwise sought to take advantage of post-war conditions.

never recognized the right of the negro to govern the white men, and we never will. We have never believed him to be equal to the white man, and we will not submit to his gratifying lust on our wives and daughters without lynching him.[30] I would to God the last one of them was in Africa and that none of them had ever been brought to our shores. . . .

I want to ask permission in this connection to print a speech which I made in the constitutional convention of South Carolina when it convened in 1895, in which the whole carpetbag regime and the indignities and wrongs heaped upon our people, the robberies which we have suffered, and all the facts and figures there brought out are incorporated, and let the whole of the facts go to the country. I am not ashamed to have those facts go to the country. They are our justification for the present situation in our State. . . .

---

[30] Estimates of lynchings vary. According to the Tuskegee Institute, from 1882-1968, 4,745 lynchings occurred in the United States. Of this number, 3,446 or 73 percent of the victims were Black. Lynching peaked in the early 1890s. In 1892, 230 were recorded. See https://goo.gl/e7NVTY. Lisa D. Cook, "Converging to a National Lynching Database: Recent Developments," (2011) describes and analyzes different databases of lynching incidents. Available at https://goo.gl/QvpcRf.

CHAPTER 17

Reconstructing the West: Grant's Peace Policy

A. President Ulysses S. Grant, First Annual Message, December 6, 1869

B. Ely S. Parker, Report of the Commissioner of Indian Affairs, December 23, 1869

C. President Ulysses S. Grant, Speech to Red Cloud and Red Dog, May 28, 1872

D. Ely S. Parker to Harriet Converse, 1885

E. Susan La Flesche, M.D., "The Home Life of the Indian," June 1892

*P*rior to the Civil War, relations between Americans and the native population had been marked by encroachment on Indian land, some cooperation, occasional alliances against common enemies, misunderstanding, violence, expulsions from traditional lands, treaties, promises, missionary work, and more violence. After the war ended, the United States had to address again the question of what to do about Native Americans. President Grant hoped for something better than what history had so far recorded. He inaugurated what came to be called Grant's peace policy (Documents A, B, and C). Documents D and E, written by Native Americans (as was Document B), explain some of the changes that occurred in Native life, both individually and collectively, because of or despite Grant's efforts. For more information on Ely Parker, see illustration on page A.

Study Questions

A. What reasons does President Grant give for his Indian policy? What are its key elements? What is Ely Parker's criticism of the attitude of "good men" and Christians toward the Indians? How would he have responded to the efforts of the Women's National Indian Association described in Document E? What did Parker mean when he said that all his life he had occupied a false position? What was the cause of this? Do Parker and Susan La Flesche have the same attitude to the changes that have occurred in Indian life?

B. In what ways are the efforts of the federal government after the Civil War to deal with former slaves and Native Americans alike or dissimilar?

C. Compare the attitudes and policies towards Native Americans expressed
here with those of the earliest European colonizers in Volume 1, Chapter 1.
What similarities or differences do you see in their underlying assumptions
about the role of the native population in the future of what would become
the United States?

A. President Ulysses S. Grant, First Annual Message, December 6, 1869[1]

... The building of railroads, and the access thereby given to all the agricultural and mineral regions of the country, is rapidly bringing civilized settlements into contact with all the tribes of Indians. No matter what ought
to be the relations between such settlements and the aborigines, the fact
is they do not harmonize well, and one or the other has to give way in the
end. A system which looks to the extinction of a race is too horrible for a
nation to adopt without entailing upon itself the wrath of all Christendom
and engendering in the citizen a disregard for human life and the rights of
others, dangerous to society. I see no substitute for such a system, except in
placing all the Indians on large reservations, as rapidly as it can be done, and
giving them absolute protection there. As soon as they are fitted for it they
should be induced to take their lands in severalty and to set up Territorial
governments for their own protection. For full details on this subject I call
your special attention to the reports of the Secretary of the Interior and the
Commissioner of Indian Affairs....

B. Ely S. Parker, Report of the Commissioner of Indian Affairs, December 23, 1869[2]

Sir: As required by law, I have the honor to submit this, my first annual report
of our Indian Affairs and relations during the past year, with accompanying
documents.

---

[1] *The Papers of Ulysses S. Grant*, ed. John Y. Simon (Carbondale: Southern Illinois
University Press, 1994), 18–44. Available online from: Gerhard Peters and John T.
Woolley, *The American Presidency Project.* https://goo.gl/QnB9kL.
[2] *Report of the Commissioner of Indian Affairs, made to the Secretary of the Interior for
the year 1869* (Washington: Government Printing Office, 1870), 3–6. Available from
Internet Archives at https://goo.gl/e5urvE. Ely S. Parker (1828–1895) was a Seneca
Indian who studied to be a lawyer, was not allowed to become one because Native
Americans at that time were not citizens (in 1924 by act of Congress they became so),

Among the reports of the superintendents and agents herewith, there will be found information, with views and suggestions of much practical value, which should command the earnest attention of our legislators, and all others who are concerned for the future welfare and destiny of the remaining original inhabitants of our country. The question is still one of the deepest interest, "What shall be done for the amelioration and civilization of the race?" For a long period in the past, great and commendable efforts were made by the government to accomplish these desirable ends, but the success was never commensurate with the means employed. Of late years a change of policy was seen to be required, as the cause of failure, the difficulties to be encountered, and the best means of overcoming them, became better understood. The measures to which we are indebted for an improved condition of affairs are the concentration of the Indians upon suitable reservations, and the supplying them with means for engaging in agricultural and mechanical pursuits for their education and moral training. As a result, the clouds of ignorance and superstition in which many of these people were so long enveloped, have disappeared, and the light of Christian civilization seems to have dawned upon their moral darkness, and opened upon a brighter future. Much, however, remains to be done for the multitude yet in their savage state, and I can but earnestly invite the serious consideration of those whose duty it is to legislate in their behalf, to the justice and importance of promptly fulfilling all treaty obligations and the wisdom of placing at the disposal of the department adequate funds for the purpose, and investing it with powers to adopt the requisite measures for the settlement of all tribes, when practicable, upon tracts of land to be set apart for their use and economy. I recommend that in addition to the reservations already established, there be others provided for the wild and roving tribes of New Mexico, Arizona and Nevada; also for the more peaceable bands in the southern part of California. These tribes, excepting the Navahos in the Territory of New Mexico, who under the Treaty of 1868, have a home in the western part of the Territory to which they have been removed, have no treaty relations with the government, and if placed upon reservations, it will be necessary that Congress, by appropriating legislation, provide for their wants, until they become capable of taking care

---

then became an engineer, met Ulysses S. Grant while working in Galena, IL, joined the Union Army during the Civil War, and became Grant's secretary. He was present at Appomattox when Lee surrendered (see illustration on page A). After the war, Parker served as Commissioner of Indian Affairs (1869–1871). He was accused of misusing funds, resigned, but was later cleared. Document D refers to this episode.

of themselves. In the other Territories, as also in Oregon and the northern part of California, the existing reservations are sufficient to accommodate all the Indians within their bounds; indeed, the number might with advantage be reduced; but in Montana there is urgent need for the setting apart permanently suitable tracts for the Blackfeet and other tribes, who claim large portions of that Territory and are parties to treaties entered into with them last year by Commissioner W. J. Cullen, which were submitted to the United States Senate, but have not been finally acted upon by that body. Should the treaties be ratified, the required reservations will be secured, greatly to the benefit of both Indians and citizens.

Before entering upon a resume of affairs of the respective superintendencies of agencies for the past year, I will here briefly notice several matters of interest which in their bearing upon the management of our Indian relations, are likely to work out judging from what has been the effect so far, the most beneficial results.

Under an act of Congress approved April 10, 1868, two million dollars[3] were appointed to enable the President to maintain peace among and with various tribes, bands and parties of Indians; to promote their civilization; bring them, when practicable, upon reservations, and to relieve their necessities, and encourage their efforts at self-support. The Executive is also authorized to organize a Board of Commissioners, to consist of not more than ten persons, selected from among men eminent for their intelligence and philanthropy, to serve without pecuniary compensation, and who, under his direction, shall exercise joint control with the Secretary of the Interior over the disbursement of this large fund. . . .

In regard to the fund of two million dollars referred to, it may be remarked that it has enabled the department to a great extent to carry out the purpose for which it was appropriated. There can be no question but that mischief has been prevented and suffering either relieved or warded off from numbers who otherwise by force or circumstances would have been led into difficulties and extreme want. By the timely supplies of subsistence and clothing furnished, and the adoption of measures for their benefit, the tribes from whom the greatest trouble was apprehended have been kept comparatively quiet, and some advance it is to be hoped, made in the direction of their permanent settlement in the localities assigned to them, and their entering

---

[3] A sum equivalent to $33 million in 2017. Two million was 0.5 percent of the Federal budget in 1868. An equivalent percentage of the budget in 2017 would be roughly 18,000,000,000.

upon a new course of life. The subsistence they receive is furnished through the agency of the commissary department of the Army, with, it is believed, greater economy and more satisfaction than could have resulted had the mode heretofore been followed. In this connection I desire to call attention to the fact that the number of wild Indians and others, also not provided for by treaty stipulations, whose precarious condition requires that something should be done for relief and who are thrown under the immediate charge of the department, is increasing. It is therefore, a matter of serious consideration and urgent necessity that means be offered to properly care for them. For this purpose, in my judgment there should be annually appropriated by Congress, a large contingent fund similar to that in question, and subject to the same control. I accordingly recommend that the subject be brought to the attention of Congress.

With a view of more efficiency in the management of affairs of the respective superintendencies and agencies, the Executive has inaugurated a change of policy whereby a different class of men from those heretofore selected, have been appointed to duty as superintendents and agents. There are doubtless just grounds for it, as great and frequent complaints have been made for years past, of either the dishonesty or inefficiency of many of these officers. Members of the Society of Friends,[4] recommended by the society, now hold these positions in the Northern superintendency, embracing all Indians in Nebraska; and in the Central, embracing tribes residing in Kansas, together with the Kiowas, Comanches, and other tribes in the Indian country. Other superintendencies and agencies, excepting that of Oregon and two agencies there, are filled by Army officers detailed for such duty. The experiment has not been sufficiently tested to enable me to say definitively that it is a success, for but a short time has elapsed since these Friends and officers entered upon duty; but so far as I can learn, the plan works advantageously, and will probably prove a positive benefit to the service, and the indications are that the interests of the government and the Indians will be subserved by an honest and faithful discharge of duty, fully answering the expectations entertained by those who regard the measure as wise and proper.

I am pleased to have it to remark that there is now a perfect understanding between the officers of this department and those of the military, with respect to their relative duties and responsibilities in reference to the Indian affairs. In this matter with the approbation of the President and yourself

---

[4] the Quakers, one of several religious groups through which much of Grant's Indian policy was administered

a circular letter was addressed to this office in June last to all superintendents and agents, defining the policy of the government in its treatments of
the Indians, as comprehended in their general terms, viz[5]: that they should
be secured their legal rights; located, when practicable, upon reservations;
assisted in agricultural pursuits and the arts of civilized life and that Indians
who should fail or refuse to come in and locate in permanent abodes provided
for them, must be subject wholly to the control and supervision of military
authorities, to be treated as friendly or hostile as circumstances might justify. The War Department concurring, issued orders upon the subject for
the information and guidance of the proper military officers, and the result
has been harmony of action between [the] two departments, no conflict of
opinion having arisen as to the duty, power and responsibility of either.

Arrangements now, as heretofore, will doubtless be required with tribes
desiring to be settled upon reservations for the relinquishment of their rights
to the lands claimed by them, and for assistance in sustaining themselves in
a new position, but I am of the opinion that they should not be of a treaty
nature. It has become a matter of serious import whether the treaty system
in use ought longer to be continued. In my judgment it should not. A treaty
involves the idea of a compact between two or more sovereign powers, each
possessing of sufficient authority and force to compel a compliance with the
obligations incurred. The Indian tribes of the United States are not sovereign
nations, capable of making treaties, as none of them have an organized government of such inherent strength as would secure a faithful obedience of its
people in the observance of compacts of this character. They are held to be
the wards of the government, and the only title the law concedes to them to
the lands they occupy or claim is a mere possessory one. But because treaties
have been made with them generally for the extinguishment of their supposed absolute title to land inhabited by them, or over which they roam, they
have become falsely impressed with the notion of national independence. It
is time that this idea should be dispelled, and that the government cease the
cruel farce of thus dealing with its helpless and ignorant wards. Many good
men, looking at this matter only from a Christian point of view, will perhaps
say that the poor Indian has been greatly wronged and ill-treated; that this
whole county was once his of which he has been despoiled, and that he has
been driven from place to place until he has hardly left to him a spot where
to lay his head. This indeed may be philanthropic and humane, but the stern
letter of the law admits of no such conclusion, and great injury has been done

---

[5] that is to say

by the government deluding these people into the belief of their being independent sovereignties, while they were at the same time recognized only as its dependents and wards. As civilization advances and their possessions of land are required for settlement, such legislation should be granted to them as a wise, liberal and just government ought to extend to its subjects holding their dependent relation. In regard to the treaties now in force, justice and humanity require that they be promptly and faithfully executed, so that the Indians may not have the cause of complaint, or reason to violate their obligation by acts of violence and robbery. . . .

C. President Ulysses S. Grant, Speech to Red Cloud and Red Dog, May 28, 1872[6]

I am very glad to see you here again, and to hear that you have tried so hard to carry out the promises made by you when you were here before—to keep the peace between your people and the whites. . . .

We want to do for you and your people all we can to advance and help them, and to enable them to become self-supporting. The time must come when, with the great growth of population here, the game will be gone, and your people will then have to resort to other means of support; and while there is time we would like to teach you new modes of living that will secure you in the future and be a safe means of livelihood.

I want to see the Indians get upon land where they can look forward to permanent homes for themselves and their children. The matter of the location of your agency we want to make agreeable to you, and also to the white people, and to regulate this you must speak to the Secretary of the Interior. I want you to have your talk with him. He tells me all that is said to him, and he speaks for me.

I do not want you and your people to go beyond the territory which has been guaranteed to you by treaty stipulations, except with your full consent; but I am going to suggest to you for your thought and reflection a movement—not for you to decide upon today, nor this year necessarily, but

---

[6] "The Indians at the White House," *The Evening Star*, May 28, 1872. Available at https://goo.gl/x5d18q. Red Cloud (1822–1909) was a leader of the Lakota Sioux, who accepted the reservation system, following Red Cloud's War, which included an engagement with a detachment under the command of William Fetterman (the Sioux killed the entire detachment). A rough contemporary of Red Cloud, Red Dog was another Sioux leader.

for you to think about taking into consideration the advantages that will be gained by it—and if you all consent I will state what we propose to do for you.

If, at any time, you feel like moving to what is known as the Cherokee country[7]—which is a large territory, with an admirable climate, where you would never suffer from the cold and where you could have lands set apart to remain exclusively your own—we would set apart a large tract of land that would belong to you and your children. We would at first build houses for your chiefs and principal men, and send men among your people to instruct them so they could have houses for shelter. We would send you large herds of cattle and sheep to live upon, and to enable you to raise stock. To this end we would send, if you so desire, Indians who have been accustomed to live with white men, who would instruct you in growing and raising stock until you know how to do so yourselves. We would establish schools, so that your children would learn to read and to write, and to speak the English language, the same as white people, and in this way you and your people would be prepared, before the game is gone, to live comfortably and securely.

I say this only for you to think about and talk about to your people. Whenever you are ready to avail yourself of this offer, then you can talk to us, and we will do what I say. All the treaty obligations we have entered into we shall keep with you unless it is with your own consent that the change is made, or so long as you keep those obligations yourself.

Any reply that you wish to make you can make to the Secretary of the Interior. This you can put off until you have thought over the subject.

D. Ely S. Parker to Harriet Converse, 1885[8]

Dear Gayaneshaoh,[9]

The outpouring of your terrific wrath against certain Christian practices,

---

[7] Grant is probably referring to Oklahoma, to which the U.S. government had relocated many tribes, including the Cherokee.

[8] *Publications of the Buffalo Historical Society, Volume VIII*, ed. Frank H. Severance (Buffalo, NY: Buffalo Historical Society, 1905), 524–527. The source does not give the date of the letter from which the first excerpt is taken. Other sources date the second letter excerpted here to 1885. We have supplied the salutation to the first letter, not present in the source, although the source notes that this was Parker's customary greeting (522).

[9] Parker addressed Converse by her Indian name, which means "The Law Bearer," according to the *Encyclopedia of the Haudenosaunee (Iroquois Confederacy)*, ed. Bruce Elliott Johansen and Barbara Alice Mann (Westport, CT: Greenwood Press,

beliefs and propositions for the amelioration and improvement of certain unchristian people who live on reservations where the English language is not spoken, and where "vice and barbarism" are rampant, was duly received yesterday. The Bishop is right in his reference to the remnants of the Six Nations[10] being yet "deplorably subject to individual disability, disadvantages and wrong arising from their tribal condition," in all except the last proposition. The disabilities, disadvantages and wrongs do not result, however, either primarily, consequently or ultimately from their tribal condition and native inheritances, but solely, wholly and absolutely from the unchristian treatment they have always received from Christian white people who speak the English language, who read the English Bible and who are Pharisaically[11] divested of all the elements of vice and barbarism. The tenacity with which the remnants of this people have adhered to their tribal organizations and religious traditions is all that has saved them thus far from inevitable extinguishment. When they abandon their birthright for a mess of Christian pottage[12] they will then cease to be a distinctive people. It is useless though to discuss this question, already prejudiced and predetermined by a granitic[13] Christian hierarchy from whose judgments and decisions there seems to be no appeal....

Dear Gayaneshaoh,

On reading your last note I was greatly amused,—and why? Because what I have written heretofore has been taken *literatim et verbatim*[14] and a character given me to which I am no more entitled than the man in the moon! I am credited or charged with being "great," "powerful" and finally crowned as "good"! Oh, my guardian genius, why should I be so burdened with what I am not now and never expect to be! Oh, indeed, would that I could feel a "kindling touch from that pure flame"[15] which a fair and ministering angel

---

2000), 63. Converse (1836–1903) befriended Parker and became an advocate for the Seneca, who adopted her into the tribe.

[10] The nations that made up the Iroquois Confederacy. The Seneca were one of these.

[11] a reference to Pharisees, or those thought to be self-righteous or hypocritical

[12] Genesis 25:29–34. See Chapter 20, Document A.

[13] hardened and inflexible, like granite rock

[14] literally and word for word

[15] Parker quotes the first line of William Wordsworth's "Siege of Vienna Raised by John Sobieski" (1816).

would endow me with in the exuberance of prejudiced enthusiasm, and which compels me to sit in sackcloth and ashes....

And why all this commotion of the spirit? Because I am an ideal or a myth and not my real self. I have lost my identity and I look about me in vain for my original being. I never was "great" and never expect to be. I never was "powerful" and would not know how to exercise power were it placed in my hands for use. And that I am "good" or ever dreamed of attaining that blissful condition of being is simply absurd....

All my life I have occupied a false position. As a youth my people voted me a genius and loudly proclaimed that Hawenneyo[16] had destined me to be their savior and gave public thanksgiving for the great blessing they believed had been given them, for unfortunately just at this period they were engaged in an almost endless and nearly hopeless litigated contest for their New York homes and consequently for their very existence.

For many years I was a constant visitor at the State and Federal capitals either seeking legislative relief or in attendance at State and Federal courts. Being only a mere lad, the pale-faced officials with whom I came in contact flattered me and declared that one so young must be extraordinarily endowed to be charged with the conduct of such weighty affairs. I pleased my people in eventually bringing their troubles to a successful and satisfactory termination. I prepared and had approved by the proper authorities a code of laws and rules for the conduct of affairs among themselves and settled them for all time or, for so long as Hawenneyo should let them live.

They saw all this and that it was good. They no longer wanted me nor gave me credit for what had been done. A generation had passed and another grown up since I began to work for them. The young men were confident of their own strength and abilities and needed not the brawny arm of experience to fight their battles for them, nor the wisdom brought about by years of training to guide them any longer. The War of the Rebellion had broken out among the pale-faces, a terrible contest between the slaveholding and non-slaveholding sections of the United States. I had, through the Hon. Wm. H. Seward, personally tendered my services for the non-slaveholding interest.[17] Mr. Seward in short said to me that the struggle in which I wished to assist, was an affair between white men and one in which the Indian was not called on to act. "The fight must be made and settled by the white men alone,"

---

[16] Great Spirit
[17] William Seward (1801–1872) was the United States Secretary of State from 1861-1869.

he said. "Go home, cultivate your farm, and we will settle our own troubles without any Indian aid."

I did go home and planted crops and myself on the farm, sometimes not leaving it for four and six weeks at a time. But the quarrel of the whites was not so easily or quickly settled. It was not a wrangle of boys, but a struggle of giants and the country was being racked to its very foundations.

Then came to me in my forest home a paper bearing the great red seal of the War Department at Washington. It was an officer's commission in the Army of the United States. The young Indian community had settled in their untutored minds that because I had settled quietly, willingly and unconcernedly in the earning of my living by the sweat of my brow, I was not, therefore, a genius or a man of mind. That they were in truth correct, they did not know, jealousy and envy having prompted the idea and utterance. But now this paper coming from the great Government at Washington offering to confer honors for which I had not served an apprenticeship, nor even asked for, revived among the poor Indians the idea that I was after all a genius and great and powerful, though to them not perceptible. They pleaded with me not to leave them, but to remain as their counsellor, adviser and chief, and that they would be powerless and lost without my presence. They tacitly acknowledged my genius, greatness, and power, and which I did not. When I explained that I was going into the war with a splendid protest of sacrificing my life, as much for their food as for the maintenance of the principles of the Constitution and laws of the United States, and upholding the Union flag in its purity, honor and supremacy over this whole country, they silently and wisely bowed their heads and wept in assent as to the inevitable. I bade them farewell, commended them to the care and protection of Hawenneyo and left them, never expecting to return.

I went from the East to the West and from the West to the East again. They heard of me in great battles and they knew of my association with the great commander of all the Union armies and how I upheld the right arm of his strength, and they said, "How great and powerful is our chief!"

The quarrel between the white men ended and the great commander with his military family settled in Washington, where the great council fire of his nation was annually lighted and blazed in all its glory and fury. As an humble member of this military family I was the envy of many pale-faced subordinate embryo generals who said in whispers, "Parker must be a genius, he is so great and powerful."

In a few years my military chieftain was made head and front of the whole American people, and in his partiality he placed me at the head of the management of the Indian Affairs of the United States. I was myself an Indian and presumably understood them, their wants and the manipulation of their affairs generally. Then, again went out among the whites and Indians the words, "Parker must be a genius, he is so great and powerful." The Indians were universally pleased, and they all were willing to be quiet and remain at peace, and were even asking to be taught civilization and Christianity. I stopped and put an end to all wars either among themselves or with their white brothers, and I sent professed Christian teachers among them. But these things did not suit that class of whites who waxed rich and fat from the plundering of the poor Indians, nor were there teacherships enough to give places to all the hungry and impecunious Christians. Then was the cry raised by all who believed themselves injured or unprovided for: "Nay! this Parker is an Indian genius; he is grown too great and powerful; he doth injure our business and taketh the bread from the mouths of our families and the money from out of our pockets, now, therefore, let us write and put him out of power, so that we may feast as heretofore."

They made their onslaught on my poor innocent head and made the air foul with their malicious and poisonous accusations. They were defeated, but it was no longer a pleasure to discharge patriotic duties in the face of foul slander and abuse. I gave up a thankless position to enjoy my declining days in peace and quiet. But my days are not all peace and quiet. I am pursued by a still small voice constantly echoing, "Thou art a genius, great and powerful," and even my little cousin, the restless Snipe,[18] has with her strong, piping voice echoed the refrain, "Thou art great, powerful and good.". . .

Your cousin,
Donehogawa, The Wolf[19]

E. Susan La Flesche, M.D., The Home Life of the Indian, June 1892[20]

The home life of the Indian of to-day is essentially the same as the home life of the Indian of thirty years ago. Any progress he may have made is due to

---

[18] a small bird

[19] Donehogawa was one of Parker's Indian names, translated as Keeper of the Western Door of the Long House of the Iroquois. He was a member of the Wolf clan.

[20] *The Indian's Friend*, A Monthly Published by the Women's National Indian Association, Vol. IV, Philadelphia, June 1892, No. 1. Susan La Flesche (1865–1915) was an Omaha Indian and thought to be the first Native American woman to become a

change of environment, produced by the coming of white people, and the consequent passing away of old customs.

The daily routine of home life is the same, the aforesaid change produced by environment being shown by the fact that in place of the tepee the Indian once occupied, he now lives in a frame house and can boast of a well, a stable, a few fruit trees and a vegetable garden. The fact that in place of hunting wild game over the prairies, he now farms and raises good crops of corn, wheat, and oats makes but little difference in the internal workings of the home.

Long ago the Indian had a removable house suited to his requirements, a tepee or tent which was made of buckskin or canvas stretched over a pyramid formed by means of poles tied together at the top with buckskin, a house easy to carry around with him in his nomadic journeyings.

When the tribe found a place where they could settle down and live eight months in the year they built mud lodges as their permanent residences. These are dome-shaped, the frame work consisting of poles, willow branches and rushes, and from base to apex it is covered with sod several inches thick. They have wide entranceways, several feet long and high enough to permit a tall person to stand upright. They are like tunnels leading into the lodge, which is circular in form. Light and air enter by means of a large circular opening in the top of the dome, this also serving as a means of exit for the smoke. The lodge is well ventilated—warm in winter and cool in summer. Several families live in them at a time, and the only two or three now left on this reservation are used for holding councils, public gatherings and dances, as they can accommodate over a hundred people.

How often as children we used to climb upon these lodges and pick the sunflowers and grasses growing on them. Near sunset the old men would sit up on these lodges where they could pursue their meditations undisturbed and alone, and I remember looking at them reverently as I played around with the other children, for I regarded them with a great deal of awe, for to me they seemed so wise.

Trodden by hundreds of feet the earthen floor is almost as hard as stone, and coming in from the hot dusty road how gratefully cool it felt to our little

---

doctor. She was educated at a Quaker school, one of those established under Grant's Peace Policy. She also attended the Hampton Institute, established after the war to educate freed slaves, and the Women's Medical College of Pennsylvania. She received financial assistance for her education from the Women's National Indian Association (see n. 21). Following medical school, La Flesche became a medical missionary to the Omaha.

bare feet as we played in and out, riding our make-believe horse made of sunflower stalks. In the center is a little hollow where the fire is built and all the cooking is done. Around this place we used to gather to listen to thrilling stories of battles with the dreaded Sioux, buffalo hunts and *ghost stories*. When it came to the last I used to look up fearfully at the opening above, for fear I should see a dog looking down, for it is a superstition among the Indians that if a dog looks down through this opening into the lodge some one of the company is sure to die soon. If such a thing happened the dog was killed immediately. It was always a relief to see the blue sky and stars looking down.

After a while the Indians built log houses of only one room, the roof covered with turf.

Now, on this reservation we have almost every family living in a neat frame house, one story or one story and a half high, wainscoted, plastered or papered inside; very clean and neatly painted outside. The premises are clear of rubbish.

These houses are built by the Indians with their own money, but the desire to own such houses was started several years ago when the "Connecticut Home-Building Fund" started the Home-Building Department of the Women's National Indian Association.[21] The seed then sown has borne fruit here and elsewhere. Whether you enter with me into a tent, a mud-lodge or log house, or one of these neat frame houses you would see the same home-life going on in every one of them.

There is little variation, one day of the week being almost the same as another.

The family usually arise early—in the summer about sunrise, but in winter the breakfast is usually considerably delayed, for they follow suntime. In most cases the hostess arises and builds the fire, gets the water and cooks the simple meal. Very few have had bread, but it is now getting to be the general rule in many families to make light bread. They have biscuit made with soda or baking powder, and sometimes "fried cakes," light brown in color and very appetizing. Coffee, sometimes fresh beef, for, in this country where there are thousands of head of cattle it is hard to get beef; sometimes fruit, dried, and in the summer potatoes and beans. You can see that their diet is very simple. The food is divided and put on plates, the coffee is poured out into cups and then the food is handed around to each individual. Usually after the meal is

---

[21] The Women's National Indian Association, founded in 1879, sought to Christianize Native Americans and help them assimilate. There were several affiliated State Associations, including one in Connecticut, which established a building fund.

over the dishes are put away in a little cupboard. If it is summer the husband and men in the family go out to their work and the wife cleans up the house and begins to get the noon-meal. It is the same as breakfast. They do not do very much sewing for their clothes are simply and quickly made. The houses on the reservation are far apart and the women cannot very well pass away the time by gossip with the neighbors, as some of our white friends have the *privilege* of doing. What a deprivation is this! Let us all be thankful for our privileges.

The evening meal is simple, and the time between that and the retiring hour is spent in talking over the events of the day or in telling news. We have no telegraph lines or telephones, but news has a wonderfully quick way of travelling from one house to another. Rumors on a reservation are the same as rumors anywhere else. When they reach the end (?)[22] of their journey they have received quite an addition, and a wise person will credit only one third of the story as truth.

There are no books, pictures or recreations save the dances, and no games except cards which are used for gambling. A narrow life in some respects. The Indians are passionately fond of their children; having no books, pictures or recreations in their home life, they lavish all attention on their children. There are some cases where the step-father or step-mother, as the case may be, makes no difference whatever between their children and the step-children. They *show* their affection for their children also.

Some ask the absurd question, "Do the Indians really love their wives?" The Indians are *human beings* just as the white people are, and there are Indian men who are just as careful, watchful and affectionate to their wives as anyone would wish to see anywhere. They do not make an outward show of their affection, but I know from personal observation that they are truly devoted to each other. One day I had to pull a young woman's tooth, and as the husband was a strong muscular man I was in hopes he would support her head for me. He sent for his brother to do it and when he saw me take the forceps up he beat a hasty retreat. I heard him walking up and down in the other room, and when they told him I was through he appeared with such a happy relieved look on his face and thanked me so earnestly. I could not help but be glad for him that she was through with her suffering. There are many instances like this that I know of. Of course, there are some cases entirely different, and where there is no happiness. But so we find it wherever we go in this world.

---

[22] The parenthetical question mark is in the original.

Indian women no longer stand in the background. Few work in the fields or do heavy work. Where it used to be the lot of the women to provide the wood, now the men get it in almost all cases. Even in so small a thing as walking or riding where the woman had to walk behind or ride in the back of the wagon, now she walks beside her husband, and in vehicles you see the woman riding beside her husband on the seat.

The old customs are fast disappearing and in place of the Indian of twenty years ago, who lived in a tent and supported himself by hunting wild game, we have an independent man who is earning his bread by his own toil, living in a frame house and learning very fast how to transact business like white people. The wife standing beside her husband shows only his true advancement, and the home is happier for this progress.

CHAPTER 18

Urban Growth: The Pullman Strike

A. United States Strike Commission, *Report on the Chicago Strike*,
   June–July 1894, December 10, 1894
B. "King Debs," *Harper's Weekly*, July 14, 1894
C. Associate Justice David Brewer, *In re Debs*, May 7, 1895
D. Eugene V. Debs, "Liberty: Speech at Battery D, Chicago,"
   On Release from Woodstock Jail, November 22, 1895

A recession in 1893 led the Pullman Sleeping Car Company to reduce the wages of its workers. When it reduced wages, it did not reduce rents in the company housing it supplied its workers. As a result, the workers went on strike on May 11, 1894. Eugene V. Debs had recently organized the American Railway Union (ARU). Although at first reluctant to get involved, he eventually seized on the Pullman strike as an opportunity to organize Pullman workers and add them to the ARU's members. The Pullman Company refused to recognize the union. To make the strike effective, Debs organized a boycott of any train that had a Pullman car. Other labor leaders and labor organizations opposed the boycott, but ARU members around the country were able to disrupt interstate rail traffic, including that which carried the US mail. (See Document B for one example of the public perception this created of Debs and his union.)

To get the mail moving, President Grover Cleveland ordered US attorneys and the Army to deal with the strike, which had included acts of violence against trains and other railroad property. (The Governor of Illinois, seeing the strike as a state and local matter, claimed that Cleveland had no constitutional right to do so.) A federal court issued an injunction barring the union from hindering railroad traffic. Debs ignored the injunction. He was arrested on federal contempt and conspiracy charges. The conspiracy charge was dropped, as Debs mentions (Document D), but he was ordered to jail for contempt for ignoring the injunction. His attorneys appealed. The Supreme Court decided unanimously (Document C) in favor of the US government and the power of the Federal courts to issue an injunction against the strike.

The Supreme Court's decision was a setback for labor, as the courts proved willing in ensuing years to issue the injunctions that the Supreme Court had approved.

*As Document A argues, however, outside the courts organized labor was finding
its place in American life. In a conciliatory move, six days after the Pullman strike
ended, Congress passed and Cleveland signed a law that established Labor Day,
a national holiday honoring workingmen. In 1932, the Norris-LaGuardia Act
gave unions full freedom of association and outlawed the kind of injunctions the
Supreme Court had approved to end the Pullman strike. Public opinion toward
unions changed in part because of the growing perception of the power of the
so-called trusts. On the trusts, see footnote 3 below and illustration on page B.*

Study Questions

A. What arguments do the authors of the Strike Commission report use to
justify the activities of labor unions? What union activities do they argue are
illegitimate? Does the Supreme Court decision in *In re Debs* take a different
view? Where does the court say that workingmen and unions should look
for redress of their grievances? Do you think that Debs was right that he was
denied his rights?

B. Are there similarities between the struggles of unions, women, and
African-Americans to gain recognition and protection of their rights? What
role have the courts and legislation played in each case? Why did both labor
and civil rights leaders (see Chapter 26) appeal to the Declaration of Independence? What is the connection between the Declaration and the rights
claims made by workingmen, women, and African Americans? Could those
claims be made without the Declaration?

C. Compare the attitudes about labor presented here with those in Volume 1,
Chapter 10. What similarities or differences do they seem to reflect the same
set of underlying assumptions about the role of the government in the economic relationships between labor and management?

A. United States Strike Commission, *Report on the Chicago Strike*, June–July 1894, December 10, 1894[1]

The commission has tried to find the drift of public opinion as to strike,
boycotts, and labor disputes upon railroads, and to find their remedy. The

---

[1] U.S. Strike Commission, Report of the Chicago Strike of June–July 1894 by the
United States Strike Commission (Washington D.C.: Government Printing Office,
1894).

invitation freely extended in this direction has brought before the commission many expressions of views, orally and by written communications. A condensation of these latter is presented with this report. In reaching its conclusions the commission has endeavored, after careful consideration, to give due weight to the many suggestions and arguments presented. It is encouraging to find general concurrence, even among labor leaders, in condemning strikes, boycotts, and lockouts as barbarisms unfit for the intelligence of this age, and as economically considered, very injurious and destructive forces. Whether won or lost is broadly immaterial. They are war—internecine war—and call for progress to a higher plane of education and intelligence in adjusting the relations of capital and labor. These barbarisms waste the products of both capital and labor, defy law and order, disturb society, intimidate capital, convert industrial paths where there ought to be plenty into highways of poverty and crime, bear as their fruit the arrogant flush of victory and the humiliating sting of defeat, and lead to preparations for greater and more destructive conflicts. Since nations have grown to the wisdom of avoiding disputes by conciliation, and even of settling them by arbitration, why should capital and labor in their dependence upon each other persist in cutting each other's throats as a settlement of differences? Official reports show that much progress has been made in the more sane direction of conciliation and arbitration even in America. Abroad they are in advance of us in this policy. Were our population as dense and opportunities as limited as abroad, present industrial conditions would keep us much more disturbed than we now are by contests between capital and labor.

In England, prior to 1824, it was conspiracy and felony for labor to unite for purposes now regarded there by all classes as desirable for the safety of the Government, of capital, and for the protection of the rights of labor.[2] All industrial labor is there, as a rule, covered by unions trained to greater conservatism through many disastrous conflicts under harsh conditions and surroundings. Capital abroad prefers to deal with these unions rather than with individuals or mobs, and from their joint efforts in good faith at conciliation and arbitration much good and many peaceful days have resulted. In fifteen of our States arbitration in various forms is now provided by law;

---

[2] Based on English common law, American law considered organized labor a conspiracy among workers to hinder the free competition for labor. This view began to change with some state court decisions in the first half of the nineteenth century. As the excerpt from In Re Debs in this chapter indicates, the U.S. government presented the efforts of labor to shut down rail traffic during the Pullman strike as a conspiracy.

the United States and eleven States have sanctioned labor organizations by statute. Some of our courts, however, are still poring over the law reports of antiquity in order to construe conspiracy out of labor unions. We also have employers who obstruct progress by perverting and misapplying the law of supply and demand, and who, while insisting upon individualism for workmen, demand that they shall be let alone to combine as they please and that society and all its forces shall protect them in their resulting contentions.

The general sentiment of employers, shared in by some of the most prominent railroad representatives we have heard, is now favorable to organization among employees. It results in a clearer presentation and calmer discussion of differences, instills mutual respect and forbearance, brings out the essentials, and eliminates misunderstandings and immaterial matters. To an ordinary observer, argument to sustain the justice and necessity of labor unions and unity of action by laborers is superfluous.

The rapid concentration of power and wealth, under stimulating legislative conditions, in persons, corporations, and monopolies has greatly changed the business and industrial situation. Our railroads were chartered upon the theory that their competition would amply protect shippers as to rates, etc., and employees as to wages and other conditions. Combination[3] has largely destroyed this theory, and has seriously disturbed the natural working of the laws of supply and demand, which, in theory, are based upon competition for labor between those who "demand" it as well as among those who supply it. The interstate commerce act and railroad-commission legislation in over thirty States are simply efforts of the people to free themselves from the results of this destruction of competition by combination. Labor is likewise affected by this progressive combination. While competition among railroad employers of labor is gradually disappearing, competition among those who supply labor goes on with increasing severity. For instance, as

---

[3] Control by one or more people over a number of firms operating in the same area of the economy, in this case railroads. A "Trust" was a way of establishing a combination. Shareholders in different corporations transferred their shares to one corporate entity that held them (hence, a "holding company"). A trust could be used to establish a monopoly over an area of the economy. For this reason, "trust busting" became part of the U.S. government's effort to ensure free markets in the United States. This paragraph in the Strike Commission's report described the effect of combinations or trusts on labor. *In re Debs* below referred to the American Railway Union effort to organize other unions to shut down railroad traffic as a "combination." See illustration on page B.

we have shown, there is no longer any competitive demand among the 24 railroads at Chicago for switchmen. They have ceased competing with each other; they are no longer 24 separate and competing employers; they are virtually one. To be sure, this combination has not covered the whole field of labor supply as yet, but it is constantly advancing in that direction. Competition for switchmen's labor still continues with outside employers, among whom, again, we find a like tendency to eliminate competitive demand for labor by similar combination. In view of this progressive perversion of the laws of supply and demand by capital and changed conditions, no man can well deny the right nor dispute the wisdom of unity for legislative and protective purposes among those who supply labor.

However men may differ about the propriety and legality of labor unions, we must all recognize the fact that we have them with us to stay and to grow more numerous and powerful. Is it not wise to fully recognize them by law; to admit their necessity as labor guides and protectors, to conserve their usefulness, increase their responsibility, and to prevent their follies and aggression by conferring upon them the privileges enjoyed by corporations, with like proper restrictions and regulations? The growth of corporate power and wealth has been the marvel of the past fifty years. Corporations have undoubtedly benefited the country and brought its resources to our doors. It will not be surprising if the marvel of the next fifty years be the advancement of labor to a position of like power and responsibility. We have heretofore encouraged the one and comparatively neglected the other. Does not wisdom demand that each be encouraged to prosper legitimately and to grow into harmonious relations of equal standing and responsibility before the law? This involves nothing hostile to the true interests and rights of either....

The commission deems recommendations of specific remedies premature. Such a problem, for instance, as universal Government ownership of railroads is too vast, many-sided, and far away, if at-tempted, to be considered as an immediate, practical remedy. It belongs to the socialistic group of public questions where Government ownership is advocated of monopolies, such as telegraphs, telephones, express companies, and municipal ownership of waterworks, gas and electric lighting, and street railways. These questions are pressing more urgently as time goes on. They need to be well studied and considered in every aspect by all citizens. Should continued combinations and consolidations result in half a dozen or less ownerships of our railroads within a few years, as is by no means unlikely, the question of Government ownership will be forced to the front, and we need to be ready to dispose of it intelligently. As combination goes on there will certainly at least have to be greater Government regulation and control of quasi-public corporations than we have now.

Whenever a nation or a state finds itself in such relation to a railroad that its investments therein must be either lost or protected by ownership, would it not be wise that the road be taken and the experiment be tried as an object lesson in Government ownership? The Massachusetts Railroad Commission, which is noted for its eminent services as a conservative pioneer in the direction of Government control of railroads through the force of public opinion, for several years urged that the experiment of State ownership be tried with the Fitchburg system, because of the large State investment in the Hoosac Tunnel. We need to fear everything revolutionary and wrong, but we need fear nothing that any nation can successfully attempt in directions made necessary by changed economic or industrial conditions. Other nations under their conditions own and operate telegraphs and railroad with varying results. Whether it is practicable for this nation to do so successfully when it becomes necessary to save an investment or when the people determine it shall be done, is an open and serious question which can not be answered fully except by actual experiment. . . .

In solving these questions, corporations seldom aid the efforts of the people or their legislators. Fear of change and the threatened loss of some power invariably make them obstructionists. They do not desire to be dealt with by any legislation; they simply want to be let alone, confident in their ability to protect themselves. Whatever is right to be done by statutes must be done by the people for their own protection and to meet the just demand that railroad labor shall have public and impartial hearing of all grievances.

The commission does not pretend to present a specific solution of these questions. Its effort is simply to present the facts; to point out that the relations of capital and labor are so disturbed as to urgently demand the attention of all thinking and patriotic citizens; to suggest a line of search for practical remedial legislation which may be followed with safety, and, finally, to urge and invite labor and railroads to hearty cooperation with the Government and the people in efforts to substitute law and reason in labor dispute for the dangers, sufferings, uncertainties, and wide-spread calamities incident to strikes, boycotts, and lockouts. . . . can we fix the hanging period?

The commission urges employers to recognize labor organizations; that such organizations be dealt with through representatives, with special reference to conciliation and arbitration when difficulties are threatened or arise. It is satisfied that employers should come in closer touch with labor and should recognize that, while the interests of labor and capital are not identical, they are reciprocal.

The commission is satisfied that if employers everywhere will endeavor to act in concert with labor; that if wages can be raised under economic conditions they can be raised voluntarily, and that if when there are reductions, reasons be given for the reduction, much friction can be avoided. It is also satisfied that if employers will consider employees as thoroughly essential to industrial success as capital, and thus take labor into consultation at proper times, much of the severity of strikes can be tempered and their number reduced.

B. "King Debs," *Harper's Weekly*, July 14, 1894[4]

See illustration on page B.

C. Associate Justice David Brewer, *In re Debs*, May 7, 1895[5]

MR. JUSTICE BREWER[6], after stating the case, delivered the opinion of the court.

The case presented by the bill[7] is this: the United States, finding that the interstate transportation of persons and property, as well as the carriage of the mails, is forcibly obstructed, and that a combination and conspiracy exists to subject the control of such transportation to the will of the conspirators, applied to one of their courts, sitting as a court of equity,[8] for an injunction to restrain such obstruction and prevent carrying into effect such conspiracy. Two questions of importance are presented: First. Are the relations of the general government to interstate commerce and the transportation of the

---

[4] King Debs—King Debs, created by William Allen Rogers in 1894. Library of Congress, LC-USZ62- 106100. https://goo.gl/UxGpFw
[5] *In re Debs*, 158 U.S. 564 (1895). Available online from Justia. https://goo.gl/efDRTw
[6] Associate Justice David Josiah Brewer (1837–1910). Appointed in 1889, Justice Brewer served on the Court until his death.
[7] a bill of complaint, not a law passed by a legislature
[8] A court of equity considers issues not adequately covered by the laws and issues decisions requiring or forbidding action. In most states and federal courts, equity and criminal courts are not separate and the term "court of equity" refers to the capacity in which a court acts. In a separate equity court, the judge is referred to as a chancellor. "Equity" and "chancellor" are terms that derive from the English legal system.

mails such as authorize a direct interference to prevent a forcible obstruction thereof. Second. If authority exists, as authority in governmental affairs
implies both power and duty, has a court of equity jurisdiction to issue an
injunction in aid of the performance of such duty.

First. What are the relations of the general government to interstate commerce and the transportation of the mails? They are those of direct supervision, control, and management. While, under the dual system which prevails
with us, the powers of government are distributed between the State and the
Nation, and while the latter is properly styled a government of enumerated
powers, yet within the limits of such enumeration, it has all the attributes of
sovereignty, and, in the exercise of those enumerated powers, acts directly
upon the citizen, and not through the intermediate agency of the State....

[*In support of this claim, Justice Brewer here cited judicial precedents as far
back as* McCulloch v. Maryland, 1819. *We have included in this excerpt only a
few of his other numerous references to and discussions of judicial precedents and
Congressional legislation.*]

Among the powers expressly given to the national government are the
control of interstate commerce and the creation and management of a post
office system for the nation. Article I, section 8, of the Constitution provides that

> the Congress shall have power... Third, to regulate commerce with
> foreign nations and among the several States, and with the Indian
> tribes.... Seventh, to establish post offices and post roads.

Congress has exercised the power granted in respect to interstate commerce in a variety of legislative acts....

As, under the Constitution, power over interstate commerce and the
transportation of the mails is vested in the national government, and Congress, by virtue of such grant, has assumed actual and direct control, it follows that the national government may prevent any unlawful and forcible
interference therewith. But how shall this be accomplished? Doubtless it is
within the competency of Congress to prescribe by legislation that any interference with these matters shall be offences against the United States, and
prosecuted and punished by indictment in the proper courts. But is that the
only remedy? Have the vast interests of the nation in interstate commerce
and in the transportation of the mails no other protection than lies in the
possible punishment of those who interfere with it?...

...The entire strength of the nation may be used to enforce in any part

URBAN GROWTH: THE PULLMAN STRIKE

of the land the full and free exercise of all national powers and the security of all rights entrusted by the Constitution to its care. The strong arm of the national government may be put forth to brush away all obstructions to the freedom of interstate commerce or the transportation of the mails. If the emergency arises, the army of the Nation, and all its militia, are at the service of the Nation to compel obedience to its laws....

... [T]he right to use force does not exclude the right of appeal to the courts for a judicial determination and for the exercise of all their powers of prevention. Indeed, it is more to the praise than to the blame of the government that, instead of determining for itself questions of right and wrong on the part of these petitioners and their associates and enforcing that determination by the club of the policeman and the bayonet of the soldier, it submitted all those questions to the peaceful determination of judicial tribunals, and involved their consideration and judgment as to the measure of its rights and powers and the correlative obligations of those against whom it made complaint. And it is equally to the credit of the latter that the judgment of those tribunals was by the great body of them respected, and the trouble which threatened so much disaster terminated.

Neither can it be doubted that the government has such an interest in the subject matter as enables it to appear as party plaintiff in this suit. It is said that equity only interferes for the protection of property, and that the government has no property interest. A sufficient reply is that the United States have a property in the mails, the protection of which was one of the purposes of this bill....

... Every government, entrusted, by the very terms of its being, with powers and duties to be exercised and discharged for the general welfare, has a right to apply to its own courts for any proper assistance in the exercise of the one and the discharge of the other, and it is no sufficient answer to its appeal to one of those courts that it has no pecuniary interest in the matter. The obligations which it is under to promote the interest of all, and to prevent the wrongdoing of one resulting in injury to the general welfare, is often, of itself, sufficient to give it a standing in court. This proposition in some of its relations has heretofore received the sanction of this court....

... [W]hile it is not the province of the government to interfere in any mere matter of private controversy between individuals, or to use its great powers to enforce the rights of one against another, yet, whenever the wrongs complained of are such as affect the public at large, and are in respect of matters which by the Constitution are entrusted to the care of the Nation and concerning which the Nation owes the duty to all the citizens of securing to them their common rights, then the mere fact that the government has no pecuniary interest in the controversy is not sufficient to exclude it from the courts or prevent it from taking measures therein to fully discharge those constitutional duties.

The national government, given by the Constitution power to regulate interstate commerce, has, by express statute, assumed jurisdiction over such commerce when carried upon railroads. It is charged, therefore, with the duty of keeping those highways of interstate commerce free from obstruction, for it has always been recognized as one of the powers and duties of a government to remove obstructions from the highways under its control. . . .

Up to a recent date, commerce, both interstate and international, was mainly by water, and it is not strange that both the legislation of Congress and the cases in the courts have been principally concerned therewith. The fact that, in recent years, interstate commerce has come mainly to be carried on by railroads and over artificial highways has in no manner narrowed the scope of the constitutional provision or abridged the power of Congress over such commerce. On the contrary, the same fullness of control exists in the one case as in the other, and the same power to remove obstruction from the one as from the other. Constitutional provisions do not change, but their operation extends to new matters as the modes of business and the habits of life of the people vary with each succeeding generation. . . . The Constitution has not changed. The power is the same. But it operates today upon modes of interstate commerce unknown to the fathers,[9] and it will operate with equal force upon any new modes of such commerce which the future may develop. It is said that seldom have the courts assumed jurisdiction to restrain by injunction in suits brought by the government, either state or national, obstructions to highways, either artificial or natural. This is undoubtedly true, but the reason is that the necessity for such interference has only been occasional. Ordinarily, the local authorities have taken full control over the matter, and by indictment for misdemeanor, or in some kindred way, have secured the removal of the obstruction and the cessation of the nuisance. . . .

That the bill filed in this case alleged special facts calling for the exercise of all the powers of the court is not open to question. The picture drawn in it of the vast interests involved, not merely of the city of Chicago and the State of Illinois, but of all the States, and the general confusion into which the interstate commerce of the country was thrown; the forcible interference with that commerce; the attempted exercise by individuals of powers

---

[9] the founding fathers—those who designed the Constitution

belonging only to government, and the threatened continuance of such invasions of public right, presented a condition of affairs which called for the fullest exercise of all the powers of the courts. If ever there was a special exigency, one which demanded that the court should do all that courts can do, it was disclosed by this bill, and we need not turn to the public history of the day, which only reaffirms with clearest emphasis all its allegations...

Again, it is objected that it is outside of the jurisdiction of a court of equity to enjoin the commission of crimes. This, as a general proposition, is unquestioned. A chancellor has no criminal jurisdiction. Something more than the threatened commission of an offence against the laws of the land is necessary to call into exercise the injunctive powers of the court. There must be some interferences, actual or threatened, with property or rights of a pecuniary nature, but when such interferences appear, the jurisdiction of a court of equity arises, and is not destroyed by the fact that they are accompanied by, or are themselves, violations of the criminal law....

Nor is there in this any invasion of the constitutional right of trial by jury. ... But the power of a court to make an order carries with it the equal power to punish for a disobedience of that order, and the inquiry as to the question of disobedience has been from time immemorial the special function of the court. And this is no technical rule. In order that a court may compel obedience to its orders, it must have the right to inquire whether there has been any disobedience thereof. To submit the question of disobedience to another tribunal, be it a jury or another court, would operate to deprive the proceeding of half its efficiency....

In brief, a court, enforcing obedience to its orders by proceedings for contempt, is not executing the criminal laws of the land, but only securing to suitors the rights which it has adjudged them entitled to....

... It surely cannot be seriously contended that the court has jurisdiction to enjoin the obstruction of a highway by one person, but that its jurisdiction ceases when the obstruction is by a hundred persons. It may be true, as suggested, that, in the excitement of passion, a mob will pay little heed to processes issued from the courts, and it may be, as said by counsel in argument, that it would savor somewhat of the puerile and ridiculous to have read a writ of injunction to Lee's army during the late civil war. It is doubtless true that *inter arma leges silent*,[10] and in the throes of rebellion or revolution, the processes of civil courts are of little avail, for the power of the courts rests on the general support of the people and their recognition of the fact that peaceful

---

[10] in time of war laws are silent

remedies are the true resort for the correction of wrongs. But does not counsel's argument imply too much? Is it to be assumed that these defendants were conducting a rebellion or inaugurating a revolution, and that they and their associates were thus placing themselves beyond the reach of the civil process of the courts? We find in the opinion of the Circuit Court a quotation from the testimony given by one of the defendants before the United States Strike Commission, which is sufficient answer to this suggestion:

> As soon as the employees found that we were arrested, and taken from the scene of action, they became demoralized, and that ended the strike. It was not the soldiers that ended the strike. It was not the old brotherhoods that ended the strike. It was simply the United States courts that ended the strike.... [N]ot by the army, and not by any other power, but simply and solely by the action of the United States courts in restraining us from discharging our duties as officers and representatives of our employees.

Whatever any single individual may have thought or planned, the great body of those who were engaged in these transactions contemplated neither rebellion nor revolution, and when, in the due order of legal proceedings, the question of right and wrong was submitted to the courts, and by them decided, they unhesitatingly yielded to their decisions. The outcome, by the very testimony of the defendants, attests the wisdom of the course pursued by the government, and that it was well not to oppose force simply by force, but to invoke the jurisdiction and judgment of those tribunals to whom, by the Constitution and in accordance with the settled conviction of all citizens, is committed the determination of questions of right and wrong between individuals, masses, and States.

It must be borne in mind that this bill was not simply to enjoin a mob and mob violence. It was not a bill to command a keeping of the peace; much less was its purport to restrain the defendants from abandoning whatever employment they were engaged in. The right of any laborer, or any number of laborers, to quit work was not challenged. The scope and purpose of the bill was only to restrain forcible obstructions of the highways along which interstate commerce travels and the mails are carried. And the facts set forth at length are only those facts which tended to show that the defendants were engaged in such obstructions.

A most earnest and eloquent appeal was made to us in eulogy of the heroic spirit of those who threw up their employment, and gave up their means of earning a livelihood, not in defense of their own rights, but in sympathy [with] and to assist others whom they believed to be wronged. We yield to none in our admiration of any act of heroism or self-sacrifice, but we may be permitted to add that it is a lesson which cannot be learnt too soon or too thoroughly that, under this government of and by the people, the means of redress of all wrongs are through the courts and at the ballot box, and that no wrong, real or fancied, carries with it legal warrant to invite as a means of redress the cooperation of a mob, with its accompanying acts of violence.

We have given to this case the most careful and anxious attention, for we realize that it touches closely questions of supreme importance to the people of this country. Summing up our conclusions, we hold that the government of the United States is one having jurisdiction over every foot of soil within its territory, and acting directly upon each citizen; that, while it is a government of enumerated powers, it has within the limits of those powers all the attributes of sovereignty; that to it is committed power over interstate commerce and the transmission of the mail; that the powers thus conferred upon the national government are not dormant, but have been assumed and put into practical exercise by the legislation of Congress; that, in the exercise of those powers, it is competent[11] for the nation to remove all obstructions upon highways, natural or artificial, to the passage of interstate commerce or the carrying of the mail; that while it may be competent for the government (through the executive branch and in the use of the entire executive power of the nation) to forcibly remove all such obstructions, it is equally within its competency to appeal to the civil courts for an inquiry and determination as to the existence and character of any alleged obstructions, and, if such are found to exist, or threaten to occur, to invoke the powers of those courts to remove or restrain such obstructions; that the jurisdiction of courts to interfere in such matter by injunction is one recognized from ancient times and by indubitable authority; that such jurisdiction is not ousted by the fact that the obstructions are accompanied by or consist of acts in themselves violations of the criminal law; that the proceeding by injunction is of a civil character, and may be enforced by proceedings in contempt; that such proceedings are not in execution of the criminal laws of the land; that the penalty for a violation of injunction is no substitute for, and no defense to, a prosecution for any criminal offences committed in the course of such violation; that the complaint filed in this case clearly showed an existing obstruction of artificial highways for the passage of interstate commerce and the transmission of

---

[11] acceptable

the mail—an obstruction not only temporarily existing, but threatening to continue; that, under such complaint, the Circuit Court had power to issue its process of injunction; that, it having been issued and served on these defendants, the Circuit Court had authority to inquire whether its orders had been disobeyed, and, when it found that they had been, then to proceed under section 725, Revised Statutes ... [to] enter the order of punishment complained of; and, finally, that, the Circuit Court having full jurisdiction in the premises, its finding of the fact of disobedience is not open to review on habeas corpus in this or any other court. ...

We enter into no examination of the act of July 2, 1890, c. 647, 26 Stat. 209,[12] upon which the Circuit Court relied mainly to sustain its jurisdiction. It must not be understood from this that we dissent from the conclusions of that court in reference to the scope of the act, but simply that we prefer to rest our judgment on the broader ground which has been discussed in this opinion, believing it of importance that the principles underlying it should be fully stated and affirmed.

The petition for a writ of habeas corpus is

Denied.

D. Eugene V. Debs, "Liberty: Speech at Battery D, Chicago," On Release from Woodstock Jail, November 22, 1895[13]

Manifestly the spirit of '76 still survives. The fires of liberty and noble aspirations are not yet extinguished. I greet you tonight as lovers of liberty and as despisers of despotism. I comprehend the significance of this demonstration and appreciate the honor that makes it possible for me to be your guest on such an occasion. The vindication and glorification of American principles of government, as proclaimed to the world in the Declaration of Independence, is the high purpose of this convocation.

Speaking for myself personally, I am not certain whether this is an occasion for rejoicing or lamentation. I confess to a serious doubt as to whether this day marks my deliverance from bondage to freedom or my doom from freedom to bondage. Certain it is, in the light of recent judicial proceedings,

---

[12] Sherman Anti-Trust Act (1890), which declared illegal "every contract, combination in the form of trust or otherwise, or conspiracy, in restraint of trade or commerce among the several States, or with foreign nations."
[13] *Debs: His Life, Writings and Speeches* (Chicago: Charles H. Kerr & Company, 1904), 337–344.

that I stand in your presence stripped of my constitutional rights as a free-man and shorn of the most sacred prerogatives of American citizenship, and what is true of myself is true of every other citizen who has the temerity to protest against corporation rule or question the absolute sway of the money power. It is not law nor the administration of law of which I complain. It is the flagrant violation of the Constitution, the total abrogation of law and the usurpation of judicial and despotic power, by virtue of which my colleagues and myself were committed to jail, against which I enter my solemn protest; and any honest analysis of the proceedings must sustain the haggard[14] truth of the indictment.

In a letter recently written by the venerable Judge Trumbull that eminent jurist[15] says: "The doctrine announced by the Supreme Court in the Debs case, carried to its logical conclusion, places every citizen at the mercy of any prejudiced or malicious federal judge who may think proper to imprison him.". . .

At this juncture I deem it proper to voice my demands for a trial by a jury of my peers. At the instigation of the railroad corporations centering here in Chicago, I was indicted for conspiracy and I insist[ed] upon being tried as to my innocence or guilt. It will be remembered that the trial last winter termi-nated very abruptly on account of a sick juror. It was currently reported at the time that this was merely a pretext to abandon the trial and thus defeat the vindication of a favorable verdict, which seemed inevitable, and which would have been in painfully embarrassing contrast with the sentence previously pronounced by Judge [William A.] Woods in substantially the same case.[16]

Whether this be true or not, I do not know. I do know, however, that I have been denied a trial,[17] and here and now I demand a hearing of my case. I am charged with conspiracy to commit a crime, and if guilty I should go to the penitentiary. All I ask is a fair trial and no favor. If the counsel for the government, alias the railroads, have been correctly quoted in the press, the case against me is "not to be pressed," as they "do not wish to appear in the light of persecuting the defendants." I repel with scorn their professed mercy. Simple justice is the demand. I am not disposed to shrink from the fullest

---

[14] The word "haggard" means careworn; Debs seems to use it to mean "threadbare" or "very thin."

[15] Trumbull was one of Debs' attorneys.

[16] Debs refers here apparently to the contempt ruling by Woods.

[17] Debs' attorneys argued, among other things, that he had been denied a trial on the contempt charge, a violation of the Sixth Amendment to the constitution.

responsibility for my acts. I have had time for meditation and reflection and I have no hesitancy in declaring that under the same circumstances I would pursue precisely the same policy. So far as my acts are concerned, I have neither apology nor regrets....

The theme tonight is personal liberty; or giving it its full height, depth and breadth—American liberty, something that Americans have been accustomed to eulogize since the foundation of the Republic, and multiplied thousands of them continue in the habit to this day because they do not recognize the truth that in the imprisonment of one man in defiance of all constitutional guarantees, the liberties of all are invaded and placed in peril. In saying this, I conjecture I have struck the keynote of alarm that has convoked this vast audience.

For the first time in the records of all the ages, the inalienable rights of man, "life, liberty and the pursuit of happiness," were proclaimed July 4, 1776.

Strike the fetters from the slave, give him liberty and he becomes an inhabitant of a new world. He looks abroad and beholds life and joy in all things around him. His soul expands beyond all boundaries. Emancipated by the genius of Liberty, he aspires to communion with all that is noble and beautiful, feels himself allied to all the higher order of intelligences, and walks abroad, redeemed from animalism, ignorance and super-stition, a new being throbbing with glorious life....

...As Americans, we have boasted of our liberties and continue to boast of them. They were once the nation's glory, and, if some have vanished, it may be well to remember that a remnant still remains. Out of prison, beyond the limits of Russian injunctions, out of reach of a deputy marshal's club, above the throttling clutch of corporations and the enslaving power of plutocracy, out of range of the government's machine guns and knowing the location of judicial traps and deadfalls, Americans may still indulge in the exaltation of liberty, though pursued through every lane and avenue of life by the baying hounds of usurped and unconstitutional power, glad if when night lets down her sable curtains, they are out of prison, though still the wage-slaves of a plutocracy which, were it in the celestial city, would wreck every avenue leading up to the throne of the Infinite by stealing the gold with which they are paved, and debauch Heaven's supreme court to obtain a decision that the command "thou shalt not steal" is unconstitutional....

...Above all, what is the duty of American workingmen whose liberties have been placed in peril? They are not hereditary bondsmen. Their fathers were free born—their sovereignty none denied and their children yet have the ballot. It has been called "a weapon that executes a free man's will as lighting does the will of God."[18] It is a metaphor pregnant with life and truth. There is nothing in our government it cannot remove or amend. It can make and unmake presidents and congresses and courts. It can abolish unjust laws and consign to eternal odium and oblivion unjust judges, strip from them their robes and gowns and send them forth unclean as lepers to bear the burden of merited obloquy as Cain with the mark of a murderer. It can sweep away trusts, syndicates, corporations, monopolies, and every other abnormal development of the money power designed to abridge the liberties of workingmen and enslave them by the degradation incident to poverty and enforced idleness, as cyclones scatter the leaves of the forest. The ballot can do all this and more. It can give our civilization its crowning glory—the cooperative commonwealth....

In the great Pullman Strike, the American Railway Union challenged the power of corporations in a way that had not previously been done, and the analyzation of this fact serves to expand it to proportions that the most conservative men of the nation regard with alarm. It must be borne in mind that the American Railway Union did not challenge the government. It threw down no gauntlet to courts or armies—it simply resisted the invasion of the rights of workingmen by corporations. It challenged and defied the power of corporations. Thrice armed with a just cause, the organization believed that justice would win for labor a notable victory, and the records proclaim that its confidence was not misplaced.

The corporations, left to their own resources of money, mendacity and malice, of thugs and ex-convicts, leeches and lawyers, would have been overwhelmed with defeat and the banners of organized labor would have floated triumphant in the breeze.

This the corporations saw and believed—hence the crowning act of infamy in which the federal courts and the federal armies participated, and which culminated in the defeat of labor....

... [T]he defeat of the American Railway Union involved questions of law, Constitution and government which, all things considered, are without a parallel in court and governmental proceedings under the Constitution of the Republic. And it is this judicial and administrative usurpation of power to override the rights of states and strike down the liberties of the people that has conferred upon the incidents connected with the Pullman strike such commanding importance as to attract the attention of men of the highest

[18] Debs paraphrases lines from the anti-slavery poem "A Word From a Petitioner," (1837) by John Pierpont.

attainments in constitutional law and of statesmen who, like Jefferson, view
with alarm the processes by which the Republic is being wrecked and a despotism reared upon its ruins....

From such reflections I turn to the practical lessons taught by this "Liberation Day" demonstration. It means that American lovers of liberty are
setting in operation forces to rescue their constitutional liberties from the
grasp of monopoly and its mercenary hirelings. It means that the people are
aroused in view of impending perils and that agitation, organization, and
unification are to be the future battle cries of men who will not part with their
birthrights and, like Patrick Henry, will have the courage to exclaim: "Give
me liberty or give me death!"[19] I have borne with such composure as I could
command the imprisonment which deprived me of my liberty. Were I a criminal; were I guilty of crimes meriting a prison cell; had I ever lifted my hand
against the life or the liberty of my fellowmen; had I ever sought to filch their
good name, I would not be here. I would have fled from the haunts of civilization and taken up my residence in some cave where the voice of my kindred
is never heard. But I am standing here without a self-accusation of crime or
criminal intent festering in my conscience, in the sunlight once more, among
my fellowmen, contributing as best I can to make this "Liberation Day" from
Woodstock prison a memorial day, realizing that, as Lowell sang:

> He's true to God who's true to man; wherever wrong is done,
> To the humblest and the weakest, 'neath the all-beholding sun.
> That wrong is also done to us, and they are slaves most base,
> Whose love of right is for themselves and not for all their race.[20]

---

[19] Henry (1736–1799) was an outspoken leader of the Patriot cause in the Virginia
House of Burgesses who allegedly ended a speech protesting the actions of Parlia-
ment against the colonies with this inflammatory remark.
[20] from James Russell Lowell, "On the Capture of Fugitive Slaves Near Washington" (1845)

CHAPTER 19

The Progressive Era: Eugenics

A. Governor Samuel W. Pennypacker, Veto of Eugenics Law, March 30, 1905
B. G. Stanley Hall, "Eugenics as a New Creed," 1911
C. New York Times, "Pastors for Eugenics," June 6, 1913
D. Supreme Court of Indiana, Judgment, November Term, 1920
E. Associate Justice Oliver Wendell Holmes, *Buck v. Bell*, May 2, 1927
F. "Better Baby Contest," Indiana State Fair, 1931

For about 30 years, from around 1900 to the late 1920s, America had an active and popular eugenics movement (see photo on page C). Supporters of eugenics argued the public good required removing from the population genes thought to cause low intelligence, or immoral, criminal or anti-social behavior. Beginning with Connecticut in 1896, states passed laws requiring medical exams before issuing marriage licenses to make sure the unfit did not reproduce. (See Document C for an effort to support such laws.) Indiana passed the first compulsory sterilization law in 1907, although other states had tried and failed before (Document A). Prominent Americans—among them Theodore Roosevelt, Stanford University President David Starr Jordan, W. E. B. Du Bois, and Margaret Sanger—supported the eugenics movement, as did such organizations as the National Federation of Women's Clubs, the National Conference of Charities and Corrections, and various religious organizations. State Fairs included Better Baby contests (Document F). As the list of its supporters indicates, eugenics was considered a progressive reform, related to the larger Progressive movement by its emphasis on the good of society and the use of science and rationality to achieve it.

Eugenics always had its critics. A referendum authorizing sterilization failed in Oregon in 1913. Some governors refused to sign eugenic legislation (Document A). Nebraska's governor vetoed a eugenics bill in 1913, writing that the legislation was "only an experiment and it seems more in keeping with the pagan age than with the teachings of Christianity. Man is more than an animal." Not every state legislature passed such legislation. Federal and state courts regularly found forced sterilization laws unconstitutional because they were cruel and unusual punishments or because the application of the laws denied equal treatment (Document D).

In addition to more conservative Protestants, Catholics and their clergy largely opposed eugenics.

Despite the opposition it faced, eugenic sterilization remained alive in part because of the Supreme Court decision Buck v. Bell (Document E), which found constitutional the sterilization of Carrie Buck by the State of Virginia. From the beginning, Buck's sterilization was intended to be a test case. Supporters of eugenics and sterilization hoped the case would reach the Supreme Court and that the Court would find sterilization constitutional. This would at once supersede all the rulings of state courts against sterilization. Buck's guardian, appointed by those intending to sterilize her, took her case to Virginia state courts and eventually the Supreme Court. (The lower Virginia court found no grounds to block the sterilization.) The Supreme Court decided that nothing in the U.S. Constitution prevented Virginia from sterilizing Buck. Eight of nine justices joined in the decision, written by Justice Oliver Wendell Holmes, perhaps the preeminent jurist of the time. Holmes' decision contained the now infamous remark, "Three generations of imbeciles are enough." The only dissent in the case came from Associate Justice Pierce Butler, a Catholic.

Sterilization continued as a legal regime even after eugenics ceased to be a popular movement. Thirty-one states eventually had sterilization programs, often adopting the language of the Virginia legislation that the Supreme Court approved, which had been drafted by a lawyer to increase its chances of meeting legal scrutiny. Sterilizations increased and did not cease until the 1960s. (The sterilization program in North Carolina lasted until 1977.) California, a leading Progressive state, sterilized about 20,000 people, a third or so of the almost 70,000 individuals sterilized in the United States.

Toward the end of his discussion of eugenics (Document B), G. Stanley Hall wrote of "the kingdom of some kind of superman" to which eugenics might lead. This remark foreshadowed the darkness of the Holocaust and reminds us that Hitler cited America's eugenics movement and laws as a precedent.

Study Questions

A. Some proponents of eugenic sterilization argued that if vaccination was an acceptable public health measure, and compulsory vaccination legal, then compulsory sterilization should be as well. Does that argument make sense? What about the claim of Justice Holmes that if young men can be conscripted to fight and possibly die for their country, then compulsory sterilization should be acceptable? Is that a good argument for forced sterilization? In the last paragraph of his opinion, Justice Holmes addressed the question of equal treatment before the law. What was his argument? Was it a good argument? How did some Christians reconcile eugenics and the moral teachings of Christianity? What does the case of the eugenics movement in the United States tell us about the relationship between science and politics?

B. A leading progressive, Albert Beveridge, argued that human efforts could regenerate the world (see Chapter 20, Document B). Is there a connection between such views and the eugenics movement?

C. In what ways are the arguments about eugenics reminiscent of the arguments in favor of slavery in Volume 1, Chapters 12 and 15? How might either set of arguments be evaluated in light of the Declaration of Independence (Appendix A)?

A. Governor Samuel W. Pennypacker, Veto of Eugenics Law, March 30, 1905[1]

Commonwealth of Pennsylvania
Executive Department
Harrisburg, March 30, 1905
To the Honorable, the Senate of the Commonwealth of Pennsylvania:

Gentlemen: I return herewith, without my approval Senate Bill No. 35, entitled, "An Act for the prevention of idiocy." This bill has what may be called with propriety an attractive title. If idiocy could be prevented by an act of assembly, we may be quite sure that such an act would have long been passed and approved in this state, and that such laws would have been enacted in all civilized countries. The subject of the act is not the prevention of idiocy, but it is to provide that in every institution in the state, entrusted with the care of idiots and imbecile children, a neurologist, a surgeon and a physician shall be authorized to perform an operation upon the inmates "for the prevention of procreation." What is the nature of the operation is not described but it is such an operation as they shall decide to be "safest and most effective." It is plain that the safest and most effective method of preventing procreation

---

[1] Harry Hamilton Laughlin, *Eugenical Sterilization in the United States* (Chicago: Psychopathic Laboratory of the Municipal Court of Chicago, December 1922), 35–36. Laughlin's book was a compendium of legislation, veto messages, and court cases concerning sterilization. Its purpose was to promote sterilization, especially by helping state legislatures pass sterilization laws that would avoid vetoes and survive court review.

would be to cut the heads off the inmates, and such authority is given by the
bill to this staff of scientific experts. It is not probable that they would resort
to this means for the prevention of procreation, but it is probable that they
would endeavor to destroy some part of the human organism. Scientists, like
all other men whose experiences have been limited to one pursuit, and whose
minds have been developed in a particular direction, sometimes need to be
restrained. Men of high scientific attainments are prone, in their love for tech-
nique, to lose sight of broad principles outside of their domain of thought. A
surgeon may possibly be so eager to advance in skill as to be forgetful of the
danger to his patient. Anatomists may be willing to gather information by
the infliction of pain and suffering upon helpless creatures, although a higher
standard of conduct would teach them that it is far better for humanity to bear
its own ills than to escape them by knowledge only secured through cruelty
to other creatures. This bill, whatever good might possibly result from it if
its provisions should become a law, violates the principles of ethics. These
feeble-minded and imbecile children have been entrusted to the institutions
by their parents or guardians for the purpose of training and instruction. It is
proposed to experiment upon them, not for their instruction, but in order to
help society in the future. It is to be done without their consent, which they
cannot give, and without the consent of their parents or guardians, who are
responsible for their welfare. It would be in contravention of the laws which
have been enacted for the establishment of these institutions. These laws
have in contemplation the training and the instruction of the children. This
bill assumes that they cannot be so instructed and trained. Moreover, the
course it is proposed to pursue would have a tendency to prevent such training and instruction. Everyone knows, whether he be a scientist or an ordinary
observer, that to destroy virility is to lessen the capacity, the energy and the
spirit which lead to effort. The bill is, furthermore, illogical in its thought.
Idiocy will not be prevented by the prevention of procreation among these
inmates. This mental condition is due to causes many of which are entirely
beyond our knowledge. It existed long before there were ever such inmates
of such institutions. If this plan is to be adopted, to make it effective it should
be carried into operation in the world at large, and not in institutions where
the inmates are watched by nurses, kept separate, and have all the care which
is likely to render procreation there very rare, if not altogether impossible.
In one of these institutions, I am reliably informed, there have only been
three births in ten years. A great objection is that the bill would encourage
experimentation upon living animals, and would be the beginning of experimentation upon living human beings, leading logically to results which can

THE PROGRESSIVE ERA: EUGENICS

readily be forecasted. The chief physician, in charge at Elwyn,[2] has candidly told us, in an article recently published upon "Heredity," that "Studies in heredity tend to emphasize the wisdom of those ancient peoples who taught that the healthful development of the individual and the elimination of the weakling was the truest patriotism—springing from an abiding sense of the fulfillment of a duty to the state."

To permit such an operation would be to inflict cruelty upon a helpless class in the community which the state has undertaken to protect. However skillfully performed, it would at times lead to peritonitis, blood poisoning, lockjaw and death. For these reasons the bill is not approved.

SAML. W. PENNYPACKER

B. G. Stanley Hall, "Eugenics as a New Creed," 1911[3]

... Galton[4] and his followers would have eugenics proclaimed as the new religion of the future, the religion of this rather than of another life. The slogan of eugenics, a new religion, the religion of this world, not of another, has caught the imagination and won the applause of many who are critical if not hostile to Christianity. It does indeed suggest a creed and a cult which modern culture and especially science and most of all those who serve the great *biologos* or spirit of life, would place as the supreme end of man. But I

---

[2] Martin W. Barr was the physician in charge of Elwyn. Elwyn was Pennsylvania's institution for disabled children, established in 1852. Pennypacker may have been quoting from Barr, *Mental Defectives: Their History, Treatment, and Training* (Philadelphia: P. Blakiston's Son & Company, 1904).

[3] G. Stanley Hall, "Eugenics: Its Ideals and What It Is Going to Do," *Religious Education* 6, 2 (June 1911): 152–159. This excerpt is from pages 156–159. G. Stanley Hall (1846–1924) was perhaps the leading psychologist of his time, when psychology was still emerging as a discipline distinct from philosophy. Raised in a religious family, Hall attended Union Theological Seminary before deciding to study psychology with William James at Harvard, where he earned a Ph. D. in psychology in 1878, the first awarded in the United States. His early teaching career was in philosophy departments at Williams and Johns Hopkins. At Johns Hopkins, he set up a psychology laboratory, perhaps the first in the United States. For many years, he was President of Clark University in Worcester, Massachusetts. Hall was a well-respected figure in American higher education and intellectual life.

[4] Francis Galton (1822–1911), an English polymath, invented the term "eugenics" to describe the effort he encouraged of improving humans through control of their breeding.

ask in closing why call it a new religion? Is not all of it simply a legitimate new
interpretation of our Christianity? Is it not all latent in our Scriptures? Was
anything more characteristic of the ancient Hebrews of Old Testament days
than their purity and to keep the purity of their blood, than duties of parents
to children and vice versa, and is there any trait more peculiar to the Jews
in our day than that they excel all races save perhaps one in fecundity? The
very covenant of Yahweh with Abraham, the great cattle-breeding sheik who
founded the Jewish nation, was that if he kept God's law his seeds should be as
the stars of heaven for multitude, as if that were indeed the chief human felic-
ity. This means according to the newest and highest psychogenetic criticism
that Jehovah's laws are at bottom those of eugenics. The supreme criterion of
virtue indeed is[:] living in every item for the interests of posterity. The world
is for the chosen, the best. It belongs to those who come after us, who will be
in number like the grains of sand upon the shore. That their seed fail not is
the supreme blessing. The entire Old Testament from the myth of Eden to the
latest prophets needs a new eugenics exegesis; while the dominant theme of
the New Testament is love, the strongest thing in the soul of man, centered
upon service and welfare of the race. Love and serve God and man; that is the
quintessence of our religion. We only need to turn a little larger proportion
of the love and service we have directed toward God, who does not need it,
to man who does, and we have eugenics, for who serves mankind so much
as he who transmits the sacred torch of heredity, which is the most precious
of all wealths and worths, undimmed to later generations by bringing more
and better men and women into the world and rearing them to the fullest
possible maturity! Every human institution, family, school, state and church
are in their last analysis, graded and measured by what they contribute to this
all-comprehendingness. I can merely say it in bare phrases here but think it
out for yourselves, think seriously; read in this field and you will see only what
has so long lay in concealed Christianity standing forth here revealed. The
beatitudes are full of it. The meek inherit the earth on the simple biological
law that over-individuation is at the expense of genesis and beyond a certain
point inversely as it. Nothing was ever so pedagogically potent in quenching
youthful passion as hell-fire when it was believed in. The better elements of
the gross phallic religions that once covered the whole earth are all retained
and sublimated in Christianity. Do you clergymen falter in your belief in
total depravity or are you unsound on the doctrine of the unpardonable sin?
If so, you only need to hear as I sometimes do youth who have lost all control
of their passions and feel that the possibilities of normal parenthood are forever lost to them or that they are tainted with venereal disease and that their

ancestry must end with them, in order to realize that the ancient makers of this new life in all the intimacy of the confessional had at their disposal both a diagnosis and a psychotherapy that we have well-nigh lost. Mr. Northcote, the author of *Christianity and Sex Problems*,[5] is right. Those who know not sex and eugenics know not the essence of Christianity.

Christianity has never said all that it meant. It is not yet all revealed to man. Scholarship on the one hand and religious experience on the other are constantly finding deeper, larger things in it, things not read into but evolved out of it. Since Darwin showed how much of the whole process of selection by which ever higher forms of life were unfolded was sexual and that many of the best things from flowers onward and play activities up were secondary sex qualities, and again since psychotherapy has shown the hither-to undreamed-of potency of this factor in human nature to make health and disease, sex also is becoming more and more long-circuited and spiritualized or literally transfigured with new potency until now we have in it almost a new organ of apperception for moral and religious experience, confirming much that some had begun to doubt and reviving much that we were well on toward forgetting. Love rules the court, the camp, the grove, for "love is God and God is love" might be the watchword of the new eugenic aspect of Christianity. To separate religion and sex does great wrong to both, for to teach sex, at least to the young, without religion is to leave out the motivation which is most practical and effective and to conceive Christianity without sex is to lose some of its choicest and deepest insights. In fine, sex and reproduction have played a more and more important role in each of the following fields, in some of which they are already dominant; in natural history since Darwin's sex selection; in anthropology and sociology from McLennan to Havelock Ellis; in criminology since Lombroso; in medicine since Krafft-Ebing, Tarnowski and Moll and the advocates of prophylaxis; in psychology beginning with Freud and his followers; in morals since Sutherland's biological ethics; in religion since Ferguson, Furlong, Inman, Morse and Northcote.[6] In all

---

[5] Hugh Northcote (1868–1933), was an Anglican priest. *Christianity and Sex Problems* appeared in 1906 (Philadelphia: F. A. Davis and Company, 1906; 2nd edition 1916).
[6] John Ferguson McLennan (1827–1881), an anthropologist who wrote about marriage; Havelock Ellis (1859–1939) a physician who studied human sexuality; Cesare Lombroso (1835–1909), a physician who argued that criminal behavior was inherited; Richard von Krafft-Ebing (1840–1902), a psychiatrist who studied sexual pathologies; Benjamin Tarnowski (1837–1906), a doctor who studied human sexuality; Albert Moll (1862–1939), a psychiatrist who studied human sexuality; Alexander Sutherland (1852–1902), author of *The Origin and Growth of the Moral Instinct* (1898).

these fields sex is a common ground of larger and larger dimensions. It gives them more interest in each other and may be destined to bring them into a new and higher unity. The time for this scientific synthesis has not yet come and may be long delayed, inevitable though it seems sooner or later. Meanwhile, eugenics draws upon all these domains and has pointed out many and will, let us hope, find out many more practical ways of improving the human stock and helping the world on towards the kingdom of some kind of superman to which the men of to-day may some day prove to be only a transition, a link which with all that absorbs us now may be lost sight of and possibly become a missing link.

C. New York Times, "Pastors for Eugenics," June 6, 1913[7]

Drs. Keigwin and Hillis Invite Richard Bennett to Speak in Churches.

The Rev. Dr. A. E. Keigwin announced a platform meeting[8] yesterday in the West End Presbyterian Church, at Amsterdam Avenue and 105th Street, for next Sunday night on the subject of eugenics. One of the speakers will be Richard Bennett, the actor.[9] The Rev. Dr. Newell Dwight Hillis is another pastor who plans to push a eugenics campaign. He arranged with Mr. Bennett yesterday for a meeting early in the Fall in Plymouth Church, Brooklyn, similar to the one to be held next Sunday night in West End Church.[10]

"Much of our public difficulty and more of our public expense to-day are due, in my judgement," said the Rev. Dr. Keigwin yesterday, "to the dense ignorance of young men and women about the weightier physical affairs of human life. I heartily approve of this present movement, and think Christian ministers may well forego vacations to push it. If we will deliver men

---

Inman is perhaps Thomas Inman (1820–1876) a physician and writer on religious topics. Morse is perhaps Josiah Morse (1879–1946), a professor of philosophy who wrote on religion, including *Pathological Aspects of Religion* (Worcester: Clark University Press, 1906). We have not identified Ferguson and Furlong.

[7] "Pastors for Eugenics," *New York Times*, June 6, 1913, 10.

[8] A meeting to establish a program of action, from which we get the phrase a political party platform, meaning the principles upon which the party will stand at an election.

[9] Richard Bennett (1870–1944) was known for impromptu speeches at the end of his theatrical productions in which he commented on social issues.

[10] Plymouth Church, in Brooklyn, had a long history of social progressivism and Christian liberal theology, having been founded by abolitionist Henry Ward Beecher in the mid-nineteenth century.

and women from the shackles of ignorance concerning themselves, we shall effect a reform that is vital to the whole human family, and especially to our own country."

The Liberal Ministers Association of New York, composed of Unitarian and Universalist pastors, and reform rabbis, among them the Rev. Drs. Wise, Magnes, Mendes, and Silverman, has appointed a Eugenics Committee, with the Rev. Edgar S. Weirs of Montclair as Chairman. It is charged to investigate the subject this Summer and report next Fall. The Rev. Dr. John Haynes Holmes, as a member of the association, said yesterday:

"What the recommendations of this committee may be I know not, but for myself I hope and shall urge that the association binds all of its members as a group to perform nothing, but health marriages. I believe in the health marriage. Both parties should present certificates, and ministers ought not to marry any who cannot. That is the ideal. The difficulty is to carry the ideal out. Eventually the State will make it a law. While we are waiting for the State to act, what are we to do? I feel it is the business of the Church to show the way because the Church has a moral responsibility. Such an important matter ought not to be left to the individual minister. Acting alone, he can accomplish little. Ministers should act in groups. Dean Sumner and the Chicago Cathedral have shown us the way."[11]

Two pastors of Fifth Avenue churches advocated the plan yesterday. Both are among the ministers who perform the largest number of fashionable marriage ceremonies. Said the Rev. Dr. Charles L. Slattery, rector of Grace Church:

"It is desirable that the personal health of each party to a marriage be certified to, but the requirement for such certificate ought to come from the State, not from the Church, because it is the function of the State to guard the health of its citizens. I am glad to see the Church take steps toward reform, and toward compelling the State to do its part."

The Brick Presbyterian Church,[12] through the decision of its pastor, the Rev. Dr. William P. Merrill, takes its stand with others. "I think the general movement to require proper conditions of health from all men and women contemplating marriage is right. The State ought to obtain the fulfillment of

---

[11] Walter Taylor Sumner (1873–1935), Dean of the Episcopal Cathedral of Saints Peter and Paul, who was for a time the head of the Chicago Vice Commission, was a leading advocate for "health marriage."

[12] A socially prominent Presbyterian Church in New York City. Henry Van Dyke (Chapter 20, Document A) was a pastor at the Brick Church.

that condition, and the Church ought to co-operate in every practical way," the pastor said yesterday.

It was said yesterday that the subject of eugenics will come into the Episcopal General Convention[13] in this city in October through the report of a committee on which are Bishop Anderson of Chicago, whose cathedral took an early stand on health marriages; Bishop Spalding of Utah, whose book on the Mormons attracted wide attention; Bishop Williams of Michigan, whose views are known to be radical; Dean Hodges of Cambridge, Dean Sumner of Chicago, Jacob A. Riis, Gifford Pinchot,[14] the Rev. J. Howard Melish of Brooklyn, and Clinton Rogers Woodruff, the head of a social welfare movement.

D. Supreme Court of Indiana, Judgement, November Term, 1920[15]

Judgment: SUPREME COURT OF INDIANA. November Term, 1920. On the 11th day of May, 1921, being the 147th judicial day of said November Term, 1920. Case No. 23709. Appealed from the Clark Circuit Court. Opinion and judgment pronounced by Associate Judge Hon. Howard L. Townsend. Appellants were enjoined from performing vasectomy on appellee, who is a prisoner in the Indiana Reformatory. The Chief Physician, Board of Managers and two chosen surgeons were proposing to act pursuant to the [Indiana sterilization statute].... In Davis v. Berry et al. (U. S. District Court, S. D.), 216 Fed. Rep. 413,[16] in passing on an Iowa statute similar to the one here in question, on page 218, the court uses this language: "The hearing is by an administrative board of officers. There is no actual hearing. There is no evidence. The proceedings are private. The public does not know what is

---

[13] The General Convention is the governing body of the Episcopal Church.
[14] Jacob August Riis (1849–1914), a Danish immigrant to the United States, was a prominent journalist and social reformer. Gifford Pinchot (1865–1946), first head of the U.S. Forest Service and Governor of Pennsylvania, was a prominent Progressive politician. Both Riis and Pinchot were close associates of Theodore Roosevelt.
[15] Laughlin, *Eugenical Sterilization in the United States*, 269.
[16] Iowa law authorized the sterilization of anyone convicted of two felonies. A federal district court in Iowa prevented the sterilization of an inmate because it held that the law violated the Fourteenth Amendment's requirement for equal protection of the law. Iowa appealed the case to the Supreme Court in 1914, but Iowa changed its law before the Court could rule and so the Court remanded the case and did not rule on it.

being done until it is done. Witnesses are not produced, or, if produced, they are not cross-examined.... The prisoner is not advised of the proceedings until ordered to submit to the operation.... Due process of law means that every person must have his day in court, and this is as old as Magna Charta; that some time in the proceeding he must be confronted by his accuser and given a public hearing." In the instant case the prisoner has no opportunity to cross-examine the experts who decide that this operation should be performed upon him. He has no chance to bring experts to show that it should not be performed; nor has he a chance to controvert the scientific question that he is of a class designated in the statute. And wholly aside from the proposition of cruel and unusual punishment, and infliction of pains and penalties by the legislative body through an administrative board, it is very plain that this act is in violation of the Fourteenth Amendment of the Federal Constitution in that it denies appellee due process. The case of Davis v. Berry, supra, is interesting in its discussion of questions other than due process.[17] It also cites the adjudicated cases in other states on similar statutes. The trial court was correct in enjoining appellant from performing, or causing to be performed, the operation of vasectomy upon appellee. Judgment of the trial court is therefore affirmed.

E. Associate Justice Oliver Wendell Holmes, *Buck v. Bell*, May 2, 1927[18]

Mr. JUSTICE HOLMES delivered the opinion of the Court.

This is a writ of error to review a judgment of the Supreme Court of Appeals of the State of Virginia affirming a judgment of the Circuit Court of Amherst County by which the defendant in error,[19] the superintendent of the State Colony for Epileptics and Feeble Minded, was ordered to perform the operation of salpingectomy upon Carrie Buck, the plaintiff in error, for

---

[17] Laughlin comments: "The court discussed at length the proposition whether or not the performance of such an operation for the punishment of crime is cruel and unusual punishment, and it is clearly apparent from reading the opinion that no doubt existed in the mind of the court but that the performance of such an operation as this for the punishment of crime was cruel and unusual punishment." Laughlin, *Eugenical Sterilization in the United States*, 212.

[18] *Buck v. Bell*, 274 U.S. 200 (1927). Available online at *Justia*. https://goo.gl/mn3RFr

[19] The party in a legal appeal. It does not mean that the defendant was wrong or guilty.

the purpose of making her sterile.[20] 143 Va. 310. The case comes here upon the contention that the statute authorizing the judgment is void under the Fourteenth Amendment as denying to the plaintiff in error due process of law and the equal protection of the laws.

Carrie Buck is a feeble minded white woman who was committed to the State Colony above mentioned in due form.[21] She is the daughter of a feeble minded mother in the same institution, and the mother of an illegitimate feeble minded child. She was eighteen years old at the time of the trial of her case in the Circuit Court, in the latter part of 1924.

An Act of Virginia, approved March 20, 1924, recites that the health of the patient and the welfare of society may be promoted in certain cases by the sterilization of mental defectives, under careful safeguard, &c.; that the sterilization may be effected in males by vasectomy and in females by sal-pingectomy, without serious pain or substantial danger to life; that the Commonwealth is supporting in various institutions many defective persons who, if now discharged, would become a menace, but, if incapable of procreating, might be discharged with safety and become self-supporting with benefit to themselves and to society, and that experience has shown that heredity plays an important part in the transmission of insanity, imbecility, &c.

The statute then enacts that, whenever the superintendent of certain institutions, including the above-named State Colony, shall be of opinion that it is for the best interests of the patients and of society that an inmate under his care should be sexually sterilized, he may have the operation performed upon any patient afflicted with hereditary forms of insanity, imbecility, &c., on complying with the very careful provisions by which the act protects the patients from possible abuse.

The superintendent first presents a petition to the special board of directors of his hospital or colony, stating the facts and the grounds for his opinion, verified by affidavit. Notice of the petition and of the time and place of the hearing in the institution is to be served upon the inmate, and also upon

---

[20] A salpingectomy is the removal of one or both Fallopian tubes.

[21] For the facts of the case, the Court relied on the Virginia trial record. Most of the facts it presented, which Justice Holmes summarized in his opinion, were wrong. For example, Buck was not feeble-minded, nor was her mother. Buck apparently became pregnant because she was raped, rather than because she was licentious. In the hearing that resulted in the decision to sterilize her, Buck was represented by someone who favored sterilization.

his guardian, and if there is no guardian, the superintendent is to apply to the Circuit Court of the County to appoint one. If the inmate is a minor, notice also is to be given to his parents, if any, with a copy of the petition. The board is to see to it that the inmate may attend the hearings if desired by him or his guardian.

The evidence is all to be reduced to writing, and, after the board has made its order for or against the operation, the superintendent, or the inmate, or his guardian, may appeal to the Circuit Court of the County. The Circuit Court may consider the record of the board and the evidence before it and such other admissible evidence as may be offered, and may affirm, revise, or reverse the order of the board and enter such order as it deems just. Finally, any party may apply to the Supreme Court of Appeals, which, if it grants the appeal, is to hear the case upon the record of the trial in the Circuit Court, and may enter such order as it thinks the Circuit Court should have entered.

There can be no doubt that, so far as procedure is concerned, the rights of the patient are most carefully considered, and, as every step in this case was taken in scrupulous compliance with the statute and after months of observation, there is no doubt that, in that respect, the plaintiff in error has had due process of law. The attack is not upon the procedure, but upon the substantive law. It seems to be contended that in no circumstances could such an order be justified. It certainly is contended that the order cannot be justified upon the existing grounds.

The judgment finds the facts that have been recited, and that Carrie Buck "is the probable potential parent of socially inadequate offspring, likewise afflicted, that she may be sexually sterilized without detriment to her general health, and that her welfare and that of society will be promoted by her sterilization," and thereupon makes the order. In view of the general declarations of the legislature and the specific findings of the Court, obviously we cannot say as matter of law that the grounds do not exist, and, if they exist, they justify the result.

We have seen more than once that the public welfare may call upon the best citizens for their lives. It would be strange if it could not call upon those who already sap the strength of the State for these lesser sacrifices, often not felt to be such by those concerned, in order to prevent our being swamped with incompetence. It is better for all the world if, instead of waiting to execute degenerate offspring for crime or to let them starve for their imbecility, society can prevent those who are manifestly unfit from continuing their kind. The principle that sustains compulsory vaccination is broad enough to cover cutting the Fallopian tubes. Jacobson v. Massachusetts, 197 U.S. 11.[22] Three generations of imbeciles are enough.

But, it is said, however it might be if this reasoning were applied generally, it fails when it is confined to the small number who are in the institutions named and is not applied to the multitudes outside. It is the usual last resort of constitutional arguments to point out shortcomings of this sort. But the answer is that the law does all that is needed when it does all that it can, indicates a policy, applies it to all within the lines, and seeks to bring within the lines all similarly situated so far and so fast as its means allow. Of course, so far as the operations enable those who otherwise must be kept confined to be returned to the world, and thus open the asylum to others, the equality aimed at will be more nearly reached.

Judgment affirmed.

MR. JUSTICE BUTLER dissents.

F. "Better Baby Contest," Indiana State Fair, 1931

See photo on page C.

---

[22] A 1905 decision by the Supreme Court that upheld a compulsory vaccination law in Massachusetts. The Court argued that "... the liberty secured by the Constitution of the United States to every person within its jurisdiction does not import an absolute right in each person to be, at all times and in all circumstances, wholly freed from restraint. There are manifold restraints to which every person is necessarily subject for the common good. On any other basis organized society could not exist with safety to its members. Society based on the rule that each one is a law unto himself would soon be confronted with disorder and anarchy." Accordingly, the Court ruled that compulsory vaccination was within the legitimate police power of the state. See *Jacobson v. Commonwealth of Massachusetts*, 197 U.S. 11, 12 (1905). https://goo.gl/fKBdgP.

Surrender of General Lee to General Grant, April 9, 1865

Louis-Mathieu Didier Guillaume, c. 1880

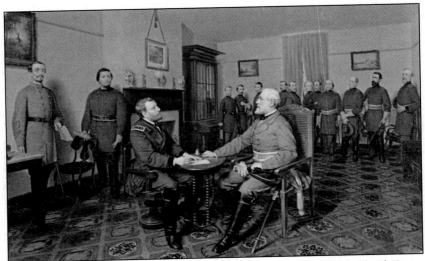

SOURCE: Appomattox Court House National Historical Park, VA. https://goo.gl/xyDhiY

Lieutenant Colonel Ely S. Parker (standing in the picture above just behind Grant's right shoulder) was a Seneca Indian who served as General Ulysses S. Grant's secretary toward the end of the war. When General Robert E. Lee arrived at the McLean House in Appomattox to surrender, he shook hands with the assembled officers. Apparently surprised to see the Native American among Grant's staff, he said reportedly, as he extended his hand to him, "I am glad to see one real American here." Parker replied, "We are all Americans."

Grant himself had intervened with civilian authorities in Washington to get an officer's commission for Parker. A grandson of a Seneca veteran of the War of 1812 (on the American side), Parker studied both law and civil engineering, opting for the latter career after being refused admittance to the New York State bar because as a tribal member, he was not a U.S. citizen. Parker had met Grant while working as a U.S. government engineer in Galena, IL in 1860. At Appomattox Courthouse on April 9, 1865, after General Grant drafted the surrender terms for the Army of Northern Virginia, Ely Parker made the emendations Grant agreed to at Lee's request and then wrote out the clean copy of the agreement.

A

King Debs

William Allen Roger, 1894

Eugene Debs sits on a railroad bridge blocking rail traffic and commerce. This magazine cover conveys a widely held view of Debs.

SOURCE: Library of Congress, LC-USZ62-106100.

The Railroad Trust

1904

SOURCE: John Moody, The Truth about The Trusts: A Description and Analysis of the American Trust Movement (New York: Moody Publishing Company, 1904). Public Domain, https://goo.gl/WMmtsY

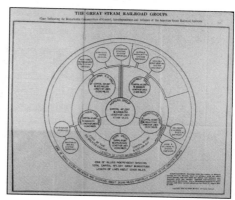

A Better Baby Contest

Indiana State Fair, 1931

SOURCE: Indiana State Archives.

"Better Baby" contests were one way that the eugenics movement became an ordinary part of American life. The NAACP organized such contests for black families in the 1920s and 1930s. Proceeds from the contests were used to combat lynching.[1]

---

[1] Gregory Michael Dorr and Angela Logan, "'Quality, Not Mere Quantity, Counts': Black Eugenics and the NAACP Baby Contests," in *A Century of Eugenics in America: From the Indiana Experiment to the Human Genome Era*, ed. Paul A. Lombardo (Bloomington, IN: Indiana University Press, 2011), 68–92.

Knights of Columbus

Lithograph by William Balfour Ker, 1917.

SOURCE: Library of Congress, Prints and Photographs Division, LC-USZC4-10131.

This poster from World War I shows religion continuing to shape American foreign policy in the years following the debate over the Philippines.

D

Photo of Texas Tenant Farmer in Marysville, California

Dorothea Lange, September 1935

LIBRARY OF CONGRESS, LC-USZ6-1026. HTTPS://goo.gl/ui5HCP

Texas tenant farmer in Marysville, California, migrant camp during the peach season. 1927 made seven thousand dollars in cotton. 1928 broke even. 1929 went in the hole. 1930 still deeper. 1931 lost everything. 1932 hit the road. 1935, fruit tramp in California.

Richard Nixon and Nikita Krushchev, The Kitchen Debate

July 24, 1959

SOURCE: Library of Congress Digital Collection, https://goo.gl/H5xk3x.

In the summer of 1959, Vice President Richard Nixon traveled to Moscow to formally open the American National Exhibit, a fair sponsored by the United States to show the Soviet people how Americans lived. Soviet Premier Nikita Khrushchev accompanied Nixon on a tour of the exhibit, with a team of journalists and photographers trailing them. The so-called Kitchen Debate was actually an unscripted series of exchanges between the two leaders about the merits and flaws of their respective economies and political systems. (One exchange came during a visit to the model American kitchen featured in the exhibit.)

Nixon and Khrushchev remained in good spirits as they argued; both leaders were mindful that their conversation was being captured using the new technology of color television and video recording. For Nixon, the encounter offered an opportunity to praise American technology, capitalism, and the high standard of living in the U.S. He observed that the debate itself showed the power and importance of free expression. For Khrushchev, the exchange allowed him to question how advanced the United States really was and to praise the communist system. The international attention the Kitchen Debate received showed the significant role that ideas and communication played in the Cold War. [This text is taken from *The Cold War: Core Documents*, edited by David Krugler (Ashland, Ohio: Ashbrook Press, 2018), 73–77.]

F

"Chief" Anderson and First Lady Eleanor Roosevelt

March 1941

SOURCE: Air Force Historical Research Agency, 234.821 v. 4.

"... Finally we went out to the aviation field, where a Civil Aeronautics unit for the teaching of colored pilots is in full swing. They have advanced training here, and some of the students went up and did acrobatic flying for us. These boys[2] are good pilots. I had the fun of going up in one of the tiny training planes with the head instructor, and seeing this interesting countryside from the air.

The days at Tuskegee have given me much to think about. To see a group of people working together for improvement of undesirable conditions is very heartening...."[3]

---

[2] In referring to the pilots as "boys," Mrs. Roosevelt is using a term universally applied to American soldiers, sailors, and airmen during World War II.

[3] Eleanor Roosevelt, *My Day: A Comprehensive, Electronic Edition of Eleanor Roosevelt's "My Day" Columns.* Online by the Eleanor Roosevelt Papers, Project of the Department of History at George Washington University. https://goo.gl/NvuBQM. Originally published as Eleanor Roosevelt, "My Day, April 1, 1941," © 1941, by United Feature Syndicate, Inc. All rights reserved. Reprinted by permission of *The Eleanor Roosevelt Papers Digital Edition* (2017).

Opposition to the Equal Rights Amendment

Florida, November 10, 1975

SOURCE: Black & white photonegative, 8 x 10 in. State Archives of Florida, Florida Memory. https://goo.gl/doUKq5. Photographed in the Florida State Capitol's Rotunda.

Reaction to the Defeat of the Amendment in the Florida Senate

1982

SOURCE: Political cartoon showing the Florida Senate result of ERA vote. 1982. Black & white photoprint, 8 x 10 in. State Archives of Florida, Florida Memory. https://goo.gl/3igTAF

CHAPTER 20

Progressive Foreign Policy:
The Philippines

A. Henry Van Dyke, *The American Birthright and the Philippine Pottage*, November 24, 1898
B. Senator Albert J. Beveridge (R-IN), Speech in the Senate in Support of an American Empire, January 9, 1900

As a result of its victory in the Spanish-American War (1898), the United States gained control of a number of former Spanish territories, principally Cuba and the Philippines. How to deal with these acquisitions immediately became a disputed issue. As the sermon by Henry Van Dyke and the speech by Senator Albert Beveridge show, the debate addressed long-standing, controversial and important questions, several of which had figured prominently in the crisis of the Civil War, a living and painful memory for Americans in the late nineteenth century. What authority over territories does the Constitution grant the federal government? What does the self-evident truth of equality proclaimed in the Declaration of Independence mean morally and politically? How should it guide the actions of the American government and people? Does it establish obligations between Americans and other peoples?

Despite their disagreement over what to do with the Philippines and the consequences of that decision for America and its people, Van Dyke and Beveridge agreed on several points. Both believed in progress and that America was a progressive nation. Both believed that there were races inferior to Americans or, more specifically, to the Anglo-Saxons whose ancestors they credited with developing the political ideals that informed the American Founding. Both saw America as a Christian nation carrying out God's plan. (Such attitudes remained part of the way Americans thought about foreign affairs in the decades following the Spanish American War. See illustration on page D.) These shared views, distinctive of the movement we call Progressivism (Beveridge was a leading Progressive), make their disagreement over the Philippines all the more instructive. Above all, their common appeal to but disagreement about the Declaration and the Constitution— above all the Declaration—deserves careful attention.

Study Questions

A. How would you describe the differences between Van Dyke and Beveridge? Why did one want to maintain control of the Philippines and the other not? How did they differ over the interpretation of the Declaration of Independence and the Constitution? Does the idea of a "living Constitution," as Beveridge puts it, have any potential limitations? Did Beveridge and Van Dyke have different understandings of self-government? If so, which one was right?

B. Is there a connection between thinking there are "inferior races," an opinion shared by Van Dyke and Beveridge, and the treatment of Carrie Buck (Chapter 19)? Is there a connection between such thinking and the discussion of civil rights for freedmen following the Civil War (Chapter 16)?

C. In what ways do the arguments for and against the Mexican-American War in Volume 1, Chapter 13 compare with the arguments for and against the Spanish-American War?

A. Henry Van Dyke, *The American Birthright and the Philippine Pottage*, November 24, 1898[1]

A Word of Explanation To the Hasty Reader

Please do not mistake the purpose of this sermon....

The sermon is against the assumption that the only way to meet our responsibilities is to annex the Philippine Islands as a permanent portion of our national domain.

It is against the abandonment of the American ideal of national growth for the European ideal of colonial conquest.

It is against the theory that it is our duty to take a share in the forcible division of the territories of the Eastern peoples, instead of using our influence for their protection and their native growth into free and intelligent States like Japan.

It is against the extension of the American frontier, by the sword, to the China Sea.

---

[1] Henry Van Dyke, *The American Birthright and the Philippine Pottage, a Sermon Preached on Thanksgiving Day by the Pastor of the Brick Church in New York City, 1898* (New York: Charles Scribner's Sons, N.D.). The text is available at https://goo.gl/YJ4JJM

It is dead against imperialism.

It is in favor of republicanism as held and taught by the authors of the Declaration of Independence....

Hebrews 12:16. "Esau, who for one morsel of meat sold his birthright."

This is the most important Thanksgiving Day that has been celebrated by the present generation of Americans. Three and thirty years have rolled away since we gave thanks for the ending of the Civil War. Never since that time has our national religious festival been observed under such brilliant sunlight of prosperity or with such portentous clouds of danger massed along the horizon.

It is a significant Thanksgiving because we have extraordinary causes for national gratitude. The first and greatest of these causes is the superabundant harvest with which, for the second year in succession, God has rewarded the patient toilers who are the strength and pride of our country....

The second cause for gratitude to-day is the new evidence that we have received of the union of the whole American people in loyalty and patriotism. The gaping wounds left by the Civil War have closed....

The third cause for gratitude is the renewal of cordial amity between the two leading nations of the world—Great Britain and the United States....

The fourth cause for thanksgiving to-day is the signal victory that has been granted to our country's arms in a war undertaken for the destruction of the ancient Spanish tyranny in the Western Hemisphere and the liberation of the oppressed people of Cuba. How reluctantly the American people took up the cross of war after thirty-three years of peace none can know except those who have read the peace-loving heart of the great silent classes, the happy, industrious, prosperous classes, of our country. The call of humanity was the only summons that could have roused them; the cause of liberty was the only cause for which they would have fought. No party, no administration could have received the loyal support of the whole people unless it had written on its banner the splendid motto: *"Not for gain, not for territory, but for freedom and human brotherhood!"* That avowal alone made the war possible and successful. For that cause alone Christians could pray with a sincere heart, and mothers give their sons to death by slaughter or disease, and lovers of liberty take up the unselfish sword.... [P]roud and glad of all that American soldiers and sailors have done this year in the cause of liberty, we present our offerings upon the solemn altar of gratitude. For the Divine guidance and protection, without which a victory so complete and swift, even over an inferior foe, could never have been won, let us give most humble and hearty thanks.

But this Thanksgiving Day is not significant alone in its causes for gratitude. It is an important day, a marked day, an immensely serious day because it finds us, suddenly and without preparation, face to face with the most momentous and far-reaching problem of our national history. . . . Can we fix the hanging periods?

Are the United States to continue as a peaceful republic, or are they to become a conquering empire? Is the result of the war with Spain to be the banishment of European tyranny from the Western Hemisphere, or is it to be the entanglement of the Western republic in the rivalries of European kingdoms? Have we set the Cubans free, or have we lost our own faith in freedom? Are we still loyal to the principles of our forefathers, as expressed in the Declaration of Independence, or are we now ready to sell the American birthright for a mess of pottage in the Philippines? . . .

. . . There is an old-fashioned document called the American Constitution which was expressly constructed to discourage the unconscious humor of such sudden changes. Before the die is cast the people must be taken fairly into the game; before the result is irrevocable the Supreme Court must pass upon the rules and the play. The question whether the American birthright is to be bartered for the Philippine pottage is still open. A brief, preliminary discussion of this question will not be out of place this morning. . . .

The proposal to annex, by force, or purchase, or forcible purchase, these distant, unwilling and semi-barbarous islands is hailed as a new and glorious departure in American history. A new word—imperialism—has been coined to define it. It is frankly confessed that it involves a departure from ancient traditions; it is openly boasted that it leaves the counsels of Washington and Jefferson far behind us forever. Because of this novelty, because of this separation from what we once counted a most precious heritage, I venture to ask whether this bargain offers any fit compensation for the loss of our American birthright?

I. Let us consider the arguments in favor of it. They may be summed up under three heads: the argument from duty, the argument from destiny, and the argument from desperation.

1. The argument from duty comes first because it is the strongest with honest and conscientious men. Undoubtedly we have incurred responsibilities by the late war, and we must meet them in a manly spirit; but certainly these responsibilities are not unlimited. They are bounded on one side by

our rights. The very question at issue is whether we have a right to deny the principles of our constitution by conquering unwilling subjects and annexing tributary colonies to our domain. On the other side our responsibilities are bounded by our abilities. It is never a duty to attempt a task which there is no prospect of performing with real usefulness. We surely owe the Filipinos the very best we can give them consistently with our other responsibilities; but it is far from being certain that the best thing we can do for them is to make them our vassals. If that were true our whole duty would not be done, the humane results of the war would not be completed, until we had annexed the misgoverned Spaniards of Spain also. No argument drawn from our duty to an oppressed and suffering race can be applied to the conquest of the Philippine Islands which does not apply with equal and even with greater force to the conquest of the Iberian Peninsula.

2. The argument from destiny is not an argument; it is a phrase. It takes for granted all that is in dispute; it clothes itself in glittering rainbows and introduces the question of debate in the disguise of a fact accomplished. "Yesterday," says a brilliant orator, "there were four great nations ruling the world and dividing up the territories of barbarous tribes—Great Britain, Russia, France and Germany—to-day there are five, for America has entered the arena of colonial conquest." But how came the great republic in that strange co-partnership? By what device was she led blindfold into that curious company? What does she there? What must she forfeit to obtain her share in the partition of spoils? That is the question. To talk of destiny is not to discuss, but to dodge, the point at issue.

3. The argument from desperation directly contradicts the argument from destiny. It presents the annexation of the Philippines, not as a glorious accomplishment, but as a hard necessity. We must do it because there is nothing else that we can do. A speaker less brilliant than the orator of the five nations, but more cautious, puts the case in a sentence: "We have got a wolf by the ears and we can't let go."[2]

The answer to this is simple. We have not got the wolf at present, though we are trying our best to get hold of him. It is absurd to say that the only way for us to get out of our difficulties is to go into the enterprise of wolf-keeping.

---

[2] Thomas Jefferson used this phrase at least twice to describe the relationship between the American people and the slaves they held. For example, he wrote "we have the wolf by the ear, and we can neither hold him, nor safely let him go. Justice is in one scale, and self-preservation in the other." Jefferson to John Holmes, April 22, 1820, commenting on the Missouri Compromise.

Nothing has yet been said or done which binds us to take permanent possession of these islands. Granting that the Philippines need a strong hand to set
them in order, it has not been shown that ours is the only hand, nor that we
must do it all alone. A protectorate for a limited time and with the purpose
of building up a firm self-government would be one of the possible solutions
of the difficulty. To pass this by and say that our only resort is to assume
sovereignty of these yet unconquered islands is merely to beg the question.

No, these contradictory arguments from duty and destiny and despair
do not touch the real spring of the movement for colonial expansion. It is the
prospect of profit that makes those distant islands gleam before our fancy as
desirable acquisitions. The argument drawn from the supposed need of creating and fortifying new outlets for our trade has the most practical force. It is
the unconscious desire of rivaling England in her colonial wealth and power
that allures us to the untried path of conquest; and this in spite of the fact
that during the last seven years, England, with all her colonies, has lost five
per cent of her export trade, while the United States, without colonies, have
gained eighteen per cent. It is a secret discontent with the part of a peaceful,
industrious, self-contained nation that urges us to take an armed hand in
the partition of the East and exchange our birthright for a mess of pottage.

II. Let us weigh the arguments against such a course.

1. It is contrary to the Constitution of the United States as interpreted by
the Supreme Court. The authority of that magnificent tribunal in which the
Anglo-Saxon ideal of the supremacy of law is forever embodied, more clearly
and powerfully than in any other human institution, is clearly against the
legitimacy of a policy of colonial expansion for this republic as now constituted. "There is certainly no power given by the constitution to the federal
government to establish or maintain colonies bordering on the United States
or at a distance, to be ruled and governed at its own pleasure.... No power
is given to acquire a territory to be held and governed permanently in that
character...."[3]

2. Every following step in the career of colonial imperialism will bring us
into conflict with our own institutions and necessitate constitutional change
or insure practical failure. Our Government, with its checks and balances,
with its prudent and conservative divisions of power, is the best in the world
for peace and self-defense; but the worst in the world for what the President

---

[3] In the printed version of this sermon, Van Dyke footnoted the source of this quotation: *Scott vs. Sanford* (1856) 60 U.S. 393, 396.

called, a few months ago, "criminal aggression."[4] We cannot compete with monarchies and empires in the game of land-grabbing and vassal ruling. We have not the machinery; and we cannot get it, except by breaking up our present system of government and building a new fabric out of the pieces. Republics have not been successful as rulers of colonies. When they have entered that career they have changed quickly into monarchies or empires. The supposed analogy between England and America is a fatal illusion. British institutions are founded, as Gladstone[5] has said, on the doctrine of inequality; American institutions are founded on the doctrine of equality. If we become a colonizing power we must abandon our institutions or be paralyzed by them. The swiftness of action, the secrecy, not to say slipperiness of policy, and the absolutism of control which are essential to success in territorial conquest and dominion are inconsistent with republicanism as America has interpreted it. Imperialism and democracy, militarism and self-government are contradictory terms. A government of the people, by the people, for the people is impregnable for defense, but impotent for conquest. When imperialism comes in at the door democracy flies out at the window. An imperialistic democracy is an impossible hybrid; we might as well speak of an atheistic religion, or a white blackness. To enter upon a career of colonial expansion with our present institutions is to court failure or to prepare for silent revolution.

3. There is an equally serious objection to the attempt to launch the United States upon the business of acquiring vassal colonies and governing distant and inferior races, in the poor outfit of our people for such a task.

It is said that we must begin or we shall never learn; the trouble is that we have already begun, but we have not learned. I am not speaking now in the spirit of pessimism or despair of the American people. No man could have a more profound confidence in their native ability, their fundamental integrity, and their ultimate common sense. It is to this common sense that I would appeal for a candid judgment of our preparation for an imperial career at the present moment.

Let us be on our guard against the flattering comparison with England.

---

[4] William McKinley (1843–1901; President 1897–1901). In his Annual Message of 1897, McKinley said that the forcible annexation of Cuba would be, according to the American moral code, "criminal aggression." He repeated this passage in his Message to Congress Requesting a Declaration of War With Spain, April 11, 1898.

[5] William Gladstone (1809–1898). He was British Prime Minister in 1868–74, 1880–85, 1886, and 1892–94.

The English people have a natural genius for governing inferior races—a steady head, an inflexible hand, and a superb self-confidence. What proof have we given of any such extraordinary genius in our dealing with inferior races? Does the comparison of the treatment of the Indians in Canada and in the United States give us a comfortable sense of pride? Is the condition of drunken and disorderly Alaska a just encouragement to larger enterprises? Is our success in treating the Chinese problem and the Negro problem so notorious that we must attempt to repeat it on a magnified scale eight thousand miles away? The rifle-shots that ring from Illinois and the Carolinas,[6] announcing a bloody skirmish of races in the very heart of the republic—are these the joyous salutes that herald our advance to rule eight millions more of black and yellow people in the islands of the Pacific Ocean?

England has a magnificent Civil Service at the foundation of her colonial empire. What have we? A recently unstarched Civil Service in New York, a Civil Service in Washington which is threatened with a new and serious crippling, and a persistent endemic of boss-rule all over the country. These things are not good guarantees that we shall send our best, our cleanest, our most educated young men to fill the offices in our distant colonies. And even if we could be sure that such men would be sent, they are more needed at home than they are abroad. We have no such domestic surplus of men and deficit of work as England has. Her tiny territory and immense population mark her necessity, even as our immense territory, not yet fully peopled nor wisely ruled, marks ours. For a country in our position to set out upon the adventure of colonial conquest promises discredit to ourselves and discomfort to our vassals. With our unsolved problems staring us in the face, our cities misgoverned and our territories neglected, the cry of to-day—not the cry of despair, but the cry of hope and courage—must be "Americans for America!"

4. Another weighty argument against the annexation of the Philippines is the frightful burden which it will almost certainly impose upon the people.

First, a burden of military service.... [T]he ranks must be kept full; and if Americans do not thirst for garrison duty in the tropics they must be compelled or bought to serve. On the one hand we see a system of conscription like that of Germany, where every man-child is born with a soldier's collar

---

[6] In October 1898, in Virden, Illinois, striking white miners had swarmed a train carrying black strikebreakers arriving from Alabama, and Pinkerton guards had fired on them. In November 1898, in Wilmington, NC. a white mob had attacked black residents, shooting some and driving others out of town, effectively wresting control of city government from Republicans who had biracial support.

around his neck; on the other hand, we see an enormous drain upon the earnings of the people, like England's annual budget of $203,000,000 for the army and navy.

Second, a burden of heavy taxation. . . .

Third, a burden of interminable and bloody strife. Expansion means entanglement; entanglement means ultimate conflict. The great nations of Europe are encamped around the China Sea in arms. If we go in among them we must fight when they blow the trumpet. . . .

. . . Colonial expansion means coming strife; the annexation of the Philippines means the annexation of a new danger to the world's peace. The acceptance of imperialism means that we must prepare to beat our ploughshares into swords and our pruning hooks into spears,[7] and be ready to water distant lands and stain foreign seas with an ever-increasing torrent of American blood. Is it for this that philanthropists and Christian preachers urge us to abandon our peaceful mission of enlightenment and thrust forward, sword in hand, into the arena of imperial conflict?

5. But the chief argument against the forcible extension of American sovereignty over the Philippines is that it certainly involves the surrender of our American birthright of glorious ideals. "This imitation of Old World methods," said one of our most powerful journals, a few months ago, "by the New World appears to us to be based upon an entire disregard, not merely of American precedence, but of American principles."[8]

I do not speak now of our word of honor, tacitly pledged to the world, when we disclaimed "Any Disposition Or Intention To Exercise Any Sovereignty, Jurisdiction Or Control Over Said Islands, Except For The Pacification Thereof."[9] . . . Pass it by.

But how can we pass by the solemn and majestic claim of our Declaration of Independence, that "Government derives its just powers from the consent of the governed?" How can we abandon the principle for which our fathers fought and died: "No taxation without representation?". . .

Anonymous patriots have written to warn me that it is a dangerous task to

---

[7] Van Dyke here reverses the famous words of Isaiah 2:4.
[8] Van Dyke footnotes the source of this statement as *The Outlook*, July 2, 1898.
[9] The language of the Teller amendment (named for its author, Senator Henry M. Teller (D–CO), 1830–1914) to the Declaration of War against Spain. The amendment was superseded by the Platt amendment (named for its author, Senator Orville H. Platt (R–CT), 1827–1905), adopted February 25, 1901. The Platt amendment established conditions for the withdrawal of U.S. forces from Cuba.

call for this discussion. It imperils popularity. The cry of to-day is: "Wherever the American flag has been raised it never must be hauled down." The man who will not join that cry may be accused of disloyalty and called a Spaniard. So be it, then. If the price of popularity is the stifling of conviction, I want none of it. If the test of loyalty is to join in every thoughtless cry of the multitude, I decline it. I profess a higher loyalty—*allegiance to the flag, not for what it covers, but for what it means.*

There is one thing that can happen to the American flag worse than to be hauled down. That is to have its meaning and its message changed.

Hitherto it has meant freedom, and equality, and self-government, and battle only for the sake of peace. Pray God its message may never be altered....

God save the birthright of the one country on earth whose ideal is not to subjugate the world but to enlighten it.

B. Senator Albert J. Beveridge, "Speech in the Senate in Support of an American Empire," January 9, 1900[10]

MR. PRESIDENT,[11] the times call for candor. The Philippines are ours forever, "territory belonging to the United States," as the Constitution calls them. And just beyond the Philippines are China's illimitable markets. We will not retreat from either. We will not repudiate our duty in the archipelago. We will not abandon our opportunity in the Orient. We will not renounce our part in the mission of our race, trustee, under God, of the civilization of the world. And we will move forward to our work, not howling out regrets like slaves whipped to their burdens but with gratitude for a task worthy of our strength and thanksgiving to Almighty God that He has marked us as His chosen people, henceforth to lead in the regeneration of the world.

This island empire is the last land left in all the oceans. If it should prove a mistake to abandon it, the blunder once made would be irretrievable. If it proves a mistake to hold it, the error can be corrected when we will. Every other progressive nation stands ready to relieve us.

---

[10] *Congressional Record*, 56th Congress, 1st Session, 9 January 1900, 704-712. Beveridge was a Republican Senator from Indiana from 1899–1911.

[11] As the Senate's web site explains, "Under the Constitution, the vice president serves as the president of the Senate and presides over the Senate's daily proceedings. In the absence of the vice president, the Senate's president pro tempore (and others designated by him) presides. As one of the Senate's constitutional officers, only the Vice President has the authority to cast a tie-breaking vote." https://goo.gl/hxLWKN

But to hold it will be no mistake. Our largest trade henceforth must be with Asia. The Pacific is our ocean. More and more Europe will manufacture the most it needs, secure from its colonies the most it consumes. Where shall we turn for consumers of our surplus? Geography answers the question. China is our natural customer. She is nearer to us than to England, Germany, or Russia, the commercial powers of the present and the future. They have moved nearer to China by securing permanent bases on her borders. The Philippines give us a base at the door of all the East.

Lines of navigation from our ports to the Orient and Australia, from the Isthmian Canal[12] to Asia, from all Oriental ports to Australia converge at and separate from the Philippines. They are a self-supporting, dividend-paying fleet, permanently anchored at a spot selected by the strategy of Providence, commanding the Pacific. And the Pacific is the ocean of the commerce of the future. Most future wars will be conflicts for commerce. The power that rules the Pacific, therefore, is the power that rules the world. And, with the Philippines, that power is and will forever be the American Republic. . . .

But if they did not command China, India, the Orient, the whole Pacific for purposes of offense, defense, and trade, the Philippines are so valuable in themselves that we should hold them. I have cruised more than 2,000 miles through the archipelago, every moment a surprise at its loveliness and wealth. I have ridden hundreds of miles on the islands, every foot of the way a revelation of vegetable and mineral riches. . . .

Here, then, senators, is the situation. Two years ago there was no land in all the world which we could occupy for any purpose. Our commerce was daily turning toward the Orient, and geography and trade developments made necessary our commercial empire over the Pacific. And in that ocean we had no commercial, naval, or military base. Today, we have one of the three great ocean possessions of the globe, located at the most commanding commercial, naval, and military points in the Eastern seas, within hail of India, shoulder to shoulder with China, richer in its own resources than any equal body of land on the entire globe, and peopled by a race which civilization demands shall be improved. Shall we abandon it?

That man little knows the common people of the republic, little understands the instincts of our race who thinks we will not hold it fast and hold it forever, administering just government by simplest methods. We may trick up devices to shift our burden and lessen our opportunity; they will avail us nothing but delay. We may tangle conditions by applying academic

---

[12] the Panama Canal

arrangements of self-government to a crude situation; their failure will drive us to our duty in the end....

... This war is like all other wars. It needs to be finished before it is stopped. I am prepared to vote either to make our work thorough or even now to abandon it. A lasting peace can be secured only by overwhelming forces in ceaseless action until universal and absolutely final defeat is inflicted on the enemy. To halt before every armed force, every guerrilla band opposing us is dispersed or exterminated will prolong hostilities and leave alive the seeds of perpetual insurrection.

Even then we should not treat. To treat at all is to admit that we are wrong. And any quiet so secured will be delusive and fleeting. And a false peace will betray us; a sham truce will curse us. It is not to serve the purposes of the hour, it is not to salve a present situation that peace should be established. It is for the tranquility of the archipelago forever. It is for an orderly government for the Filipinos for all the future. It is to give this problem to posterity solved and settled, not vexed and involved. It is to establish the supremacy of the American republic over the Pacific and throughout the East till the end of time.

It has been charged that our conduct of the war has been cruel. Senators, it has been the reverse. I have been in our hospitals and seen the Filipino wounded as carefully, tenderly cared for as our own. Within our lines they may plow and sow and reap and go about the affairs of peace with absolute liberty. And yet all this kindness was misunderstood, or rather not understood. Senators must remember that we are not dealing with Americans or Europeans. We are dealing with Orientals. We are dealing with Orientals who are Malays. We are dealing with Malays instructed in Spanish methods. They mistake kindness for weakness, forbearance for fear. It could not be otherwise unless you could erase hundreds of years of savagery, other hundreds of years of Orientalism, and still other hundreds of years of Spanish character and custom....

Mr. President, reluctantly and only from a sense of duty am I forced to say that American opposition to the war has been the chief factor in prolonging it. Had Aguinaldo[13] not understood that in America, even in the American Congress, even here in the Senate, he and his cause were supported; had he not known that it was proclaimed on the stump and in the press of a faction in the United States that every shot his misguided followers fired into the

---

[13] Emilio Aguinaldo (1869–1964) was the first President of the Philippines and the leader of opposition to American control of the islands.

breasts of American soldiers was like the volleys fired by Washington's men against the soldiers of King George, his insurrection would have dissolved before it entirely crystalized....

...It is believed and stated in Luzon, Panay, and Cebu that the Filipinos have only to fight, harass, retreat, break up into small parties, if necessary, as they are doing now, but by any means hold out until the next presidential election, and our forces will be withdrawn.

All this has aided the enemy more than climate, arms, and battle. Senators, I have heard these reports myself; I have talked with the people; I have seen our mangled boys in the hospital and field; I have stood on the firing line and beheld our dead soldiers, their faces turned to the pitiless southern sky, and in sorrow rather than anger I say to those whose voices in America have cheered those misguided natives on to shoot our soldiers down, that the blood of those dead and wounded boys of ours is on their hands, and the flood of all the years can never wash that stain away. In sorrow rather than anger I say these words, for I earnestly believe that our brothers knew not what they did.

But, senators, it would be better to abandon this combined garden and Gibraltar of the Pacific, and count our blood and treasure already spent a profitable loss than to apply any academic arrangement of self-government to these children. They are not capable of self-government. How could they be? They are not of a self-governing race. They are Orientals, Malays, instructed by Spaniards in the latter's worst estate.

They know nothing of practical government except as they have witnessed the weak, corrupt, cruel, and capricious rule of Spain. What magic will anyone employ to dissolve in their minds and characters those impressions of governors and governed which three centuries of misrule has created? What alchemy will change the Oriental quality of their blood and set the self-governing currents of the American pouring through their Malay veins? How shall they, in the twinkling of an eye, be exalted to the heights of self-governing peoples which required a thousand years for us to reach, Anglo-Saxon though we are?

Let men beware how they employ the term "self-government." It is a sacred term. It is the watchword at the door of the inner temple of liberty, for liberty does not always mean self-government. Self-government is a method of liberty—the highest, simplest, best—and it is acquired only after centuries of study and struggle and experiment and instruction and all the elements of the progress of man. Self-government is no base and common thing to be bestowed on the merely audacious. It is the degree which crowns the graduate of liberty, not the name of liberty's infant class, who have not yet mastered the alphabet of freedom. Savage blood, Oriental blood, Malay blood, Spanish example—are these the elements of self-government?

We must act on the situation as it exists, not as we would wish it....

... [W]e must never forget that in dealing with the Filipinos we deal with children.

And so our government must be simple and strong. Simple and strong! ...

Mr. President, self-government and internal development have been the dominant notes of our first century; administration and the development of other lands will be the dominant notes of our second century. And administration is as high and holy a function as self-government, just as the care of a trust estate is as sacred an obligation as the management of our own concerns. Cain was the first to violate the divine law of human society which makes of us our brother's keeper. And administration of good government is the first lesson in self-government, that exalted estate toward which all civilization tends.

Administration of good government is not denial of liberty. For what is liberty? It is not savagery. It is not the exercise of individual will. It is not dictatorship. It involves government, but not necessarily self-government. It means law. First of all, it is a common rule of action, applying equally to all within its limits. Liberty means protection of property and life without price, free speech without intimidation, justice without purchase or delay, government without favor or favorites. What will best give all this to the people of the Philippines—American administration, developing them gradually toward self-government, or self-government by a people before they know what self-government means?

The Declaration of Independence does not forbid us to do our part in the regeneration of the world. If it did, the Declaration would be wrong, just as the Articles of Confederation, drafted by the very same men who signed the Declaration, was found to be wrong. The Declaration has no application to the present situation. It was written by self-governing men for self-governing men. It was written by men who, for a century and a half, had been experimenting in self-government on this continent, and whose ancestors for hundreds of years before had been gradually developing toward that high and holy estate.

The Declaration applies only to people capable of self-government. How dare any man prostitute this expression of the very elect of self-governing peoples to a race of Malay children of barbarism, schooled in Spanish methods and ideas? And you who say the Declaration applies to all men, how dare you deny its application to the American Indian? And if you deny it to the Indian at home, how dare you grant it to the Malay abroad?

The Declaration does not contemplate that all government must have the consent of the governed. It announces that man's "inalienable rights are life, liberty, and the pursuit of happiness; that to secure these rights governments are established among men deriving their just powers from the consent of the governed; that when any form of government becomes destructive of those rights, it is the right of the people to alter or abolish it." "Life, liberty, and the pursuit of happiness" are the important things; "consent of the governed" is one of the means to those ends.

If "any form of government becomes destructive of those ends, it is the right of the people to alter or abolish it," says the Declaration. "Any forms" includes all forms. Thus the Declaration itself recognizes other forms of government than those resting on the consent of the governed. The word "consent" itself recognizes other forms, for "consent" means the understanding of the thing to which the "consent" is given; and there are people in the world who do not understand any form of government. And the sense in which "consent" is used in the Declaration is broader than mere understanding; for "consent" in the Declaration means participation in the government "consented" to. And yet these people who are not capable of "consenting" to any form of government must be governed.

And so the Declaration contemplates all forms of government which secure the fundamental rights of life, liberty, and the pursuit of happiness. Self-government, when that will best secure these ends, as in the case of people capable of self-government; other appropriate forms when people are not capable of self-government. And so the authors of the Declaration themselves governed the Indian without his consent; the inhabitants of Louisiana without their consent; and ever since the sons of the makers of the Declaration have been governing not by theory but by practice, after the fashion of our governing race, now by one form, now by another, but always for the purpose of securing the great eternal ends of life, liberty, and the pursuit of happiness, not in the savage but in the civilized meaning of those terms—life, according to orderly methods of civilized society; liberty regulated by law; pursuit of happiness limited by the pursuit of happiness by every other man.

If this is not the meaning of the Declaration, our government itself denies the Declaration every time it receives the representative of any but a republican form of government, such as that of the sultan, the czar, or other absolute autocrats, whose governments, according to the opposition's interpretation of the Declaration, are spurious governments because the people governed have not "consented" to them.

Senators in opposition are estopped from denying our constitutional power to govern the Philippines as circumstances may demand, for such power is admitted in the case of Florida, Louisiana, Alaska. How, then, is it denied in the Philippines? Is there a geographical interpretation to the Constitution? Do degrees of longitude fix constitutional limitations? Does a thousand miles of ocean diminish constitutional power more than a thousand miles of land?

The ocean does not separate us from the field of our duty and endeavor. . . .

There is in the ocean no constitutional argument against the march of the flag, for the oceans, too, are ours. . . . [T]he shores of all the continents calling us, the Great Republic before I die will be the acknowledged lord of the world's high seas. And over them the republic will hold dominion, by virtue of the strength God has given it, for the peace of the world and the betterment of man.

No; the oceans are not limitations of the power which the Constitution expressly gives Congress to govern all territory the nation may acquire. The Constitution declares that "Congress shall have power to dispose of and make all needful rules and regulations respecting the territory belonging to the United States." Not the Northwest Territory only; not Louisiana or Florida only; not territory on this continent only but any territory anywhere belonging to the nation.

The founders of the nation were not provincial. Theirs was the geography of the world. They were soldiers as well as landsmen, and they knew that where our ships should go our flag might follow. They had the logic of progress, and they knew that the republic they were planting must, in obedience to the laws of our expanding race, necessarily develop into the greater republic which the world beholds today, and into the still mightier republic which the world will finally acknowledge as the arbiter, under God, of the destinies of mankind. And so our fathers wrote into the Constitution these words of growth, of expansion, of empire, if you will, unlimited by geography or climate or by anything but the vitality and possibilities of the American people: "Congress shall have power to dispose of and make all needful rules and regulations respecting the territory belonging to the United States."

The power to govern all territory the nation may acquire would have been in Congress if the language affirming that power had not been written in the Constitution; for not all powers of the national government are expressed. Its principal powers are implied. The written Constitution is but the index of the living Constitution. Had this not been true, the Constitution would have failed; for the people in any event would have developed and progressed. And if the Constitution had not had the capacity for growth corresponding with the growth of the nation, the Constitution would and should have been abandoned as the Articles of Confederation were abandoned. For the Constitution is not immortal in itself, is not useful even in itself. The Constitution is immortal and even useful only as it serves the orderly development of the nation. The nation alone is immortal. The nation alone is sacred. The Army is its servant. The Navy is its servant. The President is its servant. This Senate is its servant. Our laws are its methods. Our Constitution is its instrument. . . .

Mr. President, this question is deeper than any question of party politics; deeper than any question of the isolated policy of our country even; deeper even than any question of constitutional power. It is elemental. It is racial. God has not been preparing the English-speaking and Teutonic peoples for a thousand years for nothing but vain and idle self-contemplation and self-admiration. No! He has made us the master organizers of the world to establish system where chaos reigns. He has given us the spirit of progress to overwhelm the forces of reaction throughout the earth. He has made us adepts in government that we may administer government among savage and senile peoples. Were it not for such a force as this the world would relapse into barbarism and night. And of all our race He has marked the American people as His chosen nation to finally lead in the regeneration of the world. This is the divine mission of America, and it holds for us all the profit, all the glory, all the happiness possible to man. We are trustees of the world's progress, guardians of its righteous peace. The judgment of the Master is upon us: "Ye have been faithful over a few things; I will make you ruler over many things."[14]

What shall history say of us? Shall it say that we renounced that holy trust, left the savage to his base condition, the wilderness to the reign of waste, deserted duty, abandoned glory, forgot our sordid profit even, because we feared our strength and read the charter of our powers with the doubter's eye and the quibbler's mind? Shall it say that, called by events to captain and command the proudest, ablest, purest race of history in history's noblest work, we declined that great commission? Our fathers would not have had it so. No! They founded no paralytic government, incapable of the simplest acts of administration. They planted no sluggard people, passive while the world's

---

[14] Matthew 25:23.

work calls them. They established no reactionary nation. They unfurled no retreating flag.

That flag has never paused in its onward march. Who dares halt it now—now, when history's largest events are carrying it forward; now, when we are at last one people, strong enough for any task, great enough for any glory destiny can bestow? How comes it that our first century closes with the process of consolidating the American people into a unit just accomplished, and quick upon the stroke of that great hour presses upon us our world opportunity, world duty, and world glory, which none but the people welded into an invisible nation can achieve or perform?

Blind indeed is he who sees not the hand of God in events so vast, so harmonious, so benign. Reactionary indeed is the mind that perceives not that this vital people is the strongest of the saving forces of the world; that our place, therefore, is at the head of the constructing and redeeming nations of the earth; and that to stand aside while events march on is a surrender of our interests, a betrayal of our duty as blind as it is base. Craven indeed is the heart that fears to perform a work so golden and so noble; that dares not win a glory so immortal....

... Pray God the time may never come when Mammon[15] and the love of ease shall so debase our blood that we will fear to shed it for the flag and its imperial destiny. Pray God the time may never come when American heroism is but a legend like the story of the Cid,[16] American faith in our mission and our might a dream dissolved, and the glory of our mighty race departed.

And that time will never come. We will renew our youth at the fountain of new and glorious deeds. We will exalt our reverence for the flag by carrying it to a noble future as well as by remembering its ineffable past. Its immortality will not pass, because everywhere and always we will acknowledge and discharge the solemn responsibilities our sacred flag, in its deepest meaning, puts upon us. And so, senators, with reverent hearts, where dwells the fear of God, the American people move forward to the future of their hope and the doing of His work....

---

[15] the demon of wealth, or the love of money that leads to evil
[16] Rodrigo Díaz de Vivar (c. 1043–1099) was a Castilian nobleman and famously successful military leader in medieval Spain, known popularly as El Cid, or "the Lord."

CHAPTER 21

What Caused the Great Depression?

A. Herbert Hoover, "Principles and Ideals of United States Government," October 22, 1928
B. Representative Jacob Milligan (D-MO), Speech on the Smoot-Hawley Tariff, July 3, 1930
C. Franklin D. Roosevelt, "The Forgotten Man," April 7, 1932
D. Franklin D. Roosevelt, Acceptance Speech at the Democratic Convention, July 2, 1932
E. Franklin D. Roosevelt, Commonwealth Club Address, September 23, 1932
F. President Herbert Hoover to Senator Simeon Fess (R-OH), February 21, 1933

*T*he farm sector of the American economy had struggled in the 1920s (See photo on page E), but overall by 1928, the United States had enjoyed eight years of unprecedented prosperity under Republican Presidents Harding and Coolidge. As the 1928 presidential race drew to a close, the Republican candidate, former Secretary of Commerce Herbert Hoover, outlined the Republicans' governing philosophy (Document A), which he credited with producing the prosperity. Seven months after Hoover took office, in October 1929, the stock market crashed. After two weeks, it recovered somewhat, but then began a long-term decline, as the American economy fell into what became known as the Great Depression.

The fall in the stock market and the resulting loss of wealth was not the sole cause of the Depression. Economists still debate what broader effect the stock market crash had on the American economy and why the Great Depression was so severe and so prolonged. Two factors that postdate the stock market crash and are part of the current debate—the decrease in foreign trade (Document B) and the failure of the banking system (Document F)—were noted by contemporaries. However, contemporaries tended to agree that the US government should ensure the soundness of the financial system by setting its own financial house in order. This meant reducing its debt by curtailing its expenditures (for example, Documents C, F) and even raising taxes, if necessary. Today, most economists would consider such measures counterproductive during a depression. High tariffs *restricting trade did not encourage recovery, and reductions in government spending removed an economic stimulus that might have helped. (Economic orthodoxy began to change with the publication of John Maynard Keynes' The General Theory of Employment, Interest and Money, in 1936, which called for governments to increase spending and deficits during a downturn.)*

Hoover responded to the economic difficulties according to the principles he had articulated in 1928. The American system was sound, he thought, and would recover with only limited assistance from the government. As the economic situation worsened, however, Hoover did propose a series of measures to deal with the crisis, including the establishment of the Reconstruction Finance Corporation (RFC), a government entity that lent money to state and local governments, banks, and other businesses.

Franklin Delano Roosevelt, the leading Democratic candidate for President in 1932, argued that the American system as championed by Hoover was not sound and needed to be changed.

In a series of speeches in 1932 (Documents C, D, and E), Roosevelt explained why he thought the Depression had occurred and what had to be done to restore the country to economic health. This was the "New Deal" that Roosevelt offered the American people (Document D).

In his final weeks in the Oval Office, as the economic crisis reached its most severe stage, Hoover argued that President-elect Roosevelt had made the situation worse by refusing to commit himself to balancing the budget and maintaining a sound currency. Hoover first offered his account verbally to one of his closest political allies, Senator Simeon Fess of Ohio. At Fess's request, Hoover put his remarks in writing in a letter he sent the Senator (Document F).

Study Questions

A. According to President Herbert Hoover, what were the major causes of the Great Depression, and what were the best ways to respond? How did Franklin D. Roosevelt's views on the causes and solutions to the economic crisis differ from Hoover's? How did the American system championed by Hoover differ from the New Deal offered by Roosevelt? How does "rugged individualism" differ from concern for "the forgotten man"? What were the different responses they offered to the "boom and bust" economic cycle? Was Roosevelt right to argue that he was following a bottom-up approach, while Hoover was following a top-down approach? What did Roosevelt mean when he said that the age of enlightened administration had come? Both Hoover and Roosevelt spoke of equality of opportunity. Did they mean the same thing by this phrase? How did each think such equality was best achieved?

B. How do the powers of the federal government implied in the New Deal compare to those Justice David Brewer described when delivering his opinion in *In re Debs* (Chapter 18, Document B)?

C. How might we evaluate these documents in light of the questions about moral virtue and market behavior raised in Volume 1, Chapter 2? What role, if any, do the authors in this chapter see for virtue in the economy? What are the consequences of neglecting to consider virtue in this context?

A. Herbert Hoover, "Principles and Ideals of the United States Government," October 22, 1928[1]

... When [*World War I*] closed, the most vital of all issues both in our own country and throughout the world was whether Governments should continue their wartime ownership and operation of many instrumentalities of production and distribution. We were challenged with a peace-time choice between the American system of rugged individualism and a European philosophy of diametrically opposed doctrines—doctrines of paternalism and state socialism. The acceptance of these ideas would have meant the destruction of self-government through centralization of government. It would have meant the undermining of the individual initiative and enterprise through which our people have grown to unparalleled greatness. ...

There is, therefore, submitted to the American people [*in the election of 1928*] a question of fundamental principle. That is: shall we depart from the principles of our American political and economic system, upon which we have advanced beyond all the rest of the world, in order to adopt methods based on principles destructive of its very foundations? And I wish to emphasize the seriousness of these proposals. I wish to make my position clear; for this goes to the very roots of American life and progress.

---

[1] Herbert Hoover, "Principles and Ideals of United States Government," October 22, 1928, *Public Papers of the Presidents of the United States—Herbert Hoover: 1929: Containing the Public Messages, Speeches, and Statements of the President, March 4 to December 31, 1929* (Washington, DC: United States Government Printing Office, 1974), 577–591. Available online at the Miller Center, University of Virginia, https://goo.gl/UWvKy1.

I should like to state to you the effect that this projection of government in business would have upon our system of self-government and our economic system. That effect would reach to the daily life of every man and woman. It would impair the very basis of liberty and freedom not only for those left outside the fold of expanded bureaucracy but for those embraced within it.

Let us first see the effect upon self-government. When the Federal Government undertakes to go into commercial business, it must at once set up the organization and administration of that business, and it immediately finds itself in a labyrinth, every alley of which leads to the destruction of self-government.

Commercial business requires a concentration of responsibility. Self-government requires decentralization and many checks and balances to safeguard liberty. Our Government to succeed in business would need become in effect a despotism. There at once begins the destruction of self-government....

The effect upon our economic progress would be even worse. Business progressiveness is dependent on competition. New methods and new ideas are the outgrowth of the spirit of adventure, of individual initiative and of individual enterprise. Without adventure there is no progress. No government administration can rightly take chances with taxpayers' money....

The Government in commercial business does not tolerate amongst its customers the freedom of competitive reprisals to which private business is subject. Bureaucracy does not tolerate the spirit of independence; it spreads the spirit of submission into our daily life and penetrates the temper of our people not with the habit of powerful resistance to wrong but with the habit of timid acceptance of irresistible might.

Bureaucracy is ever desirous of spreading its influence and its power. You cannot extend the mastery of the government over the daily working life of a people without at the same time making it the master of the people's souls and thoughts. Every expansion of government in business means that government in order to protect itself from the political consequences of its errors and wrongs is driven irresistibly without peace to greater and greater control of the nations' press and platform. Free speech does not live many hours after free industry and free commerce die.

It is a false liberalism[2] that interprets itself into the Government operation

---

[2] Liberalism here does not mean what we think of in modern terms as the opposite of conservatism. Instead, as Hoover goes on to explain, it refers to political and economic freedom.

of commercial business. Every step of bureaucratizing of the business of our country poisons the very roots of liberalism—that is, political equality, free speech, free assembly, free press, and equality of opportunity. It is the road not to more liberty, but to less liberty. Liberalism should be found not striving to spread bureaucracy but striving to set bounds to it. True liberalism seeks all legitimate freedom first in the confident belief that without such freedom the pursuit of all other blessings and benefits is vain. That belief is the foundation of all American progress, political as well as economic.

Liberalism is a force truly of the spirit, a force proceeding from the deep realization that economic freedom cannot be sacrificed if political freedom is to be preserved. Even if governmental conduct of business could give us more efficiency instead of less efficiency, the fundamental objection to it would remain unaltered and unabated. It would destroy political equality. It would increase rather than decrease abuse and corruption. It would stifle initiative and invention. It would undermine the development of leadership. It would cramp and cripple the mental and spiritual energies of our people. It would extinguish equality and opportunity. It would dry up the spirit of liberty and progress. For these reasons primarily, it must be resisted. For a hundred and fifty years liberalism has found its true spirit in the American system, not in the European systems.

I do not wish to be misunderstood in this statement. I am defining a general policy. It does not mean that our government is to part with one iota of its national resources without complete protection to the public interest. I have already stated that where the government is engaged in public works for purposes of flood control, of navigation, of irrigation, of scientific research or national defense, or in pioneering a new art, it will at times necessarily produce power or commodities as a by-product. But they must be a by-product of the major purpose, not the major purpose itself.

Nor do I wish to be misinterpreted as believing that the United States is free-for-all and devil-take-the-hind-most. The very essence of equality of opportunity and of American individualism is that there shall be no domination by any group or combination in this Republic, whether it be business or political. On the contrary, it demands economic justice as well as political and social justice. It is no system of laissez faire....

Our people have the right to know whether we can continue to solve our great problems without abandonment of our American system. I know we can. We have demonstrated that our system is responsive enough to meet any new and intricate development in our economic and business life. We have demonstrated that we can meet any economic problem and still maintain our democracy as master in its own house and that we can at the same time preserve equality of opportunity and individual freedom. . . .

The American people from bitter experience have a rightful fear that great business units might be used to dominate our industrial life and by illegal and unethical practices destroy equality of opportunity.

Years ago the Republican Administration established the principle that such evils could be corrected by regulation. It developed methods by which abuses could be prevented while the full value of industrial progress could be retained for the public. It insisted upon the principle that when great public utilities were clothed with the security of partial monopoly, whether it be railways, power plants, telephones or what not, then there must be the fullest and most complete control of rates, services, and finances by government or local agencies. It declared that these businesses must be conducted with glass pockets.[3]. . .

One of the great problems of government is to determine to what extent the Government shall regulate and control commerce and industry and how much it shall leave it alone. No system is perfect. We have had many abuses in the private conduct of business. That every good citizen resents. It is just as important that business keep out of government as that government keep out of business. . . .

And what have been the results of our American system? Our country has become the land of opportunity to those born without inheritance, not merely because of the wealth of its resources and industry but because of this freedom of initiative and enterprise. Russia has natural resources equal to ours. Her people are equally industrious, but she has not had the blessings of 150 years of our form of government and of our social system.

By adherence to the principles of decentralized self-government, ordered liberty, equal opportunity and freedom to the individual, our American experiment in human welfare has yielded a degree of well-being unparalleled in all the world. It has come nearer to the abolition of poverty, to the abolition of fear of want, than humanity has ever reached before. Progress of the past seven years is the proof of it. This alone furnishes the answer to our opponents who ask us to introduce destructive elements into the system by which this has been accomplished. . . .

My conception of America is a land where men and women may walk in ordered freedom in the independent conduct of their occupations; where they may enjoy the advantages of wealth, not concentrated in the hands of

---

[3] transparent finances

the few but spread through the lives of all, where they build and safeguard their homes, and give to their children the fullest advantages and opportunities of American life; where every man shall be respected in the faith that his conscience and his heart direct him to follow; where a contented and happy people, secure in their liberties, free from poverty and fear, shall have the leisure and impulse to seek a fuller life.

Some may ask where all this may lead beyond mere material progress. It leads to a release of the energies of men and women from the dull drudgery of life to a wider vision and a higher hope. It leads to the opportunity for greater and greater service, not alone from man to man in our own land, but from our country to the whole world. It leads to an America, healthy in body, healthy in spirit, unfettered, youthful, eager—with a vision searching beyond the farthest horizons, with an open mind sympathetic and generous. It is to these higher ideals and for these purposes that I pledge myself and the Republican Party.

B. Representative Jacob Milligan (D-MO), Speech on the Smoot-Hawley Tariff, July 3, 1930[4]

... [I]t is my opinion that it is most inopportune that the tariff bill should have become a law. We have not only a surplus of farm commodities but also a surplus in all industrial lines, hence we must have foreign markets. We cannot afford to destroy our foreign trade in order to allow the American manufacturer to plunder the pockets of the consumer....

The tariff bill was under consideration for seventeen months. During these seventeen months the President[5] had opportunity to inform Congress as to what he meant by "limited tariff revision for the benefit of agriculture." During these seventeen months the President remained mute.... So the only logical conclusion that can be reached is that the bill was entirely indorsed by the President during its making. So, I would not take credit from the President and the "Chief Manipulator" of this legislation in the Senate. I think the bill should be known as the Hoover-Grundy tariff bill.[6]

---

[4] 71st Congress, 2d session, *Congressional Record* 22, pt. 11: 12675-76.

[5] Herbert Hoover

[6] "Chief Manipulator" refers to Joseph R. Grundy, a Republican senator from Pennsylvania and president of the Pennsylvania Manufacturers' Association. Grundy had allegedly said that anyone who made campaign contributions to Republican candidates was entitled to higher tariffs in return.

The President assumed full responsibility when he signed the bill, as it could not have become law without his signature.

On the day the tariff bill became a law all grain prices fell to a new low level for the season. Wheat fell to the lowest price in a year, oats to the lowest price in eight years, rye to the lowest price reached in thirty years. Cotton fell to the lowest price in more than three years.

The steel industry reported a further decline in operations to 69 per cent of capacity.

On the day the bill passed, the Department of Commerce announced that American exports dropped in May to the lowest point in the last six years.

Stocks dropped in value $2,000,000,000 the day the President announced that he would sign the bill.

This tariff law carries a general average increase of 20.4 per cent over the Fordney-McCumber law of 1922,[7] which means an additional burden each year to the consumers of this country. The farmers are told they will benefit by this law. The facts are that every dollar of benefit given the farmer will cost him $10 because of the increase in the rate on the other than the agricultural rates....

There is an increase carried in this law upon practically every thing a person uses in everyday life from the swaddling cloth of the newborn babe to the tombstone he erects above his dead. This tariff law means an average increased cost of from fifty to one hundred dollars to every average householder in the United States each year. How the now overburdened masses can carry this additional burden I do not know.

We hear from certain quarters that prosperity is raging rampant in every corner of the land; that we are enjoying this unprecedented prosperity because Mr. Hoover is President. I am willing to give President Hoover full credit for the so-called Hoover prosperity we are not enjoying.

I understand that two new planets have been discovered and that someone suggested one be named "Hoover Prosperity" because it is invisible; the other "Farm Relief" because it is so far away.[8]

---

[7] Passed in the aftermath of World War I, the Fordney-McCumber tariff aimed primarily at restricting imports of chemical and metal products so as to give American manufacturers more time to develop innovations to compete with German manufacturers. But it also raised tariffs on agricultural imports.

[8] The farm economy of the United States had not enjoyed the general prosperity of the 1920s.

C. Franklin D. Roosevelt, "The Forgotten Man," April 7, 1932[9]

Although I understand that I am talking under the auspices of the Democratic National Committee, I do not want to limit myself to politics. I do not want to feel that I am addressing an audience of Democrats or that I speak merely as a Democrat myself. The present condition of our national affairs is too serious to be viewed through partisan eyes for partisan purposes. . . .

In my calm judgment, the Nation faces today a more grave emergency than in 1917.

It is said that Napoleon lost the battle of Waterloo because he forgot his infantry—he staked too much upon the more spectacular but less substantial cavalry. The present administration in Washington provides a close parallel. It has either forgotten or it does not want to remember the infantry of our economic army.

These unhappy times call for the building of plans that rest upon the forgotten, the unorganized but the indispensable units of economic power, for plans like those of 1917[10] that build from the bottom up and not from the top down, that put their faith once more in the forgotten man at the bottom of the economic pyramid.

Obviously, these few minutes tonight permit no opportunity to lay down the ten or a dozen closely related objectives of a plan to meet our present emergency, but I can draw a few essentials, a beginning in fact, of a planned program.

It is the habit of the unthinking to turn in times like this to the illusions of economic magic. People suggest that a huge expenditure of public funds by the Federal Government and by State and local governments will completely solve the unemployment problem. But it is clear that even if we could raise many billions of dollars and find definitely useful public works to spend these billions on, even all that money would not give employment to the seven million or ten million people who are out of work. Let us admit frankly that

---

[9] Franklin D. Roosevelt, "The Forgotten Man," April 7, 1932, *The Public Papers and Addresses of Franklin D. Roosevelt, Volume 1, The Genesis of the New Deal, 1928-1932*; with a special introduction and explanatory notes by President Roosevelt (New York: Random House, 1938), p. 624. Available at https://goo.gl/mnULoQ.

[10] Roosevelt may refer to the War Industries Board, created in 1917 and tasked to negotiate with industry so as to increase industrial production to support the U.S. effort in World War I.

it would be only a stopgap. A real economic cure must go to the killing of the bacteria in the system rather than to the treatment of external symptoms.

How much do the shallow thinkers realize, for example, that approximately one-half of our whole population, fifty or sixty million people, earn their living by farming or in small towns whose existence immediately depends on farms. They have today lost their purchasing power. Why? They are receiving for farm products less than the cost to them of growing these farm products. The result of this loss of purchasing power is that many other millions of people engaged in industry in the cities cannot sell industrial products to the farming half of the nation. This brings home to every city worker that his own employment is directly tied up with the farmer's dollar. No nation can long endure half bankrupt. Main Street, Broadway, the mills, the mines will close if half the buyers are broke.

I cannot escape the conclusion that one of the essential parts of a national program of restoration must be to restore purchasing power to the farming half of the country. Without this the wheels of railroads and of factories will not turn.

Closely associated with this first objective is the problem of keeping the home-owner and the farm-owner where he is, without being dispossessed through the foreclosure of his mortgage. His relationship to the great banks of Chicago and New York is pretty remote. The two-billion-dollar fund which President Hoover and the Congress have put at the disposal of the big banks, the railroads and the corporations of the Nation is not for him.

His is a relationship to his little local bank or local loan company. It is a sad fact that even though the local lender in many cases does not want to evict the farmer or home-owner by foreclosure proceedings, he is forced to do so in order to keep his bank or company solvent. Here should be an objective of Government itself, to provide at least as much assistance to the little fellow as it is now giving to the large banks and corporations. That is another example of building from the bottom up.

One other objective closely related to the problem of selling American products is to provide a tariff policy based upon economic common sense rather than upon politics, hot-air, and pull. This country during the past few years, culminating with the Hawley-Smoot Tariff in 1929,[11] has compelled the world to build tariff fences so high that world trade is decreasing to the vanishing point. The value of goods internationally exchanged is today less than half of what it was three or four years ago. . . .

---

[11] Document B

What we must do is this: revise our tariff on the basis of a reciprocal exchange of goods, allowing other Nations to buy and to pay for our goods by sending us such of their goods as will not seriously throw any of our industries out of balance, and incidentally making impossible in this country the continuance of pure monopolies which cause us to pay excessive prices for many of the necessities of life.

Such objectives as these three, restoring farmers' buying power, relief to the small banks and home-owners and a reconstructed tariff policy, are only a part of ten or a dozen vital factors. But they seem to be beyond the concern of a national administration which can think in terms only of the top of the social and economic structure. It has sought temporary relief from the top down rather than permanent relief from the bottom up. It has totally failed to plan ahead in a comprehensive way. It has waited until something has cracked and then at the last moment has sought to prevent total collapse.

It is high time to get back to fundamentals. It is high time to admit with courage that we are in the midst of an emergency at least equal to that of war. Let us mobilize to meet it.

D. Franklin D. Roosevelt, Acceptance Speech at the Democratic Convention, July 2, 1932[12]

... There are two ways of viewing the Government's duty in matters affecting economic and social life. The first sees to it that a favored few are helped and hopes that some of their prosperity will leak through, sift through, to labor, to the farmer, to the small business man. That theory belongs to the party of Toryism, and I had hoped that most of the Tories left this country in 1776.

But it is not and never will be the theory of the Democratic Party. This is no time for fear, for reaction or for timidity....

... [T]he people of this country want a genuine choice this year, not a choice between two names for the same reactionary doctrine. Ours must be a party of liberal thought, of planned action, of enlightened international outlook, and of the greatest good to the greatest number of our citizens....

I cannot take up all the problems today. I want to touch on a few that

---

[12] Franklin D. Roosevelt, "Address Accepting the Presidential Nomination at the Democratic National Convention in Chicago," July 2, 1932. Available online from Gerhard Peters and John T. Woolley, *The American Presidency Project*. https://goo.gl/Rff9ht.

are vital. Let us look a little at the recent history and the simple economics, the kind of economics that you and I and the average man and woman talk.

In the years before 1929 we know that this country had completed a vast cycle of building and inflation; for ten years we expanded on the theory of repairing the wastes of the War, but actually expanding far beyond that, and also beyond our natural and normal growth. Now it is worth remembering, and the cold figures of finance prove it, that during that time there was little or no drop in the prices that the consumer had to pay, although those same figures proved that the cost of production fell very greatly; corporate profit resulting from this period was enormous; at the same time little of that profit was devoted to the reduction of prices. The consumer was forgotten. Very little of it went into increased wages; the worker was forgotten, and by no means an adequate proportion was even paid out in dividends—the stockholder was forgotten.

And, incidentally, very little of it was taken by taxation to the beneficent Government of those years.

What was the result? Enormous corporate surpluses piled up—the most stupendous in history. Where, under the spell of delirious speculation, did those surpluses go? Let us talk economics that the figures prove and that we can understand. Why, they went chiefly in two directions: first, into new and unnecessary plants which now stand stark and idle; and second, into the call-money[13] market of Wall Street, either directly by the corporations, or indirectly through the banks. Those are the facts. Why blink at them?

Then came the crash. You know the story. Surpluses invested in unnecessary plants became idle. Men lost their jobs; purchasing power dried up; banks became frightened and started calling loans. Those who had money were afraid to part with it. Credit contracted. Industry stopped. Commerce declined, and unemployment mounted....

Our Republican leaders tell us economic laws—sacred, inviolable, unchangeable—cause panics which no one could prevent. But while they prate of economic laws, men and women are starving. We must lay hold of the fact that economic laws are not made by nature. They are made by human beings. Yes, when—not if—when we get the chance, the Federal Government will assume bold leadership in distress relief. For years Washington

---

[13] Unlike a loan given for a specified term, call money must be repaid when the lender requests it.

has alternated between putting its head in the sand and saying there is no large number of destitute people in our midst who need food and clothing, and then saying the States should take care of them, if there are. Instead of planning two and a half years ago to do what they are now trying to do, they kept putting it off from day to day, week to week, and month to month, until the conscience of America demanded action.

I say that while primary responsibility for relief rests with localities now, as ever, yet the Federal Government has always had and still has a continuing responsibility for the broader public welfare. It will soon fulfill that responsibility....

One word more: Out of every crisis, every tribulation, every disaster, mankind rises with some share of greater knowledge, of higher decency, of purer purpose. Today we shall have come through a period of loose thinking, descending morals, an era of selfishness, among individual men and women and among nations. Blame not governments alone for this. Blame ourselves in equal share. Let us be frank in acknowledgment of the truth that many amongst us have made obeisance to Mammon, that the profits of speculation, the easy road without toil, have lured us from the old barricades. To return to higher standards we must abandon the false prophets and seek new leaders of our own choosing.

Never before in modern history have the essential differences between the two major American parties stood out in such striking contrast as they do today. Republican leaders not only have failed in material things, they have failed in national vision, because in disaster they have held out no hope, they have pointed out no path for the people below to climb back to places of security and of safety in our American life.

Throughout the nation, men and women, forgotten in the political philosophy of the Government of the last years look to us here for guidance and for more equitable opportunity to share in the distribution of national wealth.

On the farms, in the large metropolitan areas, in the smaller cities and in the villages, millions of our citizens cherish the hope that their old standards of living and of thought have not gone forever. Those millions cannot and shall not hope in vain.

I pledge you, I pledge myself, to a new deal for the American people. Let us all here assembled constitute ourselves prophets of a new order of competence and of courage. This is more than a political campaign; it is a call to arms. Give me your help, not to win votes alone, but to win in this crusade to restore America to its own people.

E. Franklin D. Roosevelt, Commonwealth Club Address, September 23, 1932[14]

...A glance at the situation today only too clearly indicates that equality of opportunity as we have known it no longer exists. Our industrial plant is built; the problem just now is whether under existing conditions it is not over-built. Our last frontier has long since been reached, and there is practically no more free land. More than half of our people do not live on the farms or on lands and cannot derive a living by cultivating their own property. There is no safety valve in the form of a Western prairie to which those thrown out of work by the Eastern economic machines can go for a new start. We are not able to invite the immigration from Europe to share our endless plenty. We are now providing a drab living for our own people.

Our system of constantly rising tariffs has at last reacted against us to the point of closing our Canadian frontier on the north, our European markets on the east, many of our Latin-American markets to the south, and a goodly proportion of our Pacific markets on the west, through the retaliatory tariffs of those countries. It has forced many of our great industrial institutions which exported their surplus production to such countries, to establish plants in such countries, within the tariff walls. This has resulted in the reduction of the operation of their American plants, and opportunity for employment.

Just as freedom to farm has ceased, so also the opportunity in business has narrowed. It still is true that men can start small enterprises, trusting to native shrewdness and ability to keep abreast of competitors; but area after area has been pre-empted altogether by the great corporations, and even in the fields which still have no great concerns, the small man starts under a handicap. The unfeeling statistics of the past three decades show that the independent business man is running a losing race....

Clearly, all this calls for a re-appraisal of values. A mere builder of more industrial plants, a creator of more railroad systems, an organizer of more corporations, is as likely to be a danger as a help. The day of the great promoter

---

[14] Franklin D. Roosevelt, Commonwealth Club Address, September 23, 1932, *The Public Papers and Addresses of Franklin D. Roosevelt, Volume 1*, The Genesis of the New Deal, 1928–1932; with a special introduction and explanatory notes by President Roosevelt (New York : Random House, 1938), 742–756. Available online from Gerhard Peters and John T. Woolley, *The American Presidency Project*. https://goo.gl/w7G3h6.

or the financial Titan, to whom we granted anything if only he would build, or develop, is over. Our task now is not discovery or exploitation of natural resources, or necessarily producing more goods. It is the soberer, less dramatic business of administering resources and plants already in hand, of seeking to reestablish foreign markets for our surplus production, of meeting the problem of underconsumption, of adjusting production to consumption, of distributing wealth and products more equitably, of adapting existing economic organizations to the service of the people. The day of enlightened administration has come.... can we fix this hanging line?

As I see it, the task of Government in its relation to business is to assist the development of an economic declaration of rights, an economic constitutional order. This is the common task of statesman and business man. It is the minimum requirement of a more permanently safe order of things....

The Declaration of Independence discusses the problem of Government in terms of a contract. Government is a relation of give and take, a contract, perforce, if we would follow the thinking out of which it grew. Under such a contract, rulers were accorded power, and the people consented to that power on consideration that they be accorded certain rights. The task of statesmanship has always been the re-definition of these rights in terms of a changing and growing social order. New conditions impose new requirements upon Government and those who conduct Government....

The terms of that contract are as old as the Republic, and as new as the new economic order.

Every man has a right to life; and this means that he has also a right to make a comfortable living. He may by sloth or crime decline to exercise that right; but it may not be denied him. We have no actual famine or dearth; our industrial and agricultural mechanism can produce enough and to spare. Our Government formal and informal, political and economic, owes to everyone an avenue to possess himself of a portion of that plenty sufficient for his needs, through his own work.

Every man has a right to his own property; which means a right to be assured, to the fullest extent attainable, in the safety of his savings. By no other means can men carry the burdens of those parts of life which, in the nature of things, afford no chance of labor: childhood, sickness, old age. In all thought of property, this right is paramount; all other property rights must yield to it. If, in accord with this principle, we must restrict the operations of the speculator, the manipulator, even the financier, I believe we must accept the restriction as needful, not to hamper individualism but to protect it....

The Government should assume the function of economic regulation only as a last resort, to be tried only when private initiative, inspired by high responsibility, with such assistance and balance as Government can give, has finally failed. As yet there has been no final failure, because there has been no attempt; and I decline to assume that this Nation is unable to meet the situation....

Faith in America, faith in our tradition of personal responsibility, faith in our institutions, faith in ourselves demand that we recognize the new terms of the old social contract. We shall fulfill them, as we fulfilled the obligation of the apparent Utopia which Jefferson imagined for us in 1776, and which Jefferson, Roosevelt and Wilson sought to bring to realization. We must do so, lest a rising tide of misery, engendered by our common failure, engulf us all. But failure is not an American habit; and in the strength of great hope we must all shoulder our common load.

F. President Herbert Hoover to Senator Simeon Fess (R-OH), February 21, 1933[15]

... Today we are on the verge of financial panic and chaos. Fear for the policies of the new administration has gripped the country. People do not await events, they act. Hoarding of currency, and of gold, has risen to a point never before known; banks are suspending [their activities] not only in isolated instances, but in one case an entire state. Prices have fallen since last autumn below the levels which debtors and creditors can meet. Men over large areas are unable or are refusing to pay their debts. Hundreds of millions of orders placed before [the] election have been cancelled. Unemployment is increasing, there are evidences of the flight of capital from the United States to foreign countries, men have abandoned all sense of new enterprise and are striving to put their affairs in defense against disaster.

Some days before [the] election the whole economic machine began to hesitate from the upward movement of last summer and fall. For some time after [the] election it continued to hesitate but hoped for the best. As time has gone on, however, every development has stirred the fear and apprehension of the people. They have begun to realize what the abandonment of a successful program of this administration which was bringing rapid recovery last summer and fall now means and they are alarmed at possible new deal policies indicated by the current events. It is this fear that now dominates the national situation. It is not lack of resources, currency or credit.

---

[15] National Archives Catalog, Simeon D. Fess Papers, 1933. https://goo.gl/gMy7Zj.

The incidents which have produced this fear are clear. There was a delay by the President-elect of over two months in willingness to cooperate with us to bring about order from confusion in our foreign economic relations. There have been a multitude of speeches, bills, and statements of democratic members of Congress and others proposing inflation or tinkering with the currency.... Such proposals as the bills to assume Federal responsibility for billions of mortgages, loans to municipalities for public works, the Tennessee improvement and Muscle Shoals, are all of this order.[16] The proposals of Speaker Garner[17] that a constitutional government should be abandoned because the Congress, in which there will be an overwhelming majority, is unable to face reduction of expenses, has started a chatter of dictatorship. The President-elect has done nothing publicly to disavow any of these proposals.

The Democratic House has defeated a measure to increase tariffs so as to prevent invasion of goods from depreciated currency countries, thus estopping increased unemployment from this source. There have been interminable delays and threatened defeat of the Glass Banking Bill,[18] and the Bankruptcy bill.[19]

[Here Hoover recounts events of the prior 18 months, demarking five distinct periods that, he claims, oscillated between economic decline and recovery.]

The President-elect is the only man who has the power to give assurances which will stabilize [the] public mind as he alone can execute them. Those assurances should have been given before now but must be given at once if the situation is to be greatly helped. It would allay some fear and panic whereas delay will make the situation more acute.

The present administration is devoting its days and nights to put out the

---

[16] During World War I the federal government had constructed a dam and hydroelectric facility on the Tennessee River at Muscle Shoals, AL, to provide power for a munitions plant. After the war, Republicans like Hoover favored selling the facility to private industry, while Democrats and progressive Republicans argued the government should continue operating the plant to provide electricity to the rural South.

[17] John N. Garner (D-TX), the Vice-President-elect

[18] Hoover refers probably to the legislation that became the Banking Bill of 1933. This bill prohibited banks from engaging in both commercial and investment banking and established a system of insurance for bank deposits. The bill passed June 16, 1933.

[19] Hoover's reference is not clear, but may be to the Hastings-Michener Bill of 1932. See, Vincent L. Leibel, "The Chandler Act: Its Effect Upon the Law of Bankruptcy," *Fordham Law Review* 9, 3 (1940), 380–409.

fires or to localize them. I have scrupulously refrained from criticism which is
well merited, but have instead been giving repeated assurances to the country
of our desire to cooperate and help the new administration.

What is needed, if the country is not to drift into great grief, is the immediate and emphatic restoration of confidence in the future. The resources of
the country are incalculable, the available credit is ample but lenders will not
lend, and men will not borrow unless they have confidence. Instead they are
withdrawing their resources and their energies. The courage and enterprise
of the people still exist and only await release from fears and apprehension.

The day will come when the Democratic Party will endeavor to place
the responsibility for the events of this *Fifth period* on the Republican Party.
When that day comes I hope you will invite the attention of the American
people to the actual truth.

CHAPTER 22

The New Deal: Social Security

A. President Franklin D. Roosevelt, Speech to Congress on Social Security, January 17, 1935
B. Representative James W. Wadsworth (R-NY), Speech on Social Security, April 19, 1935
C. Senator Huey P. Long (D-LA), Statement on the Share Our Wealth Society, May 23, 1935

D emocrats made impressive gains in the midterm elections of 1934, which President Franklin D. Roosevelt interpreted as a popular mandate for the New Deal that he had launched upon taking office in 1933. In 1935, therefore, he placed before Congress a series of measures on a wide variety of subjects in what has become known as the "Second New Deal." Perhaps the most important of these was the Social Security Act, which provided for unemployment insurance and old-age pensions to be paid through a six percent payroll tax divided between employers and employees. The revenues generated from these payroll taxes would be more than sufficient to provide for the current elderly; the surplus would be deposited in a special fund that would—theoretically, at least—maintain the program in perpetuity. Other aspects of the plan directed that federal money would also be passed along to the states to support assistance programs for the blind, the disabled, and families with dependent children. While the benefits to the elderly would be managed at the federal level by a Social Security Administration, unemployment insurance and other assistance programs would remain under the control of the states.

The Social Security Act appeared sufficiently moderate that it aroused little real opposition, except from a few die-hard conservatives such as Republican Representative James W. Wadsworth of New York (Document B), who feared that it would destroy incentives to work and save. Others claimed that the proposed payroll tax was excessive; not only would it retard recovery, but they feared that the resulting surplus might be used to fund other attempts at New Deal "social engineering." In spite of such criticism the bill passed both houses by wide margins, and Roosevelt signed it into law on August 14, 1935.

Liberals felt the Act did not go far enough. They had hoped that the program would be funded from revenues generated by the income tax, so that it might redistribute wealth from rich to poor.

One of Roosevelt's most prominent opponents on the left was Huey P. Long, who as a popular and reform-minded Democratic governor of Louisiana took on the oil industry and built a powerful state political organization. After being elected to the U.S. Senate (in 1930, although he did not take his seat until 1932), he used his national standing to issue frequent denunciations of the wealthy and the banking system. In 1932 he supported Roosevelt's presidential campaign and supported most of the measures of the early New Deal. However, the personalities of the two men immediately clashed, and the New York patrician and the colorful, rural senator known as the "Kingfish" (after a character in the popular radio show Amos & Andy) came to loathe one another.

Long's greatest complaint about the New Deal was that to his mind it did not go far enough in reducing the great inequalities of wealth in American society. In March 1933 he proposed a series of bills that would have seized all fortunes greater than $100 million, as well as all annual income in excess of $1 million. When these laws failed—as did, indeed, everything Long proposed as senator—he established a national organization called the Share Our Wealth Society (Document C). By 1935 the society boasted 27,000 chapters nationwide, with a total membership of 7.5 million. Long hoped to use this group as a launching pad for a presidential run in 1936; however, in September 1935 he was assassinated by the son of one of his many political enemies.

Social Security has been one of the most enduring legacies of the New Deal. Roosevelt insisted on funding Social Security through payroll taxes because it would give recipients "a legal, moral, and political right to collect their pensions and their unemployment benefits. With those [payroll] taxes in there, no damn politician can ever scrap my social security program."

The program began paying out old-age benefits in 1940, when there were 159.2 taxpayers for every recipient. By 2013, however, according to the Social Security Administration, demographic patterns and longer life expectancy had changed the ratio to 2.8 taxpayers for every recipient. Without major changes, some have suggested that the Social Security system cannot remain solvent.

Study Questions

A. What does Roosevelt's Social Security plan entail? How is it to be funded? Why does the president believe it is necessary? What misgivings does Representative Wadsworth have regarding how Social Security is to be funded? Why does he think it poses a danger to the republic? How does he predict the program will develop? Have his predictions come true? How might Roosevelt respond to Wadsworth's criticisms? What does Huey Long regard as the fundamental cause of the Depression? In what ways does he think the New Deal has fallen short? What does he propose as a remedy? How does he seek to justify his program?

B. How does the New Deal compare to Reconstruction (Chapter 16) or the passage of the Civil Rights Act (Chapter 26)? What vision of the legitimate purposes and power of government are presented in each case? What connections, if any, do you see among the various policies? How does Long's understanding of what society owes to its poorest members relate to the eugenics movement's vision of what society owes to its weakest members (Chapter 19)?

C. How do the visions of a community of shared responsibility for the financial security of all presented in this chapter compare to those presented in Volume 1, Chapter 2? How do the concerns raised by conservative critics of the New Deal reflect those raised by Brutus in Volume 1, Chapter 7?

A. President Franklin D. Roosevelt, Speech to Congress on Social Security, January 17, 1935[1]

In addressing you on June 8, 1934, I summarized the main objectives of our American program. Among these was, and is, the security of the men, women, and children of the nation against certain hazards and vicissitudes of life. This purpose is an essential part of our task. In my annual message to you I promised to submit a definite program of action. This I do in the form of a report to me by a Committee on Economic Security, appointed by me for the purpose of surveying the field and of recommending the basis of legislation....

It is my best judgment that this legislation should be brought forward with

---

[1] President Franklin D. Roosevelt, Speech to Congress on Social Security, January 17, 1935, *The Public Papers and Addresses of Franklin D. Roosevelt, Volume Four, The Court Disapproves, 1935*; with a special introduction and explanatory notes by President Roosevelt (New York: Random House, 1938), 43–46. Available at https://goo.gl/Q4526x.

a minimum of delay. Federal action is necessary to, and conditioned upon, the action of States. Forty-four legislatures are meeting or will meet soon. In order that the necessary State action may be taken promptly, it is important that the Federal Government proceed speedily.

The detailed report of the Committee sets forth a series of proposals that will appeal to the sound sense of the American people. It has not attempted the impossible, nor has it failed to exercise sound caution and consideration of all of the factors concerned: the national credit, the rights and responsibilities of States, the capacity of industry to assume financial responsibilities and the fundamental necessity of proceeding in a manner that will merit the enthusiastic support of citizens of all sorts.... can we get rid of the orphans

Three principles should be observed in legislation on this subject. First, the system adopted, except for the money necessary to initiate it, should be self-sustaining in the sense that funds for the payment of insurance benefits should not come from the proceeds of general taxation. Second, excepting in old-age insurance, actual management should be left to the States subject to standards established by the Federal Government. Third, sound financial management of the funds and the reserves, and protection of the credit structure of the nation should be assured by retaining Federal control over all funds through trustees in the Treasury of the United States.

At this time, I recommend the following types of legislation looking to economic security:

1. Unemployment compensation.

2. Old-age benefits, including compulsory and voluntary annuities.

3. Federal aid to dependent children through grants to States for the support of existing mothers' pension systems and for services for the protection and care of homeless, neglected, dependent, and crippled children.

4. Additional Federal aid to State and local public-health agencies and the strengthening of the Federal Public Health Service. I am not at this time recommending the adoption of so-called "health insurance," although groups representing the medical profession are cooperating with the Federal Government in the further study of the subject and definite progress is being made.

With respect to unemployment compensation, I have concluded that the most practical proposal is the levy of a uniform Federal payroll tax, 90 percent of which should be allowed as an offset to employers contributing under a compulsory State unemployment compensation act. The purpose of this is to afford a requirement of a reasonably uniform character for all States cooperating with the Federal Government and to promote and encourage the passage of unemployment compensation laws in the States. The 10 percent not thus offset should be used to cover the costs of Federal and State administration of this broad system. Thus, States will largely administer unemployment compensation, assisted and guided by the Federal Government. An unemployment compensation system should be constructed in such a way as to afford every practicable aid and incentive toward the larger purpose of employment stabilization. This can be helped by the intelligent planning of both public and private employment. It also can be helped by correlating the system with public employment so that a person who has exhausted his benefits may be eligible for some form of public work as is recommended in this report. Moreover, in order to encourage the stabilization of private employment, Federal legislation should not foreclose the States from establishing means for inducing industries to afford an even greater stabilization of employment.

In the important field of security for our old people, it seems necessary to adopt three principles: First, noncontributory old-age pensions for those who are now too old to build up their own insurance. It is, of course, clear that for perhaps 30 years to come funds will have to be provided by the States and the Federal Government to meet these pensions. Second, compulsory contributory annuities which in time will establish a self-supporting system for those now young and for future generations. Third, voluntary contributory annuities by which individual initiative can increase the annual amounts received in old age. It is proposed that the Federal Government assume one-half of the cost of the old-age pension plan, which ought ultimately to be supplanted by self-supporting annuity plans....

The establishment of sound means toward a greater future economic security of the American people is dictated by a prudent consideration of the hazards involved in our national life. No one can guarantee this country against the dangers of future depressions but we can reduce these dangers. We can eliminate many of the factors that cause economic depressions, and we can provide the means of mitigating their results. This plan for economic security is at once a measure of prevention and a method of alleviation.

We pay now for the dreadful consequence of economic insecurity—and dearly. This plan presents a more equitable and infinitely less expensive means of meeting these costs. We cannot afford to neglect the plain duty before us. I strongly recommend action to attain the objectives sought in this report.

B. Representative James W. Wadsworth (R-NY), Speech on Social Security, April 19, 1935[2]

... I realize perfectly well that this bill is going to pass the House of Representatives ... without any substantial change, and nothing that I can say will prevent it or even tend to prevent it, in view of the determination of the majority.

It is not my purpose to discuss it in detail ... but I am going to endeavor to glance a little toward the far future and analyze some one or two things which seem to me to be susceptible of analysis, and certainly worth serious thought on the part of Members of the House regardless of their political affiliations.

First, as to the financing of the major portion of this program. As I understand it ... these funds are to be established in the Treasury Department, through the collection of payroll taxes.... The bill provides in general that those moneys shall be invested solely in the bonds of the Government of the United States or bonds guaranteed as to the principal and interest by the Government. As I read the report and have listened to the discussion on the floor, it is apparent that the proponents of this bill expect that this fund will grow from time to time, year after year, until about 1970, if I am not mistaken, the fund will approximate $32,000,000,000, every penny of which must be invested in government bonds.

It is apparent that unless the national debt of the United States goes far, far beyond $32,000,000,000 in the time over which this calculation is extended, by the time this fund has been built up to any considerable degree it will become a fund large enough to absorb at least a major portion of the national debt, and finally absorb it all....

Now, that may seem an effective and adequate way to finance the Government's financial activities in all the years to come. I am trying to look to the future. Heretofore the Government has financed its undertakings primarily and fundamentally as a result of the confidence of the individual citizen in the soundness of the Government's undertaking, but from this point on we are apparently going to abandon that philosophy of public confidence and resort to a very different practice. The Government is to impose a payroll tax through one of its agencies, collect the money into the Treasury Department, then the Treasury Department with its left hand on the proceeds of these taxes is to turn around and buy bonds of the United States Government

---

[2] *Congressional Record,* 74th Cong., 1st sess., Vol. 79, pt. 6, pp. 6060-6061. James W. Wadsworth (1877–1952) was a Republican Senator (1915–1927) and Representative (1933–1951) from New York.

issued by the right hand of the Treasury Department. Thus the Government of the United States, after this thing gets going, is no longer to be financed directly by its citizens, confident in the soundness of the Government, but it is to be financed instead by arrangements made within the bureaucracy—an undemocratic and dangerous undertaking. . . .

Now, this may not seem important at this moment. I may be old-fashioned. . . . It seems to me that we are moving away from democracy in this new and manipulative method of financing the obligations of the United States. I do not question the integrity and the honor of the men who are going to manage this fund or the men who will be Secretaries of the Treasury down through the years to come, but there is something offensive to me in the spectacle of one branch of the Treasury Department having collected a fund by taxing the working people of America, and then using that money for the floating of its own bonds. It seems to me to present the possibility of a vicious circle, and is certainly removing the financial support of the Government of the United States far from the people themselves and confining it to an inner ring, bureaucratic in character. I am trying to look ahead and visualize what that may mean in the preservation of democracy. . . .

One other thing looking toward the future. . . . I know the appeal this bill has to every human being, that it appeals to the humane instincts of men and women everywhere. We will not deny, however, that it constitutes an immense, immense departure from the traditional functions of the Federal Government for it to be projected into the field of pensioning the individual citizens of the several States. It launches the Federal Government into an immense undertaking which in the aggregate will reach dimensions none of us can really visualize and which in the last analysis, you will admit, affects millions and millions of individuals. Remember, once we pay pensions and supervise annuities, we cannot withdraw from the undertaking no matter how demoralizing and subversive it may become. Pensions and annuities are never abandoned; nor are they ever reduced. The recipients ever clamor for more. To gain their ends they organize politically. They may not constitute a majority of the electorate, but their power will be immense. On more than one occasion we have witnessed the political achievements of organized minorities. This bill opens the door and invites the entrance into the political field of a power so vast, so powerful as to threaten the integrity of our institutions and so pull the pillars of the temple down upon the heads of our descendants.

We are taking a step here today which may well be fateful. I ask you to consider it, to reexamine the fundamental philosophy of this bill, to estimate the future and ask yourselves the questions, "In what sort of country shall our grandchildren live? Shall it be a free country or one in which the citizen is a subject taught to depend upon government?"

C. Senator Huey P. Long (D-LA), Statement on the Share Our Wealth Society, May 23, 1935[3]

The Share Our Wealth Society proposes to enforce the traditions on which this country was founded, rather than to have them harmed; we aim to carry out the guaranties of our immortal Declaration of Independence and our Constitution of the United States, as interpreted by our forefathers who wrote them and who gave them to us; we will make the works and compacts of the Pilgrim fathers, taken from the Laws of God, from which we were warned never to depart, breathe into our Government again that spirit of liberty, justice, and mercy which they inspired in our founders in the days when they gave life and hope to our country. God has beckoned fullness and peace to our land; our forefathers have set the guide stakes so that none need fail to share in this abundance. Will we not have our generation, and the generations which are to come, cheated of such heritage because of the greed and control of wealth and opportunity by 600 families?

To members and well-wishers of the Share Our Wealth Society:

For 20 years I have been in the battle to provide that, so long as America has, or can produce, an abundance of the things which make life comfortable and happy, that none should own such much [sic] of the things which he does not need and cannot use as to deprive the balance of the people of a reasonable proportion of the necessities and conveniences of life. The whole line of any political thought has always been that America must face the time when the whole country would shoulder the obligation which it owes to every child born on earth—that is, a fair chance to life, liberty, and happiness....

It is not out of place for me to say that the support which I brought to Mr. Roosevelt to secure his nomination and election as President—and without which it was hardly probabl[e] he would ever have been nominated—was on the assurances which I had that he would take the proper stand for the redistribution of wealth in the campaign. He did that much in the campaign; but after his election, what then? I need not tell you the story. We have not time to cry over our disappointments, over promises which others did not keep, and over pledges which were broken....

---

[3] *Congressional Record*, 74th Cong., 1st sess., Vol. 79 (May 23, 1935), pp. 8040–43.

It is impossible for the United States to preserve itself as a republic or as a democracy when 600 families own more of this Nation's wealth—in fact, twice as much—as all the balance of the people put together. Ninety-six percent of our people live below the poverty line, while four percent own eighty-seven percent of the wealth. America can have enough for all to live in comfort and still permit millionaires to own more than they can ever spend and to have more money than they can ever use; but America cannot allow the multimillionaires and the billionaires, a mere handful of them, to own everything unless we are willing to inflict starvation upon 125,000,000 people.

We looked upon the year 1929 as the year when too much was produced for the people to consume. We were told, and we believed, that the farmers raised too much cotton and wool for the people to wear and too much food for the people to eat. Therefore, much of it went to waste, some rotted, and much of it was burned or thrown into the river or into the ocean. But, when we picked up the bulletin of the Department of Agriculture for that year 1929, we found that, according to the diet which they said everyone should eat in order to be healthy, multiplying it by 120,000,000, the number of people we had in 1929, had all of our people had the things which the Government said that [they] should eat in order to live well[? W]e did not have enough even in 1929 to feed the people. In fact, these statistics show that in some instances we had from one-third to one-half less than the people needed, particularly of milk, eggs, butter, and dried fruits.

But why in the year 1929 did it appear we had too much? Because the people could not buy the things they wanted to eat and needed to eat. That showed the need for and duty of the Government then and there, to have forced a sharing of our wealth, and a redistribution, and Roosevelt was elected on the pledge to do that very thing.

But what was done? Cotton was plowed under the ground. Hogs and cattle were burned by the millions. The same was done to wheat and corn, and farmers were paid starvation money not to raise and not to plant because of the fact that we did not want so much because of people having no money with which to buy. Less and less was produced, when already there was less produced than the people needed if they ate what the Government said they needed to sustain life. God forgive those rulers who burned hogs, threw milk in the river, and plowed under cotton while little children cried for meat and milk and something to put on their naked backs!

But the good God who placed this race on earth did not leave us without an understanding of how to meet such problems; nor did the Pilgrim fathers who landed at Plymouth in 1620 fail to set an example as to how a country and a nation of people should act under such circumstances, and our great statesman like Thomas Jefferson, Daniel Webster, Abraham Lincoln, Theodore Roosevelt, and Ralph Waldo Emerson did not fail to explain the need and necessity for following the precedents and purposes, which are necessary, even in a land of abundance, if all the people are to share the fruits produced therein. God's law commanded that the wealth of the country should be redistributed ever so often, so that none should become too rich and none should become too poor; it commanded that debts should be canceled and released ever so often, so that the human race would not be loaded with a burden which it could never pay.[4] When the Pilgrims landed at Plymouth in 1620, they established their law by compact, signed by everyone who was on board the Mayflower, and it provided that at the end of every seven years the finances of their newly formed country would be readjusted and that all debts would be released and property redistributed, so that none should starve in the land of plenty, and none should have an abundance of more than he needed.[5] These principles were preserved in the Declaration of Independence, signed in 1776, and in our Constitution. Our great statesmen, such men as James Madison, who wrote the Constitution of the United States, and Daniel Webster, its greatest exponent, admonished the generations of America to come that they must never forget to require the redistribution of wealth if they desire that their Republic should live.

And, now, what of America? Will we allow the political sports, the high heelers, the wiseacres, and those who ridicule us in our misery and poverty to keep us from organizing these societies in every hamlet so that they may bring back to life this law and custom of God and of this country? Is there a man or woman with a child born on the earth, or who expects ever to have a child born on earth, who is willing to have it raised under the present-day practices of piracy, where it comes into life burdened with debt, condemned to a system of slavery by which the sweat of its brow throughout its existence must go to satisfy the vanity and the luxury of a leisurely few, who can never be made to see that they are destroying the root and branch of the greatest country ever to have risen? Our country is calling; the laws of the Lord are

---

[4] For example, Luke 3:10-11; Proverbs 22:9; Deuteronomy 15:1-11.

[5] Long's account is inaccurate: no such clause was in the Mayflower Compact, nor was the policy motivated by the sort of redistributive philosophy he indicates. See William Bradford, *Of Plimoth Plantation: From the Original Manuscript* (Boston: Wright and Potter, State Printers, 1898), 162-164.

calling; the graces [*graves*] of our forefathers would open today if their occupants could see the bloom and flower of their creation withering and dying
because the greed of the financial masters of this country has starved and
withheld from mankind those things produced by his own labor. To hell with
the ridicule of the wise street-corner politician. Pay no attention to any news-
paper or magazine that has sold its columns to perpetuate this crime against
the people of America. Save this country. Save mankind. Who can be wrong
in such a work, and who cares what consequences may come following the
mandates of the Lord, of the Pilgrims, of Jefferson, Webster, and Lincoln?
He who falls in this fight falls in the radiance of the future. Better to make
this fight and lose than to be a party to a system that strangles humanity.

It took the genius of labor and the lives of all Americans to produce the
wealth of this land. If any man, or hundred men, wind up with all that has
been produced by 120,000,000 people, that does not mean that those hundred men produced the wealth of the country; it means that those hundred
men stole, directly or indirectly, what 125,000,000 people produced. Let no
one tell you that the money masters made this country. They did [*no*] such
thing. Very few of them ever hewed the forest; very few ever hacked a crosstie;
very few ever nailed a board; fewer of them ever laid a brick. Their fortunes
came from manipulated finance, control of government, rigging of markets,
the spider webs that have grabbed all businesses; they grab the fruits of the
land, the conveniences and the luxuries that are intended for 125,000,000
people, and run their heelers to our meetings to set up the cry, "We earned it
honestly." The Lord says they did no such thing. The voices of our forefathers
say they did no such thing. In this land of abundance, they have no right to
impose starvation, misery, and pestilence for the purpose of vaunting their
own pride and greed....

Here is the whole sum and substance of the share-our-wealth movement:

1. Every family to be furnished by the Government a homestead allowance, free of debt, of not less than one-third the average family wealth of the
country, which means, at the lowest, that every family shall have the reasonable comforts of life up to a value of from $5,000 to $6,000. No person to have
a fortune of more than 100 to 300 times the average family fortune, which
means that the limit to fortunes is between $1,500,000 and $5,000,000, with
annual capital levy taxes imposed on all above $1,000,000.

2. The yearly income of every family shall be not less than one-third of the
average family income, which means that, according to the estimates of the
statisticians of the United States Government and Wall Street, no family's
annual income would be less than from $2,000 to $[2,500]. No yearly income

shall be allowed to any person larger than from 100 to 300 times the size of the average family income, which means that no person would be allowed to earn in any year more than from $600,000 to $1,800,000, all to be subject to present income-tax laws.

3. To limit or regulate the hours of work to such an extent as to prevent overproduction; the most modern and efficient machinery would be encouraged, so that as much would be produced as possible so as to satisfy all demands of the people, but to also allow the maximum time to the workers for recreation, convenience, education, and luxuries of life.

4. An old-age pension to the persons over 60.

5. To balance agricultural production with what can be consumed according to the laws of God, which includes the preserving and storage of surplus commodities to be paid for and held by the Government for the emergencies when such are needed. Please bear in mind, however, that when the people of America have had money to buy things they needed, we have never had a surplus of any commodity. This plan of God does not call for destroying any of the things raised to eat or wear, nor does it countenance wholesale destruction of hogs, cattle, or milk.

6. To pay the veterans of our wars what we owe them and to care for their disabled.

7. Education and training for all children to be equal in opportunity in all schools, colleges, universities, and other institutions for training in the professions and vocations of life; to be regulated on the capacity of children to learn, and not on the ability of parents to pay the costs. Training for life's work to be as much universal and thorough for all walks in life as has been the training in the arts of killing.

8. The raising of revenue and taxes for the support of this program to come from the reduction of swollen fortunes from the top, as well as for the support of public works to give employment whenever there may be any slackening necessary in private enterprise.

I now ask those who read this circular to help us at once in this work of giving life and happiness to our people—not a starvation dole upon which someone may live in misery from week to week. Before this miserable system of wreckage has destroyed the life germ of respect and culture in our American people let us save what was here, merely by having none too poor and none too rich. The theory of the Share Our Wealth Society is to have enough for all, but not to have one with so much that less than enough remains for the balance of the people.

Please, therefore, let me ask you who read this document—please help this work before it is too late for us to be of help to our people. We ask you now, (1) help to get your neighbor into the work of this society and (2) help get other Share Our Wealth societies started in your county and in adjoining counties and get them to go out to organize other societies.

To print and mail out this circular costs about 60 cents per hundred, or $6 per thousand. Anyone who reads this and wants more circulars of this kind to use in the work, can get them for that price by sending the money to me, and I will pay the printer for him. Better still, if you can have this circular reprinted in your own town or city.

Let everyone who feels he wishes to help in our work start right out and go ahead. One man or woman is as important as any other. Take up the fight! Do not wait for someone else to tell you what to do. There are no high lights in this effort. We have no State managers and no city managers. Everyone can take up the work, and as many societies can be organized as there are people to organize them. One is the same as another. The reward and compensation is the salvation of humanity. Fear no opposition. "He who fails in this fight falls in the radiance of the future!"

CHAPTER 23

The Decision to Use the Atomic Bomb

A. The Scientific Panel of the Interim Committee, Recommendations on the Immediate Use of Nuclear Weapons, June 16, 1945

B. Minutes of Meetings held at the White House on Monday, June 18, 1945

C. Proclamation Defining Terms for Japanese Surrender, Potsdam, July 26, 1945

D. President Harry S. Truman, Press Release Alerting the Nation About the Atomic Bomb, August 6, 1945

E. J. R. Oppenheimer to Secretary of War Henry Stimson, August 17, 1945

*A*fter Germany's surrender on May 7, 1945, the war continued in the Pacific, as did planning for the invasion of Japan. Allied military leaders believed invasion was the only way to force the unconditional surrender for which Allied policy called (Document C). Intense bombing of Japan (on March 9-10, 1945, for example, bombs leveled nearly 16 square miles of Tokyo and killed 90,000 Japanese) had not moved Japan to surrender. Continued fighting in the Pacific (Iwo Jima, February-March, 1945; Okinawa, April-June 1945; and ongoing fighting in the Philippines) led to mounting American casualties. The experience of the invasion of Normandy June 4, 1944 also informed decision making about the use of the atomic bomb (Document B).

In May of 1945, Secretary of War Stimson set up a committee, the Interim Committee, to consider issues arising from the development of usable nuclear energy. The Interim Committee was chaired by Brigadier General Leslie Groves and J. Robert Oppenheimer, the two who led the Manhattan Project that developed the atomic bomb. Among other things, this committee considered whether and how the atomic bomb should be used. A sub-committee consisting of scientists involved in the bomb project reported on this question on June 16, 1945 (Document A). The Interim Committee recommended to Stimson on June 21 "that the weapon be used against Japan at the earliest opportunity, that it be used without warning, and that it be used on a dual target, namely, a military installation or *war plant surrounded by or adjacent to homes or other buildings most susceptible to damage."*

On June 18, 1945, President Truman met with his civilian and military advisers to consider the plan for the invasion of Japan (Document B). At the subsequent Potsdam Conference, Truman and Allied leaders warned Japan of the consequences of further resistance (Document C).

On August 6, 1945, the United States dropped an atomic bomb on Hiroshima, Japan, killing 80,000 people instantly. The American people learned about the new weapon from a White House press release (Document D). Three days later, the United States dropped a second atomic bomb on Nagasaki that killed 35,000 people. Japan surrendered unconditionally on August 14. Devastating though these attacks were, the bombing of Hiroshima and Nagasaki was not the only factor that led the Japanese to surrender unconditionally. A blockade had fully isolated Japan from outside resources by the summer of 1945 and the Russians entered the war against Japan, August 9, 1945. The latter event was a factor considered on June 18.

Shortly after the first use of the bomb, Oppenheimer wrote to Secretary of War Stimson to express his growing concern, shared by many of the scientists who worked on the Manhattan Project, about the military and political consequences of atomic weapons (Document E).

Study Questions

A. When discussing bringing the war against Japan to a close, what factors did President Truman and his military and civilian advisers consider? Did their concerns differ from those of the committee of scientists who offered advice on when and how to use the bomb? How might these different considerations have affected the decision to use the bomb? Should the points made in Document E have led to the decision *not* to drop the bomb? Is the advice given in Document A scientific advice? Why should anyone have listened to it?

B. Based on the documents in Chapter 19 (concerning Progressive advocacy of eugenics) and the documents below, what is the proper relationship between science and politics? Does politics control science or does science control politics?

C. What do both the dropping of the atomic bomb and President Washington's decision to call out the militia to end the Whiskey Rebellion (Volume 1, Chapter 8) tell us about the evolving understanding of executive power in the United States?

A. Recommendations on the Immediate Use of Nuclear Weapons, the Scientific Panel of the Interim Committee, June 16, 1945[1]

You have asked us to comment on the initial use of the new weapon. This use, in our opinion, should be such as to promote a satisfactory adjustment of our international relations. At the same time, we recognize our obligation to our nation to use the weapons to help save American lives in the Japanese war.

(1) To accomplish these ends we recommend that before the weapons are used not only Britain, but also Russia, France, and China be advised that we have made considerable progress in our work on atomic weapons, and that we would welcome suggestions as to how we can cooperate in making this development contribute to improved international relations.

(2) The opinions of our scientific colleagues on the initial use of these weapons are not unanimous: they range from the proposal of a purely technical demonstration to that of the military application best designed to induce surrender. Those who advocate a purely technical demonstration would wish to outlaw the use of atomic weapons, and have feared that if we use the weapons now our position in future negotiations will be prejudiced. Others emphasize the opportunity of saving American lives by immediate military use, and believe that such use will improve the international prospects, in that they are more concerned with the prevention of war than with the elimination of this specific weapon. We find ourselves closer to these latter views; we can propose no technical demonstration likely to bring an end to the war; we see no acceptable alternative to direct military use.

(3) With regard to these general aspects of the use of atomic energy, it is clear that we, as scientific men, have no proprietary rights. It is true that we are among the few citizens who have had occasion to give thoughtful consideration to these problems during the past few years. We have, however, no claim to special competence in solving the political, social, and military problems which are presented by the advent of atomic power.

---

[1] Michael B. Stoff et al., eds., *The Manhattan Project: A Documentary Introduction to the Atomic Age* (Philadelphia: Temple University Press, 1991), 150. Available at The Atomic Bomb and the End of World War II, *The National Security Archive*. https://goo.gl/o2U9M1

B. Minutes of Meetings held at the White House on Monday, 18 June 1945 at 1530[2]

1. DETAILS OF THE CAMPAIGN AGAINST JAPAN

THE PRESIDENT stated that he had called the meeting for the purpose of informing himself with respect to the details of the campaign against Japan set out in Admiral Leahy's[3] memorandum to the Joint Chiefs of Staff of 14 June. He asked General Marshall[4] if he would express his opinion.

GENERAL MARSHALL pointed out that the present situation with respect to operations against Japan was practically identical with the situation which had existed in connection with the operations proposed against Normandy. He then read, as an expression of his views, the following digest of a memorandum prepared by the Joint Chiefs of Staff for presentation to the President ... :

Our air and sea power has already greatly reduced movement of Jap shipping south of Korea and should in the next few months cut it to a trickle if not choke it off entirely. Hence, there is no need for seizing further positions in order to block Japanese communications south of Korea.

General MacArthur and Admiral Nimitz[5] are in agreement with the Chiefs of Staff in selecting 1 November as the target date to go into Kyushu[6] because by that time:

a. If we press preparations we can be ready.

b. Our estimates are that our air action will have smashed practically every industrial target worth hitting in Japan as well as destroying huge areas in the Jap cities.

c. The Japanese Navy, if any still exists, will be completely powerless.

d. Our sea action and air power will have cut Jap reinforcement capabilities from the mainland to negligible proportions.

---

[2] "The Decision to Drop the Atomic Bomb Research File," Truman Presidential Library. https://goo.gl/goPYGA

[3] William Leahy (1875–1959) was personal Chief of Staff to Presidents Roosevelt and Truman and Chairman of the Joint Chiefs of Staff (the title and position was not customary before he served in this role).

[4] General George C. Marshall, Army Chief of Staff

[5] Douglas MacArthur (1880–1964) was Supreme Commander of Allied Forces in the Southwest Pacific Area. Chester Nimitz (1885–1966) was the Commander of the Pacific fleet.

[6] the most southwesterly of the islands that make up Japan

Important considerations bearing on the 1 November date rather than a later one are the weather and cutting to a minimum Jap time for preparation of defenses. If we delay much after the beginning of November the weather situation in the succeeding months may be such that the invasion of Japan, and hence the end of the war, will be delayed for up to 6 months....

The Kyushu operation is essential to a strategy of strangulation and appears to be the least costly worthwhile operation following Okinawa. The basic point is that a lodgment in Kyushu is essential, both to tightening our strangle hold of blockade and bombardment on Japan, and to forcing capitulation by invasion of the Tokyo Plain.

We are bringing to bear against the Japanese every weapon and all the force we can employ and there is no reduction in our maximum possible application of bombardment and blockade, while at the same time we are pressing invasion preparations. It seems that if the Japanese are ever willing to capitulate short of complete military defeat in the field they will do it when faced by the completely hopeless prospect occasioned by (1) destruction already wrought by air bombardment and sea blockade, coupled with (2) a landing on Japan indicating the firmness of our resolution, and also perhaps coupled with (3) the entry or threat of entry of Russia into the war.

With reference to clean-up of the Asiatic mainland, our objective should be to get the Russians to deal with the Japs in Manchuria (and Korea if necessary) and to vitalize the Chinese to a point where, with assistance of American air power and some supplies, they can mop out their own country.

Casualties. Our experience in the Pacific war is so diverse as to casualties that it is considered wrong to give any estimate in numbers. Using various combinations of Pacific experience, the War Department staff reaches the conclusion that the cost of securing a worthwhile position in Korea would almost certainly be greater than the cost of the Kyushu operation. Points on the optimistic side of the Kyushu operation are that: General MacArthur has not yet accepted responsibility for going ashore where there would be disproportionate casualties. The nature of the objective area gives room for maneuver, both on the land and by sea. As to any discussion of specific operations, the following data are pertinent:

Campaign	U.S. Casualties Killed, wounded, missing	Jap Casualties Killed and Prisoners (Not including wounded)	Ratio U.S. to Jap
Leyte	17,000	78,000	1:4.6
Luzon	31,000	156,000	1:5.0
Iwo Jima	20,000	25,000	1:1.25
Okinawa	34,000 (Ground) 7,700 (Navy)	81,000 (not a complete count)	1:2
Normandy (1st 30 days)	42,000	—	—

The record of General MacArthur's operations from 1 March 1944 through 1 May 1945 shows 13,742 U.S. killed compared to 310,165 Japanese killed, or a ratio of 22 to 1.

There is reason to believe that the first 30 days in Kyushu should not exceed the price we have paid for Luzon.[7] It is a grim fact that there is not an easy, bloodless way to victory in war and it is the thankless task of the leaders to maintain their firm outward front which holds the resolution of their subordinates....

An important point about Russian participation in the war is that the impact of Russian entry on the already hopeless Japanese may well be the decisive action levering them into capitulation at that time or shortly thereafter if we land in Japan....

GENERAL MARSHALL said that he had asked General MacArthur's opinion on the proposed operation and had received from him the following telegram, which General Marshall then read:

"I believe the operation presents less hazards of excessive loss than any other that has been suggested and that its decisive effect will eventually save lives by eliminating wasteful operations of nondecisive character. I regard the operation as the most economical one in effort and lives that is possible. In this respect it must be remembered that the several preceding months will involve practically no losses in ground troops and that sooner or later a decisive ground attack must be made. The hazard and loss will be greatly lessened if an attack is launched from Siberia sufficiently ahead of our target date to commit the enemy to major combat. I most earnestly recommend no change in OLYMPIC.[8] Additional subsidiary attacks will simply build up our final total casualties."

---

[7] One of the islands that make up the Philippines

[8] Operation Olympic was the first part of Operation Downfall, the invasion of Japan.

GENERAL MARSHALL said that it was his personal view that the operation against Kyushu was the only course to pursue. He felt that air power alone was not sufficient to put the Japanese out of the war. It was unable alone to put the Germans out. General Eaker and General Eisenhower[9] both agreed to this. Against the Japanese, scattered through mountainous country, the problem would be much more difficult than it had been in Germany. He felt that this plan offered the only way the Japanese could be forced into a feeling of utter helplessness. The operation would be difficult but not more so than the assault in Normandy. He was convinced that every individual moving to the Pacific should be indoctrinated with a firm determination to see it through.

ADMIRAL KING[10] agreed with General Marshall's views and said that the more he studied the matter, the more he was impressed with the strategic location of Kyushu, which he considered the key to the success of any siege operations. He pointed out that within three months the effects of air power based on Okinawa will begin to be felt strongly in Japan. It seemed to him that Kyushu followed logically after Okinawa. It was a natural setup. It was his opinion that we should do Kyushu now, after which there would be time to judge the effect of possible operations by the Russians and the Chinese. The weather constituted quite a factor. So far as preparation was concerned, we must aim now for Tokyo Plain; otherwise we will never be able to accomplish it. If preparations do not go forward now, they cannot be arranged for later. Once started, however, they can always be stopped if desired.

GENERAL MARSHALL agreed that Kyushu was a necessity and pointed out that it constituted a landing in the Japanese homeland. Kyushu having been arranged for, the decision as to further action could be made later.

THE PRESIDENT inquired if a later decision would not depend on what the Russians agree to do. It was agreed that this would have considerable influence.

THE PRESIDENT then asked Admiral Leahy for his views of the situation.

ADMIRAL LEAHY recalled that the President had been interested in knowing what the price in casualties for Kyushu would be and whether or

---

[9] Ira C. Eaker (1896–1987) was Deputy Commander of the Army Air Forces and Chief of the Air Staff. Dwight Eisenhower (1890–1969) was Supreme Allied Commander in Europe.

[10] Earnest King (1878–1956) was Chief of Naval Operations.

not that price could be paid. He pointed out that the troops on Okinawa had lost 35 percent in casualties. If this percentage were applied to the number of troops to be employed in Kyushu, he thought from the similarity of the fighting to be expected that this would give a good estimate of the casualties to be expected. He was interested therefore in finding out how many troops are to be used in Kyushu.

ADMIRAL KING called attention to what he considered an important difference in Okinawa and Kyushu. There had been only one way to go on Okinawa. This meant a straight frontal attack against a highly fortified position. On Kyushu, however, landings would be made on three fronts simultaneously and there would be much more room for maneuver. It was his opinion that a realistic casualty figure for Kyushu would lie somewhere between the number experienced by General MacArthur in the operations on Luzon and the Okinawa casualties.

GENERAL MARSHALL pointed out that the total assault troops for the Kyushu campaign were shown in the memorandum prepared for the President as 766,700. He said, in answer to the President's question as to what opposition could be expected on Kyushu, that it was estimated at eight Japanese divisions or about 350,000 troops. He said that divisions were still being raised in Japan and that reinforcement from other areas was possible but it was becoming increasingly difficult and painful.

THE PRESIDENT asked about the possibility of reinforcements for Kyushu moving south from the other Japanese islands.

GENERAL MARSHALL said that it was expected that all communications with Kyushu would be destroyed.

ADMIRAL KING described in some detail the land communications between the other Japanese islands and Kyushu and stated that as a result of operations already planned, the Japanese would have to depend on sea shipping for any reinforcement.

ADMIRAL LEAHY stressed the fact that Kyushu was an island. It was crossed by a mountain range, which would be difficult for either the Japanese or the Americans to cross. The Kyushu operation, in effect, contemplated the taking of another island from which to bring increased air power against Japan.

THE PRESIDENT expressed the view that it was practically creating another Okinawa closer to Japan, to which the Chiefs of Staff agreed.

THE PRESIDENT then asked General Eaker for his opinion of the operation as an air man.

GENERAL EAKER said that he agreed completely with the statements made by General Marshall in his digest of the memorandum prepared for the President. He had just received a cable in which General Arnold also expressed complete agreement. He stated that any blockade of Honshu was dependent upon airdromes on Kyushu; that the air plan contemplated employment of 40 groups of heavy bombers against Japan and that these could not be deployed without the use of airfields on Kyushu. He said that those who advocated the use against Japan of air power alone overlooked the very impressive fact that air casualties are always much heavier when the air faces the enemy alone and that these casualties never fail to drop as soon as the ground forces come in. Present air casualties are averaging 2 percent per mission, about 30 percent per month. He wished to point out and to emphasize that delay favored only the enemy and he urged that there be no delay.

THE PRESIDENT said that as he understood it the Joint Chiefs of Staff, after weighing all the possibilities of the situation and considering all possible alternative plans were still of the unanimous opinion that the Kyushu operation was the best solution under the circumstances.

The Chiefs of Staff agreed that this was so.

THE PRESIDENT then asked the Secretary of War for his opinion.

MR. STIMSON agreed with the Chiefs of Staff that there was no other choice. He felt that he was personally responsible to the President more for political than for military considerations. It was his opinion that there was a large submerged class in Japan who do not favor the present war and whose full opinion and influence had never yet been felt. He felt sure that this submerged class would fight and fight tenaciously if attacked on their own ground. He was concerned that something should be done to arouse them and to develop any possible influence they might have before it became necessary to come to grips with them.

THE PRESIDENT stated that this possibility was being worked on all the time. He asked if the invasion of Japan by white men would not have the effect of more closely uniting the Japanese.

MR. STIMSON thought there was every prospect of this. He agreed with the plan proposed by the Joint Chiefs of Staff as being the best thing to do, but he still hoped for some fruitful accomplishment through other means.

THE PRESIDENT then asked for the views of the Secretary of the Navy.

MR. FORRESTAL pointed out that even if we wished to besiege Japan for a year or a year and a half, the capture of Kyushu would still be essential. Therefore, the sound decision is to proceed with the operation against Kyushu. There will still be time thereafter to consider the main decision in the light of subsequent events.

MR. McCLOY[11] said he felt that the time was propitious now to study closely all possible means of bringing out the influence of the submerged group in Japan which had been referred to by Mr. Stimson.

THE PRESIDENT stated that one of his objectives in connection with the coming conference[12] would be to get from Russia all the assistance in the war that was possible. To this end he wanted to know all the decisions that he would have to make in advance in order to occupy the strongest possible position in the discussions.

ADMIRAL LEAHY said that he could not agree with those who said to him that unless we obtain the unconditional surrender of the Japanese that we will have lost the war. He feared no menace from Japan in the foreseeable future, even if we were unsuccessful in forcing unconditional surrender. What he did fear was that our insistence on unconditional surrender would result only in making the Japanese desperate and thereby increase our casualty lists. He did not think that this was at all necessary.

THE PRESIDENT stated that it was with that thought in mind that he had left the door open for Congress to take appropriate action with reference to unconditional surrender. However, he did not feel that he could take any action at this time to change public opinion on the matter.

THE PRESIDENT said he considered the Kyushu plan all right from the military standpoint and, so far as he was concerned, the Joint Chiefs of Staff could go ahead with it; that we can do this operation and then decide as to the final action later.

The conversation then turned on the situation in China. . . .

C. Proclamation Defining Terms for Japanese Surrender, Potsdam, July 26, 1945[13]

We—the President of the United States, the President of the National Government of the Republic of China, and the Prime Minister of Great Britain, representing the hundreds of millions of our countrymen, have conferred and agree that Japan shall be given an opportunity to end this war.

The prodigious land, sea and air forces of the United States, the British

---

[11] John J. McCloy (1895–1989) was Assistant Secretary of War.

[12] Potsdam Conference

[13] *Foreign Relations of the United States, Diplomatic Papers, The Conference of Berlin (Potsdam Conference), 1945,* Volume II, 1474–76. Available online from Digital Collections, University of Wisconsin–Madison Libraries. https://goo.gl/ND2XHC

Empire and of China, many times reinforced by their armies and air fleets from the west, are poised to strike the final blows upon Japan. This military power is sustained and inspired by the determination of all the Allied Nations to prosecute the war against Japan until she ceases to resist.

The result of the futile and senseless German resistance to the might of the aroused free peoples of the world stands forth in awful clarity as an example to the people of Japan. The might that now converges on Japan is immeasurably greater than that which, when applied to the resisting Nazis, necessarily laid waste to the lands, the industry and the method of life of the whole German people. The full application of our military power, backed by our resolve, will mean the inevitable and complete destruction of the Japanese armed forces and just as inevitably the utter devastation of the Japanese homeland.

The time has come for Japan to decide whether she will continue to be controlled by those self-willed militaristic advisers whose unintelligent calculations have brought the Empire of Japan to the threshold of annihilation, or whether she will follow the path of reason.

Following are our terms. We will not deviate from them. There are no alternatives. We shall brook no delay.

There must be eliminated for all time the authority and influence of those who have deceived and misled the people of Japan into embarking on world conquest, for we insist that a new order of peace, security and justice will be impossible until irresponsible militarism is driven from the world.

Until such a new order is established and until there is convincing proof that Japan's war-making power is destroyed, points in Japanese territory to be designated by the Allies shall be occupied to secure the achievement of the basic objectives we are here setting forth.

The terms of the Cairo Declaration shall be carried out and Japanese sovereignty shall be limited to the islands of Honshu, Hokkaido, Kyushu, Shikoku and such minor islands as we determine.[14]

The Japanese military forces, after being completely disarmed, shall be permitted to return to their homes with the opportunity to lead peaceful and productive lives.

We do not intend that the Japanese shall be enslaved as a race or destroyed

---

[14] In the 1943 Cairo Declaration, the United States, Britain, and China had pledged to eject Japanese forces from all conquered lands, including China, Korea, and Pacific Islands.

as a nation, but stern justice shall be meted out to all war criminals, including those who have visited cruelties upon our prisoners. The Japanese Government shall remove all obstacles to the revival and strengthening of democratic tendencies among the Japanese people. Freedom of speech, of religion, and of thought, as well as respect for the fundamental human rights shall be established.

Japan shall be permitted to maintain such industries as will sustain her economy and permit the exaction of just reparations in kind, but not those which would enable her to re-arm for war. To this end, access to, as distinguished from control of, raw materials shall be permitted. Eventual Japanese participation in world trade relations shall be permitted.

The occupying forces of the Allies shall be withdrawn from Japan as soon as these objectives have been accomplished and there has been established in accordance with the freely expressed will of the Japanese people a peacefully inclined and responsible government.

We call upon the government of Japan to proclaim now the unconditional surrender of all Japanese armed forces, and to provide proper and adequate assurances of their good faith in such action. The alternative for Japan is prompt and utter destruction.

D. President Harry S. Truman, Press Release Alerting the Nation About the Atomic Bomb, August 6, 1945[15]

THE WHITE HOUSE
Washington, D.C.

STATEMENT BY THE PRESIDENT OF THE UNITED STATES

Sixteen hours ago, an American airplane dropped one bomb on Hiroshima and destroyed its usefulness to the enemy. That bomb had more power than 20,000 tons of TNT. It had more than two thousand times the blast power of the British "Grand Slam" which is the largest bomb ever yet used in the history of warfare.

The Japanese began the war from the air at Pearl Harbor. They have been repaid many fold. And the end is not yet. With this bomb we have now added

---

[15] Press release by the White House, August 6, 1945, Ayers Papers, U.S. Army Press releases, Truman Library. https://goo.gl/XgYovr

a new and revolutionary increase in destruction to supplement the growing power of our armed forces. In their present form these bombs are now in production and even more powerful forms are in development.

It is an atomic bomb. It is a harnessing of the basic power of the universe. The force from which the sun draws its power has been loosed against those who brought war to the Far East.

Before 1939, it was the accepted belief of scientists that it was theoretically possible to release atomic energy. But no one knew any practical method of doing it. By 1942, however, we knew that the Germans were working feverishly to find a way to add atomic energy to the other engines of war with which they hoped to enslave the world. But they failed. We may be grateful to Providence that the Germans got the V-1's and V-2's[16] late and in limited quantities and even more grateful that they did not get the atomic bomb at all.

The battle of the laboratories held fateful risks for us as well as the battles of the air, land, and sea, and we have now won the battle of the laboratories as we have won the other battles.

Beginning in 1940, before Pearl Harbor, scientific knowledge useful in war was pooled between the United States and Great Britain, and many priceless helps to our victories have come from that arrangement. Under that general policy the research on the atomic bomb was begun. With American and British scientists working together we entered the race of discovery against the Germans.

The United States had available the large number of scientists of distinction in the many needed areas of knowledge. It had the tremendous industrial and financial resources necessary for the project and they could be devoted to it without undue impairment of other vital war work. In the United States the laboratory work and the production plants, on which a substantial start had already been made, would be out of reach of enemy bombing, while at that time Britain was exposed to constant air attack and was still threatened with the possibility of invasion. For these reasons Prime Minister Churchill and President Roosevelt agreed that it was wise to carry on the project here.

We now have two great plants and many lesser works devoted to the production of atomic power. Employment during peak construction numbered 125,000 and over 65,000 individuals are even now engaged in operating the plants. Many have worked there for two and a half years. Few know what they have been producing. They see great quantities of material going in and they see nothing coming out of these plants, for the physical size of the explosive

---

[16] V1 and V2 were missiles used by the Germans for long range bombing.

charge is exceedingly small. We have spent two billion dollars on the greatest scientific gamble in history—and won.

But the greatest marvel is not the size of the enterprise, its secrecy, nor its cost, but the achievement of scientific brains in putting together infinitely complex pieces of knowledge held by many men in different fields of science into a workable plan. And hardly less marvelous has been the capacity of industry to design and of labor to operate, the machines and methods to do things never done before so that the brainchild of many minds came forth in physical shape and performed as it was supposed to do. Both science and industry worked under the direction of the United States Army, which achieved a unique success in managing so diverse a problem in the advancement of knowledge in an amazingly short time. It is doubtful if such another combination could be got together in the world. What has been done is the greatest achievement of organized science in history. It was done under pressure and without failure.

We are now prepared to obliterate more rapidly and completely every productive enterprise the Japanese have above ground in any city. We shall destroy their docks, their factories, and their communications. Let there be no mistake; we shall completely destroy Japan's power to make war.

It was to spare the Japanese people from utter destruction that the ultimatum of July 26 was issued at Potsdam.[17] Their leaders promptly rejected that ultimatum. If they do not now accept our terms they may expect a rain of ruin from the air, the like of which has never been seen on this earth. Behind this air attack will follow sea and land forces in such number and power as they have not yet seen and with the fighting skill of which they are already well aware.

The Secretary of War, who has kept in personal touch with all phases of the project, will immediately make public a statement giving further details.

His statement will give facts concerning the sites at Oak Ridge near Knoxville, Tennessee, and at Richland, near Pasco, Washington, and an installation near Santa Fe, New Mexico. Although the workers at the sites have been making materials to be used producing the greatest destructive force in history they have not themselves been in danger beyond that of many other occupations, for the utmost care has been taken of their safety.[18]

The fact that we can release atomic energy ushers in a new era in man's

---

[17] See Document C.
[18] Researchers from the Los Alamos Historical Document Retrieval and Assessment project being led by the Centers for Disease Control and Prevention (CDC)

understanding of nature's forces. Atomic energy may in the future supplement the power that now comes from coal, oil, and falling water, but at present it cannot be produced on a basis to compete with them commercially.
Before that comes there must be a long period of intensive research. It has
never been the habit of the scientists of this country or the policy of this government to withhold from the world scientific knowledge. Normally, therefore, everything about the work with atomic energy would be made public.

But under the present circumstances it is not intended to divulge the
technical processes of production or all the military applications, pending
further examination of possible methods of protecting us and the rest of the
world from the danger of sudden destruction.

I shall recommend that the Congress of the United States consider
promptly the establishment of an appropriate commission to control the
production and use of atomic power within the United States. I shall give
further consideration and make further recommendations to the Congress as
to how atomic power can become a powerful and forceful influence towards
the maintenance of world peace.

E. J. R. Oppenheimer to Secretary of War Henry Stimson, August 17, 1945[19]

From: J. R. Oppenheimer
To: Henry Stimson, Secretary of War
Date: August 17, 1945

Dear Mr. Secretary:

The Interim Committee has asked us to report in some detail on the scope
and program of future work in the field of atomic energy. One important
phase of this work is the development of weapons; and since this is the problem which has dominated our war time activities, it is natural that in this field
our ideas should be most definite and clear, and that we should be most confident of answering adequately the questions put to us by the committee. In
examining these questions we have, however, come on certain quite general
conclusions, whose implications for national policy would seem to be both
more immediate and more profound than those of the detailed technical

---

reported in 2007 that civilians living near the test site in the White Sands desert of
New Mexico were exposed to high levels of radiation.

[19] https://goo.gl/zyQJro

recommendations to be submitted. We, therefore, think it appropriate to present them to you at this time.

1. We are convinced that weapons quantitatively and qualitatively far more effective than now available will result from further work on these problems. This conviction is motivated not alone by analogy with past developments, but by specific projects to improve and multiply the existing weapons, and by the quite favorable technical prospects of the realization of the super bomb.

2. We have been unable to devise or propose effective military counter-measures for atomic weapons. Although we realize that future work may reveal possibilities at present obscure to us, it is our firm opinion that no military countermeasures will be found which will be adequately effective in preventing the delivery of atomic weapons.

The detailed technical report in preparation will document these conclusions, but hardly alter them.

3. We are not only unable to outline a program that would assure to this nation for the next decades hegemony in the field of atomic weapons; we are equally unable to insure that such hegemony, if achieved, could protect us from the most terrible destruction.

4. The development, in the years to come, of more effective atomic weapons, would appear to be a most natural element in any national policy of maintaining our military forces at great strength; nevertheless we have grave doubts that this further development can contribute essentially or permanently to the prevention of war. We believe that the safety of this nation—as opposed to its ability to inflict damage on an enemy power—cannot lie wholly or even primarily in its scientific or technical prowess. It can be based only on making future wars impossible. It is our unanimous and urgent recommendation to you that, despite the present incomplete exploitation of technical possibilities in this field, all steps be taken, all necessary international arrangements be made, to this one end.

5. We should be most happy to have you bring these views to the attention of other members of the Government, or of the American people, should you wish to do so.

Very sincerely,

J. R. Oppenheimer

CHAPTER 24

Containment and the Truman Doctrine

A. George F. Kennan to the Secretary of State, February 22, 1946
B. Walter Lippmann, *The Cold War*, 1947
C. President Harry Truman, Address of the President of the United States (Truman Doctrine), March 12, 1947
D. Henry Wallace, Critique of the Truman Doctrine, March 13, 1947

Allies during the Second World War, the United States and the Soviet Union fell out quickly once it ended. By late 1945 and early 1946, concern had already arisen about Soviet attitudes and actions in Europe. In response to a request from the State Department, in February 1946, George Kennan (1904–2005), the Chargé at the American Embassy in Moscow, sent a telegram (Document A) that offered an explanation for Soviet actions. Quickly dubbed the "Long Telegram," its analysis and recommendations, along with a version that Kennan published in the journal Foreign Affairs under the pseudonym Mr. X, became the basis for the policy of containment that in one way or another guided America's actions toward the Soviet Union until the end of the Cold War. A manifestation of containment was the so-called Truman Doctrine announced by President Truman about a year after Kennan sent his response to Washington (Document C). Like containment, the Truman Doctrine became a fundamental part of America's response to the confrontation with the Soviet Union. From the beginning, both containment and the Truman Doctrine had critics (Documents B and D). As the Cold War continued, it became a struggle not just between two political and military powers but between two ways of life or which of the two could better meet human needs. Even the quality of American and Soviet kitchens and what that represented could be part of the debate (see photo on page F).

Study Questions

A. What were the arguments for and against containment and the Truman Doctrine? Why did Kennan think that a political regime that thought it had to destroy the United States in order to survive could be contained? If the

Soviet Union could be contained, did that mean it did not have the character that Kennan ascribed to it?

B. Compare the documents below with those in Chapter 20. Do the documents show the same understanding of America's place in the world and how it should deal with other countries and foreign populations?

C. Do the arguments for and against containment of the Soviet Union recall earlier arguments for and against the containment of slavery hinted at by the documents in Volume 1, Chapters 12, 13, 15? How do the arguments for and against containment and the Truman Doctrine differ from the arguments made about the war with Mexico (Volume 1, Chapter 13)?

A. George F. Kennan to the Secretary of State, February 22, 1946[1]

I. Basic features of postwar Soviet outlook, as put forward by official propaganda machine.

A. The USSR still lives in antagonistic "capitalist encirclement" with which in the long run there can be no permanent peaceful coexistence. As stated by Stalin in 1927 to a delegation of American workers:

> In course of further development of international revolution, there will emerge two centers of world significance: a socialist center, drawing to itself the countries which tend toward socialism, and a capitalist center, drawing to itself the countries that incline toward capitalism. Battle between these two centers for command of world economy will decide fate of capitalism and of communism in entire world.

B. Capitalist world is beset with internal conflicts inherent in nature of capitalist society. These conflicts are insoluble by means of peaceful compromise. Greatest of them is that between England and US.

C. Internal conflicts of capitalism inevitably generate wars. Wars thus generated may be of two kinds: intracapitalist wars between two capitalist

---

[1] "The Chargé in the Soviet Union (Kennan) to the Secretary of State, February 22, 1946," Document 475, *The Foreign Relations of the United States, 1946, Vol. VI, Eastern Europe, the Soviet Union* (Washington, D.C.: U.S. Department of State, Office of the Historian, 1969).

states, and wars of intervention against socialist world. Smart capitalists, vainly seeking escape from inner conflicts of capitalism, incline toward latter.

D. Intervention against USSR, while it would be disastrous to those who undertook it, would cause renewed delay in progress of Soviet socialism and must therefore be forestalled at all costs.

E. Conflicts between capitalist states, though likewise fraught with danger for USSR, nevertheless hold out great possibilities for advancement of socialist cause, particularly if USSR remains militarily powerful, ideologically monolithic, and faithful to its present brilliant leadership.

F. It must be borne in mind that capitalist world is not all bad. In addition to hopelessly reactionary and bourgeois elements, it includes (1) certain wholly enlightened and positive elements united in acceptable communistic parties, and (2) certain other elements (now described for tactical reasons as progressive or democratic) whose reactions, aspirations and activities happen to be "objectively" favorable to interests of the USSR. These last must be encouraged and utilized for Soviet purposes.

G. Among negative elements of bourgeois-capitalist society, most dangerous of all are those whom Lenin called false friends of the people, namely moderate Socialist or Social Democratic leaders (in other words, non-Communist left-wing). These are more dangerous than out-and-out reactionaries, for latter at least march under their true colors, whereas moderate left-wing leaders confuse people by employing devices of socialism to serve interests of reactionary capital.

So much for premises. To what deductions do they lead from standpoint of Soviet policy? To the following:

A. Everything must be done to advance relative strength of USSR as factor in international society. Conversely, no opportunity must be missed to reduce strength and influence, collectively as well as individually, of capitalist powers.

B. Soviet efforts, and those of Russia's friends abroad, must be directed toward deepening and exploiting of differences and conflicts between capitalist powers. If these eventually deepen into an "imperialist" war, this war must be turned into revolutionary upheavals within the various capitalist countries.

C. "Democratic-progressive" elements abroad are to be utilized to bring pressure to bear on capitalist governments along lines agreeable to Soviet interests.

D. Relentless battle must be waged against Socialist and Social Democratic leaders abroad.

II. Background of outlook.

Before examining ramifications of this party line in practice, there are certain aspects of it to which your attention should be drawn.

First, it does not represent natural outlook of Russian people. Latter are, by and large, friendly to outside world, eager for experience of it, eager to measure against it talents they are conscious of possessing, eager above all to live peace and enjoy fruits of their own labor....

Second, please note that premises on which this party line is based are for most part simply not true. Experience has shown that peaceful and mutually profitable coexistence of capitalist and socialist states is entirely possible....

Falseness of these premises, every one of which predates recent war, was amply demonstrated by that conflict itself. Anglo-American differences did not turn out to be major differences of Western world. Capitalist countries, other than those of Axis, showed no disposition to solve their differences by joining in crusade against USSR. Instead of imperialist war turning into civil wars and revolutions, USSR found itself obliged to fight side by side with capitalist powers for an avowed community of aims.

Nevertheless, all these theses, however baseless and disproven, are being boldly put forward again today. What does this indicate? It indicates that the Soviet party line is not based on any objective analysis of the situation beyond Russia's borders; that it has, indeed, little to do with conditions outside of Russia; that it arises mainly from basic inner-Russian necessities which existed before recent war and exist today.

At the bottom of the Kremlin's neurotic view of world affairs is traditional and instinctive Russian sense of insecurity. Originally, this was insecurity of a peaceful agricultural people trying to live on vast exposed plain in neighborhood of fierce nomadic peoples. To this was added, as Russia came into contact with economically advanced West, fear of more competent, more powerful, more highly organized societies in that area....

It was no coincidence that Marxism, which had smoldered ineffectively for half a century in Western Europe, caught hold and blazed for first time in Russia. Only in this land which had never known a friendly neighbor or indeed any tolerant equilibrium of separate powers, either internal or international, could a doctrine thrive which viewed economic conflicts of society as insoluble by peaceful means. After establishment of Bolshevist regime,

Marxist dogma, rendered even more truculent and intolerant by Lenin's interpretation, became a perfect vehicle for sense of insecurity with which Bolsheviks, even more than previous Russian rulers, were afflicted.[2]. . .

It should not be thought from above that Soviet party line is necessarily disingenuous and insincere on part of all those who put it forward. Many of them are too ignorant of outside world and mentally too dependent to question self-hypnotism, and have no difficulty making themselves believe what they find it comforting and convenient to believe. Finally, we have the unsolved mystery as to who, if anyone, in this great land actually receives accurate and unbiased information about outside world. In an atmosphere of Oriental secretiveness and conspiracy which pervades this government, possibilities for distorting or poisoning sources and currents of information are infinite. . . .

III. Projection of Soviet outlook in practical policy on official level.

We have now seen nature and background of the Soviet program. What may we expect of its practical implementations?

Soviet policy is conducted on two planes: (1) official plane represented by actions undertaken officially in the name of the Soviet government; and (2) subterranean plane of actions undertaken by agencies for which the Soviet government does not admit responsibility.

Policy promulgated on both planes will be calculated to serve basic policies A to D outlined in "I." Actions taken on different planes will differ considerably, but will dovetail into each other in purposes, timing, and effect.

On official plane, we must look for following:

A. Internal policy devoted to increasing in every way strength and prestige of Soviet state; intensive military-industrialization; maximum development of armed forces; great displays to impress outsiders; continued secretiveness about internal matters, designed to conceal weaknesses and to keep opponents in dark.

B. Wherever it is considered timely and promising, efforts will be made to advance official limits of Soviet power. For the moment, these efforts are restricted to certain neighboring points conceived of here as being of

---

[2] The Bolshevik Party, led by Vladimir Lenin (1870–1924), was the precursor to the Communist Party of the Soviet Union. They billed themselves as the people's party; the word Bolshevik literally means "the majority," in Russian.

immediate strategic necessity, such as northern Iran, Turkey, possibly Born-holm.[3] However, other points may at any time come into question, if and as concealed Soviet political power is extended to new areas. Thus a "friendly" Persian government might be asked to grant Russia a port on Persian Gulf. Should Spain fall under Communist control, question of Soviet base at Gibraltar Strait might be activated. But such claims will appear on official level only when unofficial preparation is complete.

C. Russians will participate officially in international organizations where they see opportunity of extending Soviet power or of inhibiting or diluting power of others. Moscow sees in [the United Nations] not the mechanism for a permanent and stable world society founded on mutual interest and aims of all nations, but an arena in which aims just mentioned can be favorably pursued....

D. Toward colonial areas and backward or dependent peoples, Soviet policy, even on official plane, will be directed toward weakening of power and influence and contacts of advanced Western nations, on theory that insofar as this policy is successful, there will be created a vacuum which will favor communist-Soviet penetration. Soviet pressure for participation in trusteeship arrangements thus represents a desire to be in a position to complicate and inhibit exertion of Western influence at such points rather than to provide major channel for exerting of Soviet power. Latter motive is not lacking, but for this Soviets prefer to rely on other channels than offi-cial trusteeship arrangements. Thus we may expect to find Soviets asking for admission everywhere to trusteeship or similar arrangements and using levers thus acquired to weaken Western influence among such peoples....

IV. Following may be said as to what we may expect by way of implemen-tation of basic Soviet policies on unofficial, or subterranean, plane; i.e., on plane for which Soviet government accepts no respon-sibility.

Agencies utilized for promulgation of policies on this plane are the following:

A. Inner central core of Communist parties in other countries. While many of the persons who compose this category may also appear and act in unrelated public capacities, they are in reality working closely together as an underground operating directorate of world communism, a concealed

---

[3] Bornhom is an island in the Baltic Sea east of Copenhagen and south of Sweden.

Comintern[4] tightly coordinated and directed by Moscow. It is important to remember that this inner core is actually working on underground lines, despite legality of parties with which it is associated.

B. Rank and file of Communist parties. Note distinction is drawn between these and persons defined in paragraph A. . . . As a rule they are used to penetrate, and to influence or dominate, as the case may be, other organizations less likely to be suspected of being tools of Soviet government, with a view to accomplishing their purposes through front organizations, rather than by direct action as a separate political party.

C. A wide variety of national associations or bodies which can be dominated or influenced by such penetration. These include: labor unions, youth leagues, women's organizations, racial societies, religious societies, social organizations, cultural groups, liberal magazines, publishing houses, etc.

D. International organizations which can be similarly penetrated through influence over various national components. . . .

It may be expected that the component parts of this far-flung apparatus will be utilized, in accordance with their individual suitability, as follows:

To undermine general political and strategic potential of major Western powers. Efforts will be made in such countries to disrupt national self-confidence, to hamstring measures of national defense, to increase social and industrial unrest, to stimulate all forms of disunity. All persons with grievances, whether economic or racial, will be urged to seek redress not in mediation and compromise, but in defiant violent struggle for destruction of other elements of society. Here poor will be set against rich, black against white, young against old, newcomers against established residents, etc.

On unofficial plane particularly violent efforts will be made to weaken power and influence of Western powers over colonial, backward, or dependent peoples. On this level, no holds will be barred. Mistakes and weaknesses of Western colonial administration will be mercilessly exposed and exploited. Liberal opinion in Western countries will be mobilized to weaken colonial policies. Resentment among dependent peoples will be stimulated. And while latter are being encouraged to seek independence of Western powers, Soviet-dominated puppet political machines will be undergoing

---

[4] The Communist International or Comintern (1919–1943) advocated worldwide communism. Through the Comintern the Soviet Union controlled communist parties in other countries, supporting them financially, including the Communist Party of the United States.

preparation to take over domestic power in respective colonial areas when independence is achieved.

Where individual governments stand in path of Soviet purposes pressure will be brought for their removal from office. This can happen where governments directly oppose Soviet foreign policy aims (Turkey, Iran), where they seal their territories off against Communist penetration (Switzerland, Portugal), or where they compete too strongly, like Labor government in England, for moral domination among elements which it is important for Communists to dominate. (Sometimes, two of these elements are present in a single case. Then Communist opposition becomes particularly shrill and savage.) ...

Everything possible will be done to set major Western powers against each other....

In general, all Soviet efforts on unofficial international plane will be negative and destructive in character, designed to tear down sources of strength beyond reach of Soviet control. This is only in line with basic Soviet instinct that there can be no compromise with rival power and that constructive work can start only when Communist power is dominant. But behind all this will be applied insistent, unceasing pressure for penetration and command of key positions in administration and especially in police apparatus of foreign countries. The Soviet regime is a police regime par excellence, reared in the dim half-world of Tsarist police intrigue, accustomed to think primarily in terms of police power. This should never be lost sight of in gauging Soviet motives.

V. Practical deductions from standpoint of US policy

In summary, we have here a political force committed fanatically to the belief that with US there can be no permanent modus vivendi, that it is desirable and necessary that the internal harmony of our society be disrupted, our traditional way of life be destroyed, the international authority of our state be broken, if Soviet power is to be secure. This political force has complete power of disposition over energies of one of the world's greatest peoples and resources of the world's richest national territory, and is borne along by deep and powerful currents of Russian nationalism. In addition, it has an elaborate and far-flung apparatus for exertion of its influence in other countries, an apparatus of amazing flexibility and versatility, managed by people whose experience and skill in underground methods are presumable without parallel in history. Finally, it is seemingly inaccessible to considerations of reality in its basic reactions. For it, the vast fund of objective fact about human society is not, as with us, the measure against which outlook is constantly being tested and reformed, but a grab bag from which individual items are selected arbitrarily and tendentiously to bolster an outlook already preconceived. This is admittedly not a pleasant picture. Problem of how to cope with this force is undoubtedly greatest task our diplomacy has ever faced and probably the greatest it will ever have to face. It should be the point of departure from which our political general staff work at the present juncture should proceed. It should be approached with same thoroughness and care as solution of major strategic problem in war, and if necessary, with no smaller outlay in planning effort. I cannot attempt to suggest all the answers here. But I would like to record my conviction that the problem is within our power to solve—and that without recourse to any general military conflict. And in support of this conviction there are certain observations of a more encouraging nature I should like to make:

(One) Soviet power, unlike that of Hitlerite Germany, is neither schematic nor adventuristic. It does not work by fixed plans. It does not take unnecessary risks. Impervious to logic of reason, and it is highly sensitive to logic of force. For this reason it can easily withdraw—and usually does—when strong resistance is encountered at any point. Thus, if the adversary has sufficient force and makes clear his readiness to use it, he rarely has to do so. If situations are properly handled there need be no prestige-engaging showdowns.

(Two) Gauged against Western world as a whole, Soviets are still by far the weaker force. Thus, their success will really depend on degree of cohesion, firmness, and vigor which Western world can muster. And this is factor which it is within our power to influence.

(Three) Success of Soviet system, as form of internal power, is not yet finally proven. It has yet to be demonstrated that it can survive supreme test of successive transfer of power from one individual or group to another. Lenin's death was first such transfer, and its effects wracked Soviet state for fifteen years after. Stalin's death or retirement will be second. But even this will not be final test. Soviet internal system will now be subjected, by virtue of recent territorial expansions, to a series of additional strains which once proved severe tax on Tsardom. We here are convinced that never since termination of the civil war[5] have the mass of Russian people been emotionally

---

[5] 1917–1922, a conflict following the Russian Revolution between the Bolsheviks, who had seized power, and those who opposed them.

farther removed from doctrines of Communist Party than they are today. In Russia, party has now become a great and—for the moment—highly success-ful apparatus of dictatorial administration, but it has ceased to be a source of emotional inspiration. Thus, internal soundness and permanence of move-ment need not yet be regarded as assured.

(Four) All Soviet propaganda beyond Soviet security sphere is basically negative and destructive. It should therefore be relatively easy to combat it by any intelligent and really constructive program.

For these reasons I think we may approach calmly and with good heart the problem of how to deal with Russia. As to how this approach should be made, I only wish to advance, by way of conclusion, the following comments:

1. Our first step must be to apprehend, and recognize for what it is, the nature of the movement with which we are dealing. We must study it with the same courage, detachment, objectivity, and the same determination not to be emotionally provoked or unseated by it, with which a doctor studies unruly and unreasonable individuals.

2. We must see that our public is educated to realities of Russian situa-tion. I cannot overemphasize the importance of this. Press cannot do this alone. It must be done mainly by government, which is necessarily more experienced and better informed on practical problems involved.... Can we fix the orphans?

3. Much depends on health and vigor of our own society. World commu-nism is like malignant parasite which feeds only on diseased tissue. This is the point at which domestic and foreign policies meet. Every courageous and incisive measure to solve internal problems of our own society, to improve self-confidence, discipline, morale, and community spirit of our own people, is a diplomatic victory over Moscow worth a thousand diplomatic notes and joint communiqués. If we cannot abandon fatalism and indifference in face of deficiencies of our own society, Moscow will profit—Moscow cannot help profiting by them in its foreign policies.

4. We must formulate and put forward for other nations a much more positive and constructive picture of the sort of world we would like to see than we have put forward in the past. It is not enough to urge the people to develop political processes similar to our own. Many foreign peoples, in Europe at least, are tired and frightened by experiences of the past, and are less interested in abstract freedom than in security. They are seeking guid-ance rather than responsibilities. We should be better able than the Russians to give them this. And unless we do, the Russians certainly will.

5. Finally, we must have courage and self-confidence to cling to our own methods and conceptions of human society. After all, the greatest danger that can befall us in coping with this problem of Soviet communism is that we shall allow ourselves to become like those with whom we are coping.

B. Walter Lippmann, *The Cold War*, 1947[6]

My objection . . . to the policy of containment is not that it seeks to confront the Soviet power with American power, but that the policy is misconceived, and must result in a misuse of American power. For as I have sought to show, it commits this country to a struggle which has for its objective nothing more substantial than the hope that in ten or fifteen years the Soviet power will, as the result of long frustration, "break up" or "mellow." In this prolonged struggle the role of the United States is, according to Mr. X, to react "at a series of constantly shifting geographical and political points" to the encroachments of the Soviet power.[7]

The policy, therefore, concedes to the Kremlin the strategical initiative as to when, where and under what local circumstances the issue is to be joined. It compels the United States to meet the Soviet pressure at these shifting geographical and political points by using satellite states, puppet governments and agents which have been subsidized and supported, though their effectiveness is meager and their reliability uncertain. By forcing us to expend our energies and our substance upon these dubious and unnatural allies on the perimeter of the Soviet Union, the effect of the policy is to neglect our natural allies in the Atlantic community, and to alienate them.

They are alienated also by the fact that they do not wish to become, like the nations of the perimeter, the clients of the United States in whose affairs

---

[6] Walter Lippmann, *The Cold War: A Study in US Foreign Policy* (New York: Harper, 1947), 29–31, 35, 37–39. Lippmann (1889–1974) was perhaps the most prominent journalist and public intellectual of his day.

[7] Lippmann quotes from the article that Kennan published in *Foreign Affairs* in 1947, "The Sources of Soviet Conduct," which was based on his "long telegram" and which included the sentence "In the light of the above, it will be clearly seen that the Soviet pressure against the free institutions of the western world is something that can be contained by the adroit and vigilant application of counter-force at a series of constantly shifting geographical and political points, corresponding to the shifts and maneuvers of Soviet policy. . . ." This sentence gave the policy Kennan proposed its name, "containment."

we intervene, asking as the price of our support that they take the directives of their own policy from Washington. They are alienated above all by the prospect of war, which could break out by design or accident, by miscalculation or provocation, if at any of these constantly shifting geographical and political points the Russians or Americans became so deeply engaged that no retreat or compromise was possible. In this war their lands would be the battlefield. Their peoples would be divided by civil conflict. Their cities and their fields would be the bases and the bridgeheads in a total war which, because it would merge into a general civil war, would be as indecisive as it was savage....

I am contending that the American diplomatic effort should be concentrated on the problem created by the armistice—which is on how the continent of Europe can be evacuated by the three non-European armies which are now inside Europe. This is the problem which will have to be solved if the independence of the European nations is to be restored. Without that there is no possibility of a tolerable peace. But if these armies withdraw, there will be a very different balance of power in the world than there is today, and one which cannot easily be upset. For the nations of Europe, separately and in groups, perhaps even in unity, will then, and then only, cease to be the stakes and the pawns of the Russian-American conflict....

The terms of the problem were defined at Yalta[8] in the winter of 1945. There, with a victory over Germany in sight, Roosevelt, Churchill, and Stalin made a military settlement which fixed the boundaries where the converging armies were to meet, and were to wait while the governments negotiated the terms of peace which would provide for the withdrawal of the armies. The crucial issue in the world today is whether the Yalta military boundary, which was intended to be provisional for the period of the armistice, is to become the political boundary of two hostile coalitions....

The Yalta military boundary was the datum line from which the diplomatic settlement of the war had necessarily to begin. It was, I believe, at this juncture that American diplomacy became confused, lost sight of the primary and essential objective, and became entangled in all manner of secondary issues and disputes in the Russian borderlands.

The British and the Americans, of course, could not accept the permanent

---

[8] President Roosevelt, Prime Minister of Great Britain Winston Churchill, and Premier Joseph Stalin met at the Yalta Conference, February 4–11, 1945 to discuss the post-war reorganization of Europe.

division of the European continent along the Yalta line. They could not accept a settlement in which Poland, Czechoslovakia, Yugoslavia, Hungary, Rumania and Bulgaria would lose all independence and become incorporated as Soviet republics in the U.S.S.R. They had a debt of honor to the countless patriots in those lands. They realized that if the frontiers of the Soviet system were extended as far west as the middle of Germany and Austria, then not only Germany and Austria but all western Europe might fall within the Russian sphere of influence and be dominated by the Soviet Union.

Thus for the best of reasons and with the best of motives they came to the conclusion that they must wage a diplomatic campaign to prevent Russia from expanding her sphere, to prevent her from consolidating it, and to compel her to contract it. But they failed to see clearly that until the Red Army evacuated eastern Europe and withdrew to the frontiers of the Soviet Union, none of these objectives could be achieved....

For if, and only if, we can bring about the withdrawal of the Red Army from the Yalta line to the new frontier of the Soviet Union—and simultaneously, of course, the withdrawal of the British and American armies from continental Europe—can a balance of power be established which can then be maintained. For after the withdrawal, an attempt to return would be an invasion—an open, unmistakable act of military aggression. Against such an aggression, the power of the United States to strike the vital centers of Russia by air and by amphibious assault would stand as the opposing and deterrent force. And until treaties are agreed to which bring about the withdrawal of the Red Army, the power of the United States to strike these vital centers would be built up for the express purpose of giving weight to our policy of ending the military occupation of Europe.

All the other pressures of the Soviet Union at the "constantly shifting geographical and political points," which Mr. X is so concerned about—in the Middle East and in Asia—are, I contend, secondary and subsidiary to the fact that its armed forces are in the heart of Europe. It is to the Red Army in Europe, therefore, and not to ideologies, elections, forms of government, to socialism, to communism, to free enterprise, that a correctly conceived and soundly planned policy should be directed.

C. President Harry Truman, Address of the President of the United States (Truman Doctrine), March 12, 1947[9]

The gravity of the situation which confronts the world today necessitates my appearance before a joint session of the Congress.

The foreign policy and the national security of this country are involved.

One aspect of the present situation, which I wish to present to you at this time for your consideration and decision, concerns Greece and Turkey....

The Greek Government has . . . asked for the assistance of ex-perienced American administrators, economists and technicians to in-sure that the financial and other aid given to Greece shall be used effectively in creating a stable and self-sustaining economy and in im-proving its public administration.

The very existence of the Greek state is today threatened by the terrorist activities of several thousand armed men, led by Communists, who defy the government's authority at a number of points, particularly along the northern boundaries. A Commission appointed by the United Nations Security Council is at present investigating disturbed conditions in northern Greece and alleged border violations along the frontier between Greece on the one hand and Albania, Bulgaria, and Yugoslavia on the other.

Meanwhile, the Greek Government is unable to cope with the situation. The Greek army is small and poorly equipped. It needs supplies and equipment if it is to restore the authority of the government through-out Greek territory.

. . .

The British Government, which has been helping Greece, can give no further financial or economic aid after March 31. Great Britain finds itself under the necessity of reducing or liquidating its commitments in several parts of the world, including Greece.

We have considered how the United Nations might assist in this crisis. But the situation is an urgent one requiring immediate action, and the United

---

[9] *Congressional Record*, 80th Congress, First Session, Document 171, 1–4. Available at "The Truman Doctrine and the Beginning of the Cold War," Elsey Papers, Truman Library. https://goo.gl/Zvw3pu. The policy expressed in this speech, in particular Truman's claim that "I believe that it must be the policy of the United States to support free peoples who are resisting attempted subjugation by armed minorities or by outside pressures," soon became known as the "Truman Doctrine."

Nations and its related organizations are not in a position to extend help of the kind that is required. . . .

Greece's neighbor, Turkey, also deserves our attention.

The future of Turkey as an independent and economically sound state is clearly no less important to the freedom-loving peoples of the world than the future of Greece. The circumstances in which Turkey finds itself today are considerably different from those of Greece. Turkey has been spared the disasters that have beset Greece. And during the war, the United States and Great Britain furnished Turkey with material aid. Nevertheless, Turkey now needs our support.

Since the war Turkey has sought financial assistance from Great Britain and the United States for the purpose of effecting that modernization necessary for the maintenance of its national integrity.

That integrity is essential to the preservation of order in the Middle East.

The British government has informed us that, owing to its own difficulties, it can no longer extend financial or economic aid to Turkey.

As in the case of Greece, if Turkey is to have the assistance it needs, the United States must supply it. We are the only country able to provide that help.

I am fully aware of the broad implications involved if the United States extends assistance to Greece and Turkey, and I shall discuss these implications with you at this time.

One of the primary objectives of the foreign policy of the United States is the creation of conditions in which we and other nations will be able to work out a way of life free from coercion. This was a fundamental issue in the war with Germany and Japan. Our victory was won over countries which sought to impose their will, and their way of life, upon other nations.

To ensure the peaceful development of nations, free from coercion, the United States has taken a leading part in establishing the United Nations, The United Nations is designed to make possible lasting freedom and independence for all its members. We shall not realize our objectives, however, unless we are willing to help free peoples to maintain their free institutions and their national integrity against aggressive movements that seek to impose upon them totalitarian regimes. This is no more than a frank recognition that totalitarian regimes imposed on free peoples, by direct or indirect aggression, undermine the foundations of international peace and hence the security of the United States.

The peoples of a number of countries of the world have recently had totalitarian regimes forced upon them against their will. The Government of the United States has made frequent protests against coercion and intimidation, in violation of the Yalta agreement, in Poland, Rumania, and Bulgaria. I must also state that in a number of other countries there have been similar developments.

At the present moment in world history nearly every nation must choose between alternative ways of life. The choice is too often not a free one.

One way of life is based upon the will of the majority, and is distinguished by free institutions, representative government, free elections, guarantees of individual liberty, freedom of speech and religion, and freedom from political oppression.

The second way of life is based upon the will of a minority forcibly imposed upon the majority. It relies upon terror and oppression, a controlled press and radio; fixed elections, and the suppression of personal freedoms.

I believe that it must be the policy of the United States to support free peoples who are resisting attempted subjugation by armed minorities or by outside pressures.

I believe that we must assist free peoples to work out their own destinies in their own way.

I believe that our help should be primarily through economic and financial aid which is essential to economic stability and orderly political processes.

The world is not static, and the status quo is not sacred. But we cannot allow changes in the status quo in violation of the Charter of the United Nations by such methods as coercion, or by such subterfuges as political infiltration. In helping free and independent nations to maintain their freedom, the United States will be giving effect to the principles of the Charter of the United Nations.

It is necessary only to glance at a map to realize that the survival and integrity of the Greek nation are of grave importance in a much wider situation. If Greece should fall under the control of an armed minority, the effect upon its neighbor, Turkey, would be immediate and serious. Confusion and disorder might well spread throughout the entire Middle East.

Moreover, the disappearance of Greece as an independent state would have a profound effect upon those countries in Europe whose peoples are struggling against great difficulties to maintain their freedoms and their independence while they repair the damages of war.

It would be an unspeakable tragedy if these countries, which have struggled so long against overwhelming odds, should lose that victory for which they sacrificed so much. Collapse of free institutions and loss of independence would be disastrous not only for them but for the world. Discouragement and possibly failure would quickly be the lot of neighboring peoples striving to maintain their freedom and independence.

Should we fail to aid Greece and Turkey in this fateful hour, the effect will be far reaching to the West as well as to the East.

We must take immediate and resolute action. . . .

D. Henry Wallace, Critique of the Truman Doctrine, March 13, 1947[10]

March 12, 1947, marked a turning point in American history. It is not a Greek crisis that we face, it is an American crisis. It is a crisis in the American spirit. Only the American people fully aroused and promptly acting can prevent disaster.

President Truman, in the name of democracy and humanitarianism, proposed a military lend-lease program. He proposed a loan of $400,000,000 to Greece and Turkey as a down payment on an unlimited expenditure aimed at opposing Communist expansion. He proposed, in effect, that America police Russia's every border. There is no regime too reactionary for us provided it stands in Russia's expansionist path. There is no country too remote to serve as the scene of a contest which may widen until it becomes a world war.

President Truman calls for action to combat a crisis. What is this crisis that necessitates Truman going to Capitol Hill as though a Pearl Harbor has suddenly hit us? How many more of these Pearl Harbors will there be? How can they be foreseen? What will they cost?

One year ago at Fulton, Mo., Winston Churchill called for a diplomatic offensive against Soviet Russia. By sanctioning that speech, Truman committed us to a policy of combating Russia with British sources. That policy proved to be so bankrupt that Britain can no longer maintain it. Now President

---

[10] Radio address concerning President Truman's proposed loan of $400 million to Greece and Turkey, March 13, 1947, reprinted in the *Congressional Record*, 80th Congress, First Session, Appendix, Volume 93, Part 10, (January 3, 1947—April 1, 1947), A1329. Henry Wallace (1888–1965) was President Roosevelt's Vice President and also served as his Secretary of Agriculture. He was Secretary of Commerce under President Truman until Truman fired him in 1946 for publicly disagreeing with Truman's approach to the Soviet Union. Wallace ran for President in 1948 as the Progressive Party nominee.

Truman proposes we take over Britain's hopeless task. Today Americans are asked to support the Governments of Greece and Turkey. Tomorrow we shall be asked to support the Governments of China and Argentina.

I say that this policy is utterly futile. No people can be bought. America cannot afford to spend billions and billions of dollars for unproductive purposes. The world is hungry and insecure, and the peoples of all lands demand change. President Truman cannot prevent change in the world any more than he can prevent the tide from coming in or the sun from setting. But once America stands for opposition to change, we are lost. America will become the most-hated nation in the world.

Russia may be poor and unprepared for war, but she knows very well how to reply to Truman's declaration of economic and financial pressure. All over the world Russia and her ally, poverty, will increase the pressure against us. Who among us is ready to predict that in this struggle American dollars will outlast the grievances that lead to communism? I certainly don't want to see communism spread. I predict that Truman's policy will spread communism in Europe and Asia. You can't fight something with nothing. When Truman offers unconditional aid to King George of Greece, he is acting as the best salesman communism ever had. In proposing this reckless adventure, Truman is betraying the great tradition of America and the leadership of the great American who preceded him.

When President Truman proclaims the world-wide conflict between East and West, he is telling the Soviet leaders that we are preparing for eventual war. They will reply by measures to strengthen their position in the event of war. Then the task of keeping the world at peace will pass beyond the power of the common people everywhere who want peace. Certainly it will not be freedom that will be victorious in this struggle. Psychological and spiritual preparation for war will follow financial preparation; civil liberties will be restricted; standards of living will be forced downward; families will be divided against each other; none of the values that we hold worth fighting for will be secure.

This is the time for an all-out worldwide reconstruction program for peace. This is America's opportunity. The peoples of all lands say to America: Send us plows for our fields instead of tanks and guns to be used against us. The dollars that are spent will be spent for the production of goods and will come back to us in a thousand different ways. Our programs will be based on service instead of the outworn ideas of imperialism and power politics. It is a fundamental law of life that a strong idea is merely strengthened by persecution. The way to handle communism is by what William James called the replacing power of the higher affection. In other words, we give the common man all over the world something better than communism. I believe we have something better than communism here in America. But President Truman has not spoken for the American ideal. It is now the turn of the American people to speak.

Common sense is required of all of us in realizing that helping militarism never brings peace. Courage is required of all of us in carrying out a program that can bring peace. Courage and common sense are the qualities that made America great. Let's keep those qualities now.

CHAPTER 25

Internal Security and Civil Liberties

A. Senator Joseph McCarthy (R-WI), Address to the League of
   Women Voters, Wheeling, West Virginia, February 9, 1950
B. The Internal Security Act, September 22, 1950
C. President Harry S. Truman, Veto of the Internal Security Act,
   September 22, 1950

O n January 21, 1950, a federal grand jury indicted Alger Hiss, a former State
     Department official, on perjury charges related to his spy work for the Soviet
Union during the 1930s. Also in 1950, Klaus Fuchs, who had worked on the American atomic bomb, confessed to being a Soviet spy while doing so, and implicated
others, revealing a Soviet espionage network that had acquired significant classified information about America's atomic bomb program. His confession ultimately led to the arrest, trial, and conviction of several other people, including
Julius and Ethel Rosenberg, who were executed in 1953.

Senator Joseph McCarthy (R-Wisconsin), a first-term senator, was not a
well-known figure when he spoke at an event sponsored by the League of Women
Voters in Wheeling, West Virginia, shortly after the Hiss indictment. Taking this
news as his theme, he claimed that 205 State Department employees were members of the Communist Party of the United States of America and that Secretary
of State Dean Acheson was protecting them. In subsequent speeches, McCarthy
cited different numbers—eighty-one, then fifty-seven—without providing much
corroboration. (After the Cold War, newly accessible Soviet files revealed that
over 500 Americans, including journalists and other ranking government officials
besides Hiss, had spied or worked for the Soviet Union in the 1930s and 1940s. See
John Earl Haynes, Harvey Klehr, and Alexander Vassiliev, Spies: The Rise and
Fall of the KGB in America [New Haven: Yale University Press, 2009]. McCarthy
knew nothing of this.)

Problems with McCarthy's evidence did not diminish the massive attention
he and his charges received. (Nor did the existence of a federal employee loyalty
program that President Harry Truman had implemented in 1947.) The Hiss case,
the communist victory in China (1949), the Soviet development of atomic weapons

(1949), and the outbreak and early stages of the Korean War (1950) fed the impression that the United States was losing the Cold War. According to McCarthy, subversives within the U.S. government were responsible.

McCarthy's charges, the espionage trials, and growing Cold War tension led Congress to pass the Internal Security Act on September 20, 1950. President Truman vetoed the act on September 23. His veto was overridden by both houses of Congress on the same day. Various provisions of the law were subsequently overturned by the Supreme Court or repealed by Act of Congress. As for McCarthy, some Senators opposed him early on (most prominently Margaret Chase Smith, R-Maine), but he continued to command attention for several years, summoning people to Senate hearings and publicly accusing them of disloyalty and treason. He was eventually censured by the Senate for his conduct (December 2, 1954). After that, he ceased to be an influential public figure. He died in 1957.

Study Questions

A. The Internal Security Act states that it should not be construed to restrict freedom of speech or press. Was President Truman right to think it would? Section 4a of the Act prohibits establishing a totalitarian government except by constitutional amendment. If it is wrong to vote or campaign for such a government, why would it be right to amend the Constitution to allow for one? Why does section 5 apply only to nonelective officials? If the law allows Americans to elect communists, why does it prohibit other actions intended to bring about a communist government?

B. Threats to national security also formed an important part of the backdrop of President Barack Obama's speech in Cairo (see Chapter 29). To what extent are the concerns and issues raised in these two time periods similar, and in what ways are they distinguishable? Has America learned to balance its need for security with its commitment to freedom of expression and association?

C. Would the organized dissent movements so prevalent in earlier American history have been "legal" under the terms of the National Security Act? Consider especially the Whiskey Rebellion, the Hartford Convention, and the Nullification Crisis (Volume 1, Chapters 8-9, 11). Is there a conflict between the type of "security mindset" exemplified in this chapter and a commitment to freedom of conscience (see Volume 1, Chapter 4)?

A. Senator Joseph McCarthy (R-WI), Address to the League of Women Voters, Wheeling, West Virginia, February 9, 1950[1]

Ladies and gentlemen, tonight as we celebrate the one hundred forty-first birthday of one of the greatest men [*Abraham Lincoln*] in American history, I would like to be able to talk about what a glorious day today is in the history of the world. As we celebrate the birth of this man who with his whole heart and soul hated war, I would like to be able to speak of peace in our time—of war being outlawed—and of world-wide disarmament. These would be truly appropriate things to be able to mention as we celebrate the birthday of Abraham Lincoln.

Five years after a world war has been won, men's hearts should anticipate a long peace—and men's minds should be free from the heavy weight that comes with war. But this is not such a period—for this is not a period of peace. This is a time of the cold war. This is a time when all the world is split into two vast, increasingly hostile, armed camps—a time of a great armament race....

... There is still a hope for peace if we finally decide that no longer can we safely blind our eyes and close our ears to those facts which are shaping up more and more clearly—and that is that we are now engaged in a show-down fight—not the usual war between nations for land areas or other material gains, but a war between two diametrically opposed ideologies.

The great difference between our western Christian world and the atheistic Communist world is not political, gentlemen, it is moral....

The real, basic difference, however, lies in the religion of immoralism—invented by Marx, preached feverishly by Lenin, and carried to unimaginable extremes by Stalin. This religion of immoralism, if the Red half of the world triumphs—and well it may, gentlemen—this religion of immoralism will more deeply wound and damage mankind than any conceivable economic or political system....

Today we are engaged in a final, all-out battle between communistic atheism and Christianity....

The reason why we find ourselves in a position of impotency is not because

---

[1] McCarthy spoke from a prepared text, but he apparently deviated from it at points and a tape recording was erased. This version comes from a copy provided to a Senate committee that investigated McCarthy's charges later that year. See Arthur M. Schlesinger, Jr., and Roger Bruns, eds., *Congress Investigates: A Documented History, 1792–1974*, vol. 5 (New York: Chelsea House Publishers, 1975), 3757–63.

our only powerful potential enemy has sent men to invade our shores—but rather because of the traitorous actions of those who have been treated so well by this Nation. It has not been the less fortunate, or members of minority groups who have been traitorous to this Nation—but rather those who have had all the benefits that the wealthiest Nation on earth has had to offer—the finest homes, the finest college education and the finest jobs in government we can give.

This is glaringly true in the State Department. There the bright young men who are born with silver spoons in their mouths are the ones who have been most traitorous....

...I have here in my hand a list of 205—a list of names that were made known to the Secretary of State as being members of the Communist Party and who nevertheless are still working and shaping policy in the State Department....

As you know, very recently the Secretary of State [*Dean Acheson*] proclaimed his loyalty to a man guilty[2] of what has always been considered as the most abominable of all crimes—being a traitor to the people who gave him a position of great trust—high treason....

He has lighted the spark which is resulting in a moral uprising and will end only when the whole sorry mess of twisted, warped thinkers are swept from the national scene so that we may have a new birth of honesty and decency in government.

B. The Internal Security Act of 1950, September 22, 1950[3]

AN ACT

To protect the United States against certain un-American and subversive activities by requiring registration of Communist organizations, and for other purposes.

Be it enacted by the Senate and House of Representatives of the United States of America in Congress assembled, That this Act may be cited as the "Internal Security Act of 1950."

TITLE I—SUBVERSIVE ACTIVITIES CONTROL

Section 1. (a) This title may be cited as the "Subversive Activities Control Act of 1950."

---

[2] Alger Hiss (see introductory note)
[3] U.S. Statutes at Large, 81st Cong., II Sess., Chp. 1024, p. 987-1031.

(b) Nothing in this Act shall be construed to authorize, require, or establish military or civilian censorship or in any way to limit or infringe upon freedom of the press or of speech as guaranteed by the Constitution of the United States and no regulation shall be promulgated hereunder having that effect.

Necessity for Legislation

Sec. 2. As a result of evidence adduced before various committees of the Senate and House of Representatives, the Congress hereby finds that

(1) There exists a world Communist movement which, in its origins, its development, and its present practice, is a world-wide revolutionary movement whose purpose it is, by treachery, deceit, infiltration into other groups (governmental and otherwise), espionage, sabotage, terrorism, and any other means deemed necessary, to establish a Communist totalitarian dictatorship in the countries throughout the world through the medium of a world-wide Communist organization.

(2) The establishment of a totalitarian dictatorship in any country results in the suppression of all opposition to the party in power, the subordination of the rights of individuals to the state, the denial of fundamental rights and liberties which are characteristic of a representative form of government, such as freedom of speech, of the press, of assembly, and of religious worship, and results in the maintenance of control over the people through fear, terrorism, and brutality.

(3) The system of government known as a totalitarian dictatorship is characterized by the existence of a single political party, organized on a dictatorial basis, and by substantial identity between such party and its policies and the government and governmental policies of the country in which it exists.

(4) The direction and control of the world Communist movement is vested in and exercised by the Communist dictatorship of a foreign country.

(5) The Communist dictatorship of such foreign country, in exercising such direction and control and in furthering the purposes of the world Communist movement, establishes or causes the establishment of, and utilizes, in various countries, action organizations which are not free and independent organizations, but are sections of a world-wide Communist organization and are controlled, directed, and subject to the discipline of the Communist dictatorship of such foreign country.

(6) The Communist action organizations so established and utilized in various countries, acting under such control, direction, and discipline,

endeavor to carry out the objectives of the world Communist movement by bringing about the overthrow of existing governments by any available means, including force if necessary, and setting up Communist totalitarian dictatorships which will be subservient to the most powerful existing Communist totalitarian dictatorship. Although such organizations usually designate themselves as political parties, they are in fact constituent elements of the world-wide Communist movement and promote the objectives of such movement by conspiratorial and coercive tactics, instead of through the democratic processes of a free elective system or through the freedom-preserving means employed by a political party which operates as an agency by which people govern themselves.

(7) In carrying on the[ir] activities . . . such Communist organizations . . . are organized on a secret, conspiratorial basis and operate to a substantial extent through organizations, commonly known as "Communist fronts", which in most instances are created and maintained, or used, in such manner as to conceal the facts as to their true character and purposes and their membership. One result of this method of operation is that such affiliated organizations are able to obtain financial and other support from persons who would not extend such support if they knew the true purposes of, and the actual nature of the control and influence exerted upon, such "Communist fronts". . . .

(9) In the United States those individuals who knowingly and willfully participate in the world Communist movement, when they so participate, in effect repudiate their allegiance to the United States, and in effect transfer their allegiance to the foreign country in which is vested the direction and control of the world Communist movement. . . .

(11) The agents of communism have devised clever and ruthless espionage and sabotage tactics which are carried out in many instances in form or manner successfully evasive of existing law.

(12) The Communist network in the United States is inspired and controlled in large part by foreign agents who are sent into the United States ostensibly as attachés of foreign legations, affiliates of international organizations, members of trading commissions, and in similar capacities, but who use their diplomatic or semi-diplomatic status as a shield behind which to engage in activities prejudicial to the public security.

(13) There are, under our present immigration laws, numerous aliens who have been found to be deportable, many of whom are in the subversive, criminal, or immoral classes who are free to roam the country at will without supervision or control.

(14) One device for infiltration by Communists is by procuring naturalization for disloyal aliens who use their citizenship as a badge for admission into the fabric of our society.

(15) The Communist movement in the United States is an organization numbering thousands of adherents, rigidly and ruthlessly disciplined. Awaiting and seeking to advance a moment when the United States may be so far extended by foreign engagements, so far divided in counsel, or so far in industrial or financial straits, that overthrow of the Government of the United States by force and violence may seem possible of achievement, it seeks converts far and wide by an extensive system of schooling and indoctrination....

Certain Prohibited Acts

Sec. 4. (a) It shall be unlawful for any person knowingly to combine, conspire, or agree, with any other person to perform any act which would substantially contribute to the establishment within the United States of a totalitarian dictatorship, ... the direction and control of which is to be vested in, or exercised by or under the domination or control of, any foreign government, foreign organization, or foreign individual: Provided, however, That this subsection shall not apply to the proposal of a constitutional amendment....

...

(f) Neither the holding of office nor membership in any Communist organization by any person shall constitute per se a violation of subsection (a) or subsection (c) of this section or of any other criminal statute. The fact of the registration of any person under section 7 or section 8 of this title as an officer or member of any Communist organization shall not be received in evidence against such person in any prosecution for any alleged violation of subsection (a) or subsection (c) of this section or for any alleged violation of any other criminal statute.

Employment of Members of Communist Organizations

Sec. 5. (a) When a Communist organization, as defined in paragraph (5) of section 3 of this title, is registered or there is in effect a final order of the Board requiring such organization to register, it shall be unlawful

(1) For any member of such organization, with knowledge or notice that such organization is so registered or that such order has become final

(A) in seeking, accepting, or holding any nonelective office or employment under the United States, to conceal or fail to disclose the fact that he is a member of such organization; or

(B) to hold any nonelective office or employment under the United States; or

(C) in seeking, accepting, or holding employment in any defense facility, to conceal or fail to disclose the fact that he is a member of such organization; or

(D) if such organization is a Communist-action organization, to engage in any employment in any defense facility.

(2) For any officer or employee of the United States or of any defense facility, with knowledge or notice that such organization is so registered or that such order has become final—

(A) to contribute funds or services to such organization; or

(B) to advise, counsel or urge any person, with knowledge or notice that such person is a member of such organization, to perform, or to omit to perform, any act if such act or omission would constitute a violation of any provision of subparagraph (1) of this subsection....

Denial of Passports to Members of Communist Organizations

Sec. 6. (a) When a Communist organization as defined in paragraph (5) of section 3 of this title is registered, or there is in effect a final order of the Board requiring such organization to register, it shall be unlawful for any member of such organization, with knowledge or notice that such organization is so registered or that such order has become final—

(1) to make application for a passport, or the renewal of a passport, to be issued or renewed by or under the authority of the United States; or

(2) to use or attempt to use any such passport....

Registration and Annual Reports of Communist Organizations

Sec. 7. (a) Each Communist-action organization (including any organization required, by a final order of the Board, to register as a Communist-action organization) shall ... register with the Attorney General, on a form prescribed by him ... as a Communist-action organization....

... containing the following information:

(1) The name of the organization and the address of its principal office.

(2) The name and last-known address of each individual who is ... [or] who was at any time during the period of twelve full calendar months next

preceding the filing of such statement, an officer of the organization, with the designation or title of the office so held, and with a brief statement of the duties and functions of such individual as such officer.

(3) An accounting... of all moneys received and expended (including the sources from which received and the purposes for which expended) by the organization during the period of twelve full calendar months next preceding the filing of such statement.

(4) In the case of a Communist-action organization, the name and last-known address of each individual who was a member of the organization at any time during the period of twelve full calendar months preceding the filing of such statement...

Use of the Mails and Instrumentalities of Interstate or Foreign Commerce

Sec. 10. It shall be unlawful for any organization which is registered under section 7, or for any organization with respect to which there is in effect a final order of the Board requiring it to register under section 7, or for any person acting for or on behalf of any such organization—

(1) to transmit or cause to be transmitted, through the United States mails or by any means or instrumentality of interstate or foreign commerce, any publication which is intended to be, or which it is reasonable to believe is intended to be, circulated or disseminated among two or more persons, unless such publication, and any envelope, wrapper, or other container in which it is mailed or otherwise circulated or transmitted, bears the following, printed in such manner as may be provided in regulations prescribed by the Attorney General, with the name of the organization appearing in lieu of the blank: "Disseminated by _____, a Communist organization"; or

(2) to broadcast or cause to be broadcast any matter over any radio or television station in the United States, unless such matter is preceded by the following statement, with the name of the organization being stated in place of the blank: "The following program is sponsored by _____, a Communist organization"....

Subversive Activities Control Board

Sec. 12. (a) There is hereby established a board, to be known as the Subversive Activities Control Board, which shall be composed of five members, who shall be appointed by the President, by and with the advice and consent of the Senate. Not more than three members of the Board shall be members of the same political party....

(e) It shall be the duty of the Board

(1) upon application made by the Attorney General under section 13(a) of this title, or by any organization under section 13(b) of this title, to determine whether any organization is a "Communist-action organization" within the meaning of paragraph (3) of section 3 of this title, or a "Communist-front organization" within the meaning of paragraph (4) of section 3 of this title; and

(2)... to determine whether any individual is a member of any Communist-action organization registered, or by final order of the Board required to be registered, under section 7(a) of this title....

Proceedings before Board

Sec. 13. (a) Whenever the Attorney General shall have reason to believe that any organization which has not registered under... this title is in fact an organization of a kind required to be registered under such subsection, or that any individual who has not registered under... this title is in fact required to register under such section, he shall file with the Board and serve upon such organization or individual a petition for an order requiring such organization or individual to register pursuant to such subsection or section, as the case may be....

(b) Any organization registered under... this title, and any individual registered under... this title, may, not oftener than once in each calendar year, make application to the Attorney General for the cancellation of such registration and (in the case of such organization) for relief from obligation to make further annual reports....

(c) Upon the filing of any petition pursuant to subsection (a) or subsection (b) of this section, the Board (or any member thereof or any examiner designated thereby) may hold hearings, administer oaths and affirmations, may examine witnesses and receive evidence at any place in the United States, and may require by subpoena the attendance and testimony of witnesses and the production of books, papers, correspondence, memoranda, and other records deemed relevant, to the matter under inquiry....

(d) (1) All hearings conducted under this section shall be public. Each party to such proceeding shall have the right to present its case with the assistance of counsel, to offer oral or documentary evidence, to submit rebuttal evidence, and to conduct such cross-examination as may be required for a full and true disclosure of the facts. . . .

(e) In determining whether any organization is a "Communist-action organization," the Board shall take into consideration

(1) the extent to which its policies are formulated and carried out and its activities performed, pursuant to directives or to effectuate the policies of the foreign government or foreign organization in which is vested, or under the domination or control of which is exercised, the direction and control of the world Communist movement referred to in section 2 of this title; and

(2) the extent to which its views and policies do not deviate from those of such foreign government or foreign organization; and

(3) the extent to which it receives financial or other aid, directly or indirectly, from or at the direction of such foreign government or foreign organization; . . .

. . .

(8) the extent to which its principal leaders or a substantial number of its members consider the allegiance they owe to the United States as subordinate to their obligations to such foreign government or foreign organization.

(f) In determining whether any organization is a "Communist-front organization," the Board shall take into consideration

(1) the extent to which persons who are active in its management, direction, or supervision, whether or not holding office therein, are active in the management, direction, or supervision of, or as representatives of, any Communist-action organization, Communist foreign government, or the world Communist movement referred to in section 2; and

(2) the extent to which its support, financial or otherwise, is derived from any Communist-action organization, Communist foreign govern-ment, or the world Communist movement referred to in section 2; . . .

(k) When any order of the Board requiring registration of a Com-munist organization becomes final under the provisions of. . . this title, the Board shall publish in the Federal Register the fact that such order has become final, and publication thereof shall constitute notice to all members of such organization that such order has become final.

Judicial Review

Sec. 14. (a) The party aggrieved by any order entered by the Board under subsection (g), (h), (i) or (j) of section 13 may obtain a review of such order by filing in the United States Court of Appeals for the District of Columbia, within sixty days from the date of service upon it of such order, a written petition praying that the order of the Board be set aside....

TITLE II—EMERGENCY DETENTION

Sec. 100. This title may be cited as the "Emergency Detention Act of 1950."

Findings of Fact and Declaration of Purpose

[This Title repeats the findings reported at the beginning of Title I above.]
. . .

(14) The detention of persons who there is reasonable ground to believe probably will commit or conspire with others to commit espionage or sabotage is, in a time of internal security emergency, essential to the common defense and to the safety and security of the territory, the people and the Constitution of the United States.

(15) It is also essential that such detention in an emergency involving the internal security of the Nation shall be so authorized, executed, restricted and reviewed as to prevent any interference with the constitutional rights and privileges of any persons, and at the same time shall be sufficiently effective to permit the performance by the Congress and the President of their constitutional duties to provide for the common defense, to wage war, and to preserve, protect and defend the Constitution, the Government and the people of the United States.

Declaration of "Internal Security Emergency"

Sec. 102. (a) In the event of any one of the following:

(1) Invasion of the territory of the United States or its possessions,

(2) Declaration of war by Congress, or

(3) Insurrection within the United States in aid of a foreign enemy, and if, upon the occurrence of one or more of the above, the President shall find that the proclamation of an emergency pursuant to this section is essential to the preservation, protection and defense of the Constitution, and to the common defense and safety of the territory and people of the United States, the President is authorized to make public proclamation of the existence of an "Internal Security Emergency".

(b) A state of "Internal Security Emergency" (hereinafter referred to as the "emergency") so declared shall continue in exercise until terminated by proclamation of the President or by concurrent resolution of the Congress.

Detention during Emergency

Sec. 103. (a) Whenever there shall be in existence such an emergency, the President, acting through the Attorney General, is hereby authorized to apprehend and by order detain, pursuant to the provisions of this title, each person as to whom there is reasonable ground to believe that such person probably will engage in, or probably will conspire with others to engage in, acts of espionage or of sabotage....

Detention Review Board

Sec. 105. (a) The President is hereby authorized to establish a Detention Review Board (referred to in this title as the "Board") which shall consist of nine members, not more than five of whom shall be members of the same political party, appointed by the President by and with the advice and consent of the Senate....

Sec. 109. (a) Any Board created under this title is empowered

(1) to review upon petition of any detainee any order of detention issued pursuant to section 104 (d) of this title;

(2) to determine whether there is reasonable ground to believe that such detainee probably will engage in, or conspire with others to engage in, espionage or sabotage;

(3) to issue orders confirming, modifying, or revoking any such order of detention; ...

(3) The several departments and agencies of the Government, when directed by the President, shall furnish the Board, upon its request, all records, papers, and information in their possession relating to any matter before the Board.

(f) Every detainee shall be afforded full opportunity to be represented by counsel at the preliminary hearing prescribed by this title and in all stages of the detention review proceedings, including the hearing before the Board and any judicial review, and he shall have the right at hearings of the Board to testify, to have compulsory process for obtaining witnesses in his favor, and to cross-examine adverse witnesses....

(2) Any past act or acts of espionage or sabotage committed by such person, or any past participation by such person in any attempt or conspiracy

to commit any act of espionage or sabotage, against the United States, any agency or instrumentality thereof, or any public or private national defense facility within the United States; ...

Orders of the Board

Sec. 110. (a) If upon all the testimony taken in any proceeding for the review of any order of detention issued pursuant to section 104 (d) of this title, the Board shall determine that there is not reasonable ground to believe that the detainee in question probably will engage in, or conspire with others to engage in, espionage or sabotage, the Board shall state its findings of fact and shall issue and serve upon the Attorney General or order revoking the order for detention of the detainee concerned and requiring the Attorney General, and any officer designated by him for the supervision or control of the detention of such person, to release such detainee from custody; and shall forthwith serve a copy of such order upon the detainee....

Judicial Review

Sec. 111. (a) Any petitioner aggrieved by an order of the Board denying in whole or in part the relief sought by him, or by the failure or refusal of the Attorney General to obey such order, shall be entitled to the judicial review or judicial enforcement, provided hereinafter in this section....

Separability of Provisions

Sec. 116. ... Nothing contained in this title shall be construed to suspend or to authorize the suspension of the privilege of the writ of habeas corpus.

Sam Rayburn Speaker of the House of Representatives.

Alben W. Barkley Vice President of the United States and President of the Senate.

C. President Harry S. Truman, Veto of the Internal Security Act, September 22, 1950[4]

To the House of Representatives:

---

[4] *Public Papers*, Harry S. Truman, 1945–1953, Truman Presidential Library. https://goo.gl/yZYnPU

I return herewith, without my approval, H.R. 9490, the proposed "Internal Security Act of 1950."...

It has been claimed over and over again that this is an "anti-communist" bill—a "communist control" bill. But in actual operation the bill would have results exactly the opposite of those intended....

Specifically, some of the principal objections to the bill are as follows:

1. It would aid potential enemies by requiring the publication of a complete list of vital defense plants, laboratories, and other installations.

2. It would require the Department of Justice and its Federal Bureau of Investigation to waste immense amounts of time and energy attempting to carry out its unworkable registration provisions.

3. It would deprive us of the great assistance of many aliens in intelligence matters.

4. It would antagonize friendly governments.

5. It would put the Government of the United States in the thought control business.

6. It would make it easier for subversive aliens to become naturalized as United States citizens.

7. It would give Government officials vast powers to harass all of our citizens in the exercise of their right of free speech.

Legislation with these consequences is not necessary to meet the real dangers which communism presents to our free society. Those dangers are serious, and must be met. But this bill would hinder us, not help us, in meeting them. Fortunately, we already have on the books strong laws which give us most of the protection we need from the real dangers of treason, espionage, sabotage, and actions looking to the overthrow of our Government by force and violence. Most of the provisions of this bill have no relation to these real dangers.

One provision alone of this bill is enough to demonstrate how far it misses the real target. Section 5 would require the Secretary of Defense to "proclaim" and "have published in the Federal Register" a public catalogue of defense plants, laboratories, and all other facilities vital to our national defense—no matter how secret. I cannot imagine any document a hostile foreign government would desire more....

This is only one example of many provisions in the bill which would in actual practice work to the detriment of our national security....

I repeat, the net result of this bill would be to help the communists, not to hurt them.

I therefore most earnestly request the Congress to reconsider its action. I am confident that on more careful analysis most members of Congress will recognize that this bill is contrary to the best interests of our country at this critical time.

H.R. 9490 is made up of a number of different parts. In summary, their purposes and probable effects may be described as follows:

Sections 1 through 17 are designed for two purposes. First, they are intended to force communist organizations to register and to divulge certain information about themselves—information on their officers, their finances, and, in some cases, their membership. These provisions would in practice be ineffective, and would result in obtaining no information about communists that the FBI and our other security agencies do not already have. But in trying to enforce these sections, we would have to spend a great deal of time, effort, and money—all to no good purpose.

Second, those provisions are intended to impose various penalties on communists and others covered by the terms of the bill. So far as communists are concerned, all these penalties which can be practicably enforced are already in effect under existing laws and procedures. But the language of the bill is so broad and vague that it might well result in penalizing the legitimate activities of people who are not communists at all, but loyal citizens.

Thus the net result of these sections of the bill would be: no serious damage to the communists, much damage to the rest of us. Only the communist movement would gain from such an outcome. . . .

. . . [The] provisions [of the Act] . . . [that] prevent us from admitting to our country, or to citizenship, many people who could make real contributions to our national strength. The bill would deprive our Government and our intelligence agencies of the valuable services of aliens in security operations. It would require us to exclude and to deport the citizens of some friendly noncommunist countries. . . .

Sections 100 through 117 of this bill (Title II) are intended to give the Government power, in the event of invasion, war, or insurrection in the United States in aid of a foreign enemy, to seize and hold persons who could be expected to attempt acts of espionage or sabotage, even though they had as yet committed no crime. . . . [T]he provisions in H.R. 9490 would very probably prove ineffective to achieve the objective sought, since they would not suspend the writ of habeas corpus, and under our legal system to detain a man not charged with a crime would raise serious constitutional questions unless the writ of habeas corpus were suspended. . . .

. . . Instead of striking blows at communism, [the bill] would strike blows at our own liberties and at our position in the forefront of those working for freedom in the world. At a time when our young men are fighting for freedom in Korea, it would be tragic to advance the objectives of communism in this country, as this bill would do.

Because I feel so strongly that this legislation would be a terrible mistake, I want to discuss more fully its worst features....

Most of the first seventeen sections of H.R. 9490 are concerned with requiring registration and annual reports, by what the bill calls "communist-action organizations" and "communist-front organizations," of names of officers, sources and uses of funds, and, in the case of "communist-action organizations," names of members.

The idea of requiring communist organizations to divulge information about themselves is a simple and attractive one. But it is about as practical as requiring thieves to register with the sheriff. Obviously, no such organization as the Communist Party is likely to register voluntarily.

Under the provisions of the bill .... [t]he Attorney General would have to produce proof that the organization in question was in fact a "communist-action" or a "communist-front organization." To do this he would have to offer evidence relating to every aspect of the organization's activities. The organization could present opposing evidence. Prolonged hearings would be required to allow both sides to present proof and to cross-examine opposing witnesses....

The bill lists a number of criteria for the Board to consider in deciding whether or not an organization is a "communist-action" or "communist-front" organization. Many of these deal with the attitudes or states of mind of the organization's leaders. It is frequently difficult in legal proceedings to establish whether or not a man has committed an overt act, such as theft or perjury. But under this bill, the Attorney General would have to attempt the immensely more difficult task of producing concrete legal evidence that men have particular ideas or opinions. This would inevitably require the disclosure of many of the FBI's confidential sources of information and thus would damage our national security.

If, eventually, the Attorney General should overcome these difficulties and get a favorable decision from the Board, the Board's decision could be appealed to the Courts. The Courts would review any questions of law involved, and whether the Board's findings of fact were supported by the "preponderance" of the evidence.

All these proceedings would require great effort and much time. It is almost certain that from two to four years would elapse between the Attorney General's decision to go before the Board with a case, and the final disposition of the matter by the Courts.

And when all this time and effort had been spent, it is still most likely that no organization would actually register.... [T]o frustrate the law [leaders] would... dissolve the organization and establish a new one with a different name and a new roster of nominal officers. The Communist Party has done this again and again in countries throughout the world. And nothing could be done about it except to begin all over again the long dreary process of investigative, administrative, and judicial proceedings to require registration.

Thus the net result of the registration provisions of this bill would probably be an endless chasing of one organization after another, with the communists always able to frustrate the law enforcement agencies and prevent any final result from being achieved....

Unfortunately, these provisions are not merely ineffective and unworkable. They represent a clear and present danger to our institutions.

In so far as the bill would require registration by the Communist Party itself, it does not endanger our traditional liberties. However, the application of the registration requirements to so-called communist-front organizations can be the greatest danger to freedom of speech, press and assembly, since the Alien and Sedition Laws of 1798. This danger arises out of the criteria or standards to be applied in determining whether an organization is a communist-front organization.

There would be no serious problem if the bill required proof that an organization was controlled and financed by the Communist Party before it could be classified as a communist-front organization. However, recognizing the difficulty of proving those matters, the bill would permit such a determination to be based solely upon "the extent to which the positions taken or advanced by it from time to time on matters of policy do not deviate from those" of the communist movement.

This provision could easily be used to classify as a communist-front organization any organization which is advocating a single policy or objective which is also being urged by the Communist Party or by a communist foreign government.... Thus, an organization which advocates low-cost housing for sincere humanitarian reasons might be classified as a communist-front organization because the communists regularly exploit slum conditions as one of their fifth-column techniques.

It is not enough to say that this probably would not be done. The mere fact that it could be done shows clearly how the bill would open a Pandora's box of opportunities for official condemnation of organizations and individuals for perfectly honest opinions which happen to be stated also by communists.

The basic error of these sections is that they move in the direction of suppressing opinion and belief. This would be a very dangerous course to take, not because we have any sympathy for communist opinions, but because any governmental stifling of the free expression of opinion is a long step toward totalitarianism.

There is no more fundamental axiom of American freedom than the familiar statement: In a free country, we punish men for the crimes they commit, but never for the opinions they have. And the reason this is so fundamental to freedom is not, as many suppose, that it protects the few unorthodox from suppression by the majority. To permit freedom of expression is primarily for the benefit of the majority, because it protects criticism, and criticism leads to progress.

We can and we will prevent espionage, sabotage, or other actions endangering our national security. But we would betray our finest traditions if we attempted, as this bill would attempt, to curb the simple expression of opinion. This we should never do, no matter how distasteful the opinion may be to the vast majority of our people. The course proposed by this bill would delight the communists, for it would make a mockery of the Bill of Rights and of our claims to stand for freedom in the world.

And what kind of effect would these provisions have on the normal expression of political views? Obviously, if this law were on the statute books, the part of prudence would be to avoid saying anything that might be construed by someone as not deviating sufficiently from the current communist propaganda line. And since no one could be sure in advance what views were safe to express, the inevitable tendency would be to express no views on controversial subjects.

The result could only be to reduce the vigor and strength of our political life—an outcome that the communists would happily welcome, but that free men should abhor.

We need not fear the expression of ideas—we do need to fear their suppression.

Our position in the vanguard of freedom rests largely on our demonstration that the free expression of opinion, coupled with government by popular consent, leads to national strength and human advancement. Let us not, in cowering and foolish fear, throw away the ideals which are the fundamental basis of our free society....

No considerations of expediency can justify the enactment of such a bill as this, a bill which would so greatly weaken our liberties and give aid and comfort to those who would destroy us. I have, therefore, no alternative but to return this bill without my approval, and I earnestly request the Congress to reconsider its action.

HARRY S. TRUMAN

CHAPTER 26

The Civil Rights Act, 1964

A. Langston Hughes, "Harlem," 1951
B. F. L. Shuttlesworth, N. H. Smith, Birmingham Manifesto,
   April 3, 1963
C. President John F. Kennedy, Radio and Television Report to the
   American People on Civil Rights, June 11, 1963
D. Senator Hubert Humphrey (D-MN) and Senator Strom Thurmond
   (D-SC), Debate on the Civil Rights Act, March 18, 1964
E. Associate Justice Tom C. Clark, *Atlanta Motel v. United States*,
   December 14, 1964

World War II brought African Americans closer to the mainstream of American life than ever before. Many moved out of the South to take jobs in defense industries. Others served in the still segregated military (see photo on page G). (President Truman integrated the military in 1948.) Still, they were not fully part of American life (Document B). In the 1950s, African Americans and their allies organized a movement to gain full civil rights, to realize a dream too long deferred, as Langston Hughes put it (Document A). Boycotts of white businesses, public transportation, and marches gave impetus to the movement. Reputedly one of the most segregated cities in the United States, Birmingham, Alabama became, in 1963, a center of protest and action against discrimination and the denial of civil rights (Document B). Faced with continuing discrimination and rising protests, President John F. Kennedy decided to support a new civil rights law (Document C). (Congress had passed a series of such laws during the decade following the Civil War.) On June 11, 1963, after consulting with Congressional leaders, Kennedy addressed the American people to explain why the new law was necessary. Eight days later he sent the bill to Congress.

Opponents objected to various provisions, including equal access to public accommodations, but also to what they felt was its unconstitutional extension of federal power (Document D). Supporters organized a March on Washington in August 1963, at which Martin Luther King gave his now famous "I Have a Dream Speech" (see the online collection of King's papers, https://goo.gl/FqJyqq). Stressing non-violent civil disobedience, King had become the leader of the Civil Rights movement. *Opposition in Congress was sufficient, however, to prevent passage of the law. When Lyndon Johnson became president following Kennedy's assassination in November 1963, he pushed for the new law, in part as a memorial to Kennedy. The law was passed July 2, 1964.*

A motel in Atlanta, Georgia challenged the constitutionality of the public accommodation portion of the bill. The case reached the Supreme Court, which decided in December 1964 that the provision was a constitutional exercise of the federal government's power to regulate interstate commerce (Document D). Attorneys General from Florida and Virginia had filed briefs urging that the lower court decision affirming the law be reversed, while attorneys general from California, Massachusetts and New York had filed briefs urging that it be upheld.

Study Questions

A. What are the arguments of Senators Hubert Humphrey and Strom Thurmond for and against the Civil Rights Act? Are they making the same kinds of arguments? Proponents of civil rights like Martin Luther King and Fred L. Shuttlesworth appealed to the Declaration of Independence, as well as the Constitution; Thurmond appealed soley to the Constitution and the rights it protects. Is there a conflict between the Declaration and the Constitution? How did the Supreme Court respond to those like Senator Thurmond who claimed that the Civil Rights Act violated the Fifth Amendment?

B. What is the connection between the Declaration of Independence and the rights claims made by workingmen, women, and African-Americans? Could those claims be made without the Declaration? (See Chapters 18 and 27.)

C. Consider the issues raised by the texts here in light of the discussion of the pernicious institution of slavery in Volume 1, Chapters 12 and 15; how have attitudes from the earlier time period remained in force? How have they changed?

A. "Harlem," Langston Hughes, 1951[1]

What happens to a dream deferred?

---

[1] "Harlem (2)" from *The Collected Poems of Langston Hughes* by Langston Hughes, edited by Arnold Rampersad with David Roessel, Associate Editor, copyright © 1994 by the Estate of Langston Hughes. Used by permission of Alfred A. Knopf, an

Does it dry up
like a raisin in the sun?
Or fester like a sore—
And then run?
Does it stink like rotten meat?
Or crust and sugar over—
like a syrupy sweet?

Maybe it just sags
like a heavy load.

Or does it explode?

B. F. L. Shuttlesworth, N. H. Smith, Birmingham Manifesto, April 3, 1963[2]

The patience of an oppressed people cannot endure forever. The Negro cit-izens of Birmingham for the last several years have hoped in vain for some evidence of good faith resolution of our just grievances.

Birmingham is part of the United States and we are *bona fide* citizens. Yet the history of Birmingham reveals that very little of the democratic pro-cess touches the life of the Negro in Birmingham. We have been segregated racially, exploited economically, and dominated politically. Under the lead-ership of the Alabama Christian Movement for Human Rights,[3] we sought relief by petition for the repeal of city ordinances requiring segregation and the institution of a merit hiring policy in city employment. We were rebuffed. We then turned to the system of the courts. We weathered set-back after set-back, with all of its costliness, finally winning the terminal, bus, parks and airport cases. The bus decision has been implemented begrudgingly and the

---

[2] https://goo.gl/4WmEvJ. Fred Shuttlesworth and N. H. Smith were ministers in Birmingham, Alabama active in the civil rights movement. Birmingham was the site of non-violent demonstrations against segregation and black boycotts of white businesses in 1963. The demonstrations were met with violence by police and oth-ers. In September 1963, an African American church in Birmingham was bombed, killing four young girls.
[3] Shuttlesworth, Smith and others created this organization in 1956, after the state of Alabama banned the National Association for the Advancement of Colored People.

parks decision prompted the closing of all municipally-owned recreational
facilities with the exception of the zoo and Legion Field. The airport case has
been a slightly better experience with the experience of hotel accommodations and the subtle discrimination that continues in the limousine service.

We have always been a peaceful people, bearing our oppression with
super-human effort. Yet we have been the victims of repeated violence, not
only that inflicted by the hoodlum element but also that inflicted by the
blatant misuse of police power. Our memories are seared with painful mob
experience of Mother's Day 1961 during the Freedom Rides.[4] For years, while
our homes and churches were being bombed, we heard nothing but the rant-
ings and ravings of racist city officials.

The Negro protest for equality and justice has been a voice crying in the
wilderness.[5] Most of Birmingham has remained silent, probably out of fear.
In the meanwhile, our city has acquired the dubious reputation of being the
worst big city in race relations in the United States. Last fall, for a flickering
moment, it appeared that sincere community leaders from religion, business and industry discerned the inevitable confrontation in race relations
approaching. Their concern for the city's image and commonweal of all its
citizens did not run deep enough. Solemn promises were made, pending a
postponement of direct action, that we would be joined in a suit seeking
the relief of segregation ordinances. Some merchants agreed to desegregate their restrooms as a good-faith start, some actually complying, only
to retreat shortly thereafter. We hold in our hands now, broken faith and
broken promises.

We believe in the American Dream of democracy, in the Jeffersonian
doctrine that "all men are created equal and are endowed by their Creator
with certain inalienable rights, among these being life, liberty and the pursuit of happiness."

Twice since September we have deferred our direct action thrust in order
that a change in city government would not be made in the hysteria of community crisis. We act today in full concert with our Hebraic-Christian tradition, the law of morality and the Constitution of our nation. The absence of
justice and progress in Birmingham demands that we make a moral witness

---

[4] Freedom rides were bus trips taken across the South beginning in 1961 to desegregate public interstate transportation. On May 14, 1961, Mother's Day, a mob of Klu
Klux Klan members attacked the freedom riders in Anniston, Alabama.
[5] Isaiah 40:3; Mark 1:3; John 1:23

to give our community a chance to survive. We demonstrate our faith that we believe that The Beloved Community[6] can come to Birmingham.

We appeal to the citizenry of Birmingham, Negro and white, to join us in this witness for decency, morality, self-respect and human dignity. Your individual and corporate support can hasten the day of "liberty and justice for all." This is Birmingham's moment of truth in which every citizen can play his part in her larger destiny.

—The Alabama Christian Movement for Human Rights, in behalf of the Negro community of Birmingham.

F. L. Shuttlesworth, President
N. H. Smith, Secretary

C. President John F. Kennedy, "Radio and Television Report to the American People on Civil Rights," June 11, 1963[7]

Good evening, my fellow citizens:

This afternoon, following a series of threats and defiant statements, the presence of Alabama National Guardsmen was required on the University of Alabama to carry out the final and unequivocal order of the United States District Court of the Northern District of Alabama. That order called for the admission of two clearly qualified young Alabama residents who happened to have been born Negro.

That they were admitted peacefully on the campus is due in good measure to the conduct of the students of the University of Alabama, who met their responsibilities in a constructive way.

I hope that every American, regardless of where he lives, will stop and examine his conscience about this and other related incidents. This Nation was founded by men of many nations and backgrounds. It was founded on the principle that all men are created equal, and that the rights of every man are diminished when the rights of one man are threatened.

Today we are committed to a worldwide struggle to promote and protect

---

[6] A term associated with Martin Luther King, "the beloved community" was one characterized by brotherhood rather than conflict. See https://goo.gl/LnPr2Z.
[7] John F. Kennedy: "Radio and Television Report to the American People on Civil Rights," June 11, 1963, John F. Kennedy Presidential Library, White House Audio Collections, 1961–1963, WH-194-001. Available online from Gerhard Peters and John T. Woolley, *The American Presidency Project*. https://goo.gl/2Pb6gt.

the rights of all who wish to be free. And when Americans are sent to Vietnam or West Berlin, we do not ask for whites only. It ought to be possible, therefore, for American students of any color to attend any public institution they select without having to be backed up by troops.

It ought to be possible for American consumers of any color to receive equal service in places of public accommodation, such as hotels and restaurants and theaters and retail stores, without being forced to resort to demonstrations in the street, and it ought to be possible for American citizens of any color to register and to vote in a free election without interference or fear of reprisal.

It ought to be possible, in short, for every American to enjoy the privileges of being American without regard to his race or his color. In short, every American ought to have the right to be treated as he would wish to be treated, as one would wish his children to be treated. But this is not the case.

The Negro baby born in America today, regardless of the section of the Nation in which he is born, has about one-half as much chance of completing high school as a white baby born in the same place on the same day, one-third as much chance of completing college, one-third as much chance of becoming a professional man, twice as much chance of becoming unemployed, about one-seventh as much chance of earning $10,000 a year, a life expectancy which is 7 years shorter, and the prospects of earning only half as much.

This is not a sectional issue. Difficulties over segregation and discrimination exist in every city, in every State of the Union, producing in many cities a rising tide of discontent that threatens the public safety. Nor is this a partisan issue. In a time of domestic crisis men of good will and generosity should be able to unite regardless of party or politics. This is not even a legal or legislative issue alone. It is better to settle these matters in the courts than on the streets, and new laws are needed at every level, but law alone cannot make men see right.

We are confronted primarily with a moral issue. It is as old as the scriptures and is as clear as the American Constitution.

The heart of the question is whether all Americans are to be afforded equal rights and equal opportunities, whether we are going to treat our fellow Americans as we want to be treated. If an American, because his skin is dark, cannot eat lunch in a restaurant open to the public, if he cannot send his children to the best public school available, if he cannot vote for the public officials who represent him, if, in short, he cannot enjoy the full and free life which all of us want, then who among us would be content to have the color of his skin changed and stand in his place? Who among us would then be content with the counsels of patience and delay?

One hundred years of delay have passed since President Lincoln freed the slaves, yet their heirs, their grandsons, are not fully free. They are not yet freed from the bonds of injustice. They are not yet freed from social and economic oppression. And this Nation, for all its hopes and all its boasts, will not be fully free until all its citizens are free.

We preach freedom around the world, and we mean it, and we cherish our freedom here at home, but are we to say to the world, and much more importantly, to each other that this is a land of the free except for the Negroes; that we have no second-class citizens except Negroes; that we have no class or cast system, no ghettoes, no master race except with respect to Negroes?

Now the time has come for this Nation to fulfill its promise. The events in Birmingham and elsewhere have so increased the cries for equality that no city or state or legislative body can prudently choose to ignore them.

The fires of frustration and discord are burning in every city, North and South, where legal remedies are not at hand. Redress is sought in the streets, in demonstrations, parades, and protests which create tensions and threaten violence and threaten lives.

We face, therefore, a moral crisis as a country and as a people. It cannot be met by repressive police action. It cannot be left to increased demonstrations in the streets. It cannot be quieted by token moves or talk. It is a time to act in the Congress, in your State and local legislative body and, above all, in all of our daily lives....

Next week I shall ask the Congress of the United States to act, to make a commitment it has not fully made in this century to the proposition that race has no place in American life or law. The Federal judiciary has upheld that proposition in a series of forthright cases. The executive branch has adopted that proposition in the conduct of its affairs, including the employment of Federal personnel, the use of Federal facilities, and the sale of federally financed housing.

But there are other necessary measures which only the Congress can provide, and they must be provided at this session. The old code of equity law under which we live commands for every wrong a remedy, but in too many communities, in too many parts of the country, wrongs are inflicted on Negro citizens and there are no remedies at law. Unless the Congress acts, their only remedy is in the street.

I am, therefore, asking the Congress to enact legislation giving all

Americans the right to be served in facilities which are open to the public—
hotels, restaurants, theaters, retail stores, and similar establishments.

This seems to me to be an elementary right. Its denial is an arbitrary
indignity that no American in 1963 should have to endure, but many do....

I am also asking Congress to authorize the Federal Government to participate more fully in lawsuits designed to end segregation in public education.
We have succeeded in persuading many districts to desegregate voluntarily.
Dozens have admitted Negroes without violence. Today a Negro is attend-
ing a state-supported institution in every one of our 50 States, but the pace
is very slow....

Other features will be also requested, including greater protection for
the right to vote. But legislation, I repeat, cannot solve this problem alone. It
must be solved in the homes of every American in every community across
our country.

In this respect, I want to pay tribute to those citizens North and South
who have been working in their communities to make life better for all. They
are acting not out of a sense of legal duty but out of a sense of human decency.

Like our soldiers and sailors in all parts of the world, they are meeting
freedom's challenge on the firing line, and I salute them for their honor and
their courage.

My fellow Americans, this is a problem which faces us all—in every city
of the North as well as the South. Today there are Negroes unemployed, two
or three times as many compared to whites, inadequate in education, moving into the large cities, unable to find work, young people particularly out
of work without hope, denied equal rights, denied the opportunity to eat at
a restaurant or lunch counter or go to a movie theater, denied the right to a
decent education, denied almost today the right to attend a state university
even though qualified. It seems to me that these are matters which concern
us all, not merely Presidents or Congressmen or Governors, but every citizen
of the United States.

This is one country. It has become one country because all of us and all
the people who came here had an equal chance to develop their talents....

Therefore, I am asking for your help in making it easier for us to move
ahead and to provide the kind of equality of treatment which we would want
ourselves; to give a chance for every child to be educated to the limit of his
talents.

As I have said before, not every child has an equal talent or an equal ability or an equal motivation, but they should have the equal right to develop

their talent and their ability and their motivation, to make something of themselves.

We have a right to expect that the Negro community will be responsible, will uphold the law, but they have a right to expect that the law will be fair, that the Constitution will be color blind, as Justice Harlan said at the turn of the century.[8]

This is what we are talking about and this is a matter which concerns this country and what it stands for, and in meeting it I ask the support of all our citizens.

Thank you very much.

D. Senator Hubert Humphrey (D-MN) and Senator Strom Thurmond (D–SC), Debate on the Civil Rights Act, March 18, 1964[9]

Senator Hubert Humphry:

We simply have to face up to this question: Are we as a nation now ready to guarantee equal protection of the laws as declared in our Constitution to every American regardless of his race, his color, or his creed? The time has arrived for this nation to create a framework of law in which we can resolve our problems honorably and peacefully. Each American knows that the promises of freedom and equal treatment found in the Constitution and the laws of this country are not being fulfilled for millions of our Negro

---

[8] Kennedy is referring to Justice John Marshall Harlan's (1833-1911) dissent in *Plessy v. Ferguson* (1896). In that case, the majority of the court ruled that separate facilities for whites and blacks could be considered equal; Harlan dissented, on the grounds that the law should take no recognition of race.

[9] Originally Broadcast on *CBS Reports: Filibuster—Birth Struggle of a Law*, March 18, 1964. Available at *The Civil Rights Act of 1964: A Long Struggle for Freedom*, Library of Congress. https://goo.gl/HoS9YC. Senator Hubert Humphrey (1911–1978), was the majority whip and floor manager of the bill; Senator Strom Thurmond (1902–2003) one of its staunchest opponents. Thurmond, then Governor of South Carolina, had split from the Democratic party in 1948 to help form the States' Rights Democratic Party in opposition to the civil rights policies of President Truman (Truman had established a Civil Rights Commission and ended segregation in the U.S. Military in 1948) and the Democratic Party. The Democrats, in an effort led by Hubert Humphrey, had adopted a civil rights plank in its 1948 platform—against the wishes of Truman, who feared that it would split the party. The States Rights Democratic party all but disappeared after the 1948 election, which Truman won.

citizens and for some other minority groups. Deep in our heart we know, we know that such denials of civil rights, which we have heard about, which we have witnessed, are still taking place today. And we know that as long as freedom and equality is denied to anyone, it in a sense weakens all of us. There is indisputable evidence that fellow Americans who happen to be Negro have been denied the right to vote in a flagrant fashion. And we know that fellow Americans who happen to be Negro have been denied equal access to places of public accommodation, denied in their travels the chance for a place to rest and to eat and to relax. We know that one decade after the Supreme Court's decision declaring school segregation to be unconstitutional that less than two percent of the Southern school districts are desegregated. And we know that Negroes do not enjoy equal employment opportunities. Frequently, they are the last to be hired and the first to be fired. Now the time has come for us to correct these evils, and the civil rights bill before the Senate is designed for that purpose. It is moderate, it is reasonable, it is well designed. It was passed by the House 290 to 130. It is bi-partisan, and I think it will help give us the means to help secure, for example, the right to vote for all of our people, and it will give us the means to make possible the admittance to school rooms of children regardless of their race. And it will make sure that no American will have to suffer the indignity of being refused service at a public place. This passage of the civil rights bill, to me, is one of the great moral challenges of our time. This is not a partisan issue, this is not a sectional issue, this is, in essence, a national issue, and it is a moral issue. And it must be won by the American people.

Senator Strom Thurmond:

Mr. Sevareid[10] and my colleague, Senator Humphry: This bill, in order to bestow preferential rights on a favored few, who vote in block, would sacrifice the Constitutional rights of every citizen, and would concentrate in the national government arbitrary powers, unchained by laws, to suppress the liberty of all. This bill makes a shambles of Constitutional guarantees and the Bill of Rights. It permits a man to be jailed and fined without a jury trial. It empowers the national government to tell each citizen who must be allowed to enter upon and use his property without any compensation or due process of law as guaranteed by the Constitution. This bill would take away the rights of individuals and give to government the power to decide who is to be hired, fired and promoted in private businesses. This bill would take

---

[10] Eric Sevareid, a journalist, was the debate moderator.

away the right of individuals and give to government the power to abolish the seniority rule in labor unions and in apprenticeship programs. This bill would abandon the principle of a government of laws in favor of a government of men. It would give the power in government to government bureaucrats to decide what is discrimination. This bill would open wide the door for political favoritism with federal funds. It would vest the power in various bureaucrats to give or withhold grants, loans, and contracts on the basis of who, in the bureaucrats' discretion, is guilty of the undefined crime of discrimination. It is because of these and other radical departures from our Constitutional system that the attempt is being made to railroad this bill through Congress without following normal procedures.[11] It was only after lawless riots and demonstrations sprang up all over the country that the administration, after two years in office, sent this bill to Congress where it has been made even worse. This bill is intended to appease those waging a vicious campaign of civil disobedience. The leaders of the demonstrations have already stated that passage of the bill will not stop the mobs. Submitting to intimidation will only encourage further mob violence to gain preferential treatment. The issue is whether the Senate will pay the high cost of sacrificing a precious portion of each and every individual's Constitutional rights in a vain effort to satisfy the demands of the mob. The choice is between law and anarchy. What shall rule these United States: the Constitution or the mob?

E. Associate Justice Tom C. Clark, *Atlanta Motel v. United States*, December 14, 1964[12]

Appellant,[13] the owner of a large motel in Atlanta, Georgia, which restricts its clientele to white persons, three-fourths of whom are transient interstate travelers, sued for declaratory relief and to enjoin enforcement of the Civil Rights Act of 1964, contending that the prohibition of racial discrimination in places of public accommodation affecting commerce exceeded Congress' powers under the Commerce Clause and violated other parts of the

---

[11] Thurmond refers to the legislative maneuvers of Senate Majority Leader Mike Mansfield (1903–2001; D-MT) to prevent the Civil Rights bill from being bottled up in the Judiciary Committee, which was chaired by James Eastland (D-MS), who supported segregation and opposed the bill.

[12] *Heart of Atlanta Motel, Inc. v. United States*, 379 U.S. 241 (1964). Available online from *Justia*. https://goo.gl/H2QGK3.

[13] a person, in this case, the owner of the Atlanta Motel, who applies to a higher court for a reversal of the decision of a lower court

Constitution. A three-judge District Court upheld the constitutionality of Title II, 201 (a), (b) (1) and (c) (1), the provisions attacked, and on appellees' counterclaim permanently enjoined appellant from refusing to accommodate Negro guests for racial reasons. Held:

1. Title II of the Civil Rights Act of 1964 is a valid exercise of Congress' power under the Commerce Clause as applied to a place of public accommodation serving interstate travelers....

MR. JUSTICE CLARK[14] delivered the opinion of the Court.

This is a declaratory judgment[15] action,... attacking the constitutionality of Title II of the Civil Rights Act of 1964.... In addition to declaratory relief the complaint sought an injunction restraining the enforcement of the Act and damages against appellees based on allegedly resulting injury in the event compliance was required. Appellees[16] counterclaimed for enforcement under [Section] 206 (a) of the Act and asked for a three-judge district court under 206 (b). A three-judge court, empaneled under [Section] 206 (b) as well as 28 U.S.C. 2282 (1958 ed.), sustained the validity of the Act and issued a permanent injunction on appellees' counterclaim restraining appellant from continuing to violate the Act which remains in effect on order of MR. JUSTICE BLACK, 85 S. Ct. 1. We affirm the judgment.

1. *The Factual Background and Contentions of the Parties....*

The appellant contends that Congress in passing this Act exceeded its power to regulate commerce under Art. I, §8, cl. 3, of the Constitution of the United States; that the Act violates the Fifth Amendment because appellant is deprived of the right to choose its customers and operate its business as it wishes, resulting in a taking of its liberty and property without due process of law and a taking of its property without just compensation; and, finally, that by requiring appellant to rent available rooms to Negroes against its will, Congress is subjecting it to involuntary servitude in contravention of the Thirteenth Amendment.

The appellees counter that the unavailability to Negroes of adequate accommodations interferes significantly with interstate travel, and that Congress, under the Commerce Clause, has power to remove such obstructions and restraints; that the Fifth Amendment does not forbid reasonable regulation and that consequential damage does not constitute a "taking" within the meaning of that amendment; that the Thirteenth Amendment claim

---

[14] Associate Justice Tom C. Clark (1899–1977)
[15] a judgment that establishes rights
[16] the party against whom an appeal is filed

fails because it is entirely frivolous to say that an amendment directed to the abolition of human bondage and the removal of widespread disabilities associated with slavery places discrimination in public accommodations beyond the reach of both federal and state law. . . .

. . .

3. *Title II of the Act.*

This Title is divided into seven sections beginning with 201 (a) which provides that:

"All persons shall be entitled to the full and equal enjoyment of the goods, services, facilities, privileges, advantages, and accommodations of any place of public accommodation, as defined in this section, without discrimination or segregation on the ground of race, color, religion, or national origin."

There are listed in 201 (b) four classes of business establishments, each of which "serves the public" and "is a place of public accommodation" within the meaning of 201 (a) "if its operations affect commerce, or if discrimination or segregation by it is supported by State action." The covered establishments are:

"(1) any inn, hotel, motel, or other establishment which provides lodging to transient guests, other than an establishment located within a building which contains not more than five rooms for rent or hire and which is actually occupied by the proprietor of such establishment as his residence . . . ."

4. *Application of Title II to Heart of Atlanta Motel.*

It is admitted that the operation of the motel brings it within the provisions of 201 (a) of the Act and that appellant refused to provide lodging for transient Negroes because of their race or color and that it intends to continue that policy unless restrained.

The sole question posed is, therefore, the constitutionality of the Civil Rights Act of 1964 as applied to these facts. The legislative history of the Act indicates that Congress based the Act on [*Section*] 5 [*below*] and the Equal Protection Clause of the Fourteenth Amendment as well as its power to regulate interstate commerce under Art. I, §8, cl. 3, of the Constitution. . . .

5. *The Civil Rights Cases, 109 U.S. 3 (1883), and their Application.*

In light of our ground for decision, it might be well at the outset to discuss the Civil Rights Cases . . . which declared provisions of the Civil Rights Act of 1875 unconstitutional. . . . We think [the] decision inapposite, and without precedential value in determining the constitutionality of the present Act. Unlike Title II of the present legislation, the 1875 Act broadly proscribed discrimination in "inns, public conveyances on land or water, theaters, and other places of public amusement," without limiting the categories of affected businesses to those impinging upon interstate commerce. In contrast, the applicability of Title II is carefully limited to enterprises having a direct and substantial relation to the interstate flow of goods and people, except where state action is involved. Further, the fact that certain kinds of businesses may not in 1875 have been sufficiently involved in interstate commerce to warrant bringing them within the ambit of the commerce power is not necessarily dispositive of the same question today. Our populace had not reached its present mobility, nor were facilities, goods and services circulating as readily in interstate commerce as they are today. Although the principles which we apply today are those first formulated by Chief Justice Marshall in *Gibbons v. Ogden*, 9 Wheat. 1 (1824), the conditions of transportation and commerce have changed dramatically, and we must apply those principles to the present state of commerce. The sheer increase in volume of interstate traffic alone would give discriminatory practices which inhibit travel a far larger impact upon the Nation's commerce than such practices had on the economy of another day. Finally, there is language in the Civil Rights Cases which indicates that the Court did not fully consider whether the 1875 Act could be sustained as an exercise of the commerce power. Though the Court observed that, "no one will contend that the power to pass it was contained in the Constitution before the adoption of the last three amendments [Thirteenth, Fourteenth, and Fifteenth]," the Court went on specifically to note that the Act was not "conceived" in terms of the commerce power...

Since the commerce power was not relied on by the Government and was without support in the record, it is understandable that the Court narrowed its inquiry and excluded the Commerce Clause as a possible source of power. In any event, it is clear that such a limitation renders the opinion devoid of authority for the proposition that the Commerce Clause gives no power to Congress to regulate discriminatory practices now found substantially to affect interstate commerce. We, therefore, conclude that the Civil Rights Cases have no relevance to the basis of decision here where the Act explicitly relies upon the commerce power, and where the record is filled with testimony of obstructions and restraints resulting from the discriminations found to be existing. We now pass to that phase of the case.

6. *The Basis of Congressional Action.*

While the Act, as adopted, carried no congressional findings, the record of its passage through each house is replete with evidence of the burdens that discrimination by race or color places upon interstate commerce.... This testimony included the fact that our people have become increasingly mobile with millions of people of all races traveling from State to State; that

Negroes in particular have been the subject of discrimination in transient accommodations, having to travel great distances to secure the same; that often they have been unable to obtain accommodations and have had to call upon friends to put them up overnight ... and that these conditions had become so acute as to require the listing of available lodging for Negroes in a special guidebook which was itself "dramatic testimony to the difficulties" Negroes encounter in travel.... These exclusionary practices were found to be nationwide, the Under Secretary of Commerce testifying that there is "no question that this discrimination in the North still exists to a large degree" and in the West and Midwest as well.... This testimony indicated a qualitative as well as quantitative effect on interstate travel by Negroes. The former was the obvious impairment of the Negro traveler's pleasure and convenience that resulted when he continually was uncertain of finding lodging. As for the latter, there was evidence that this uncertainty stemming from racial discrimination had the effect of discouraging travel on the part of a substantial portion of the Negro community.... This was the conclusion not only of the Under Secretary of Commerce but also of the Administrator of the Federal Aviation Agency who wrote the Chairman of the Senate Commerce Committee that it was his "belief that air commerce is adversely affected by the denial to a substantial segment of the traveling public of adequate and desegregated public accommodations."... We shall not burden this opinion with further details since the voluminous testimony presents overwhelming evidence that discrimination by hotels and motels impedes interstate travel.

7. *The Power of Congress Over Interstate Travel.*

The power of Congress to deal with these obstructions depends on the meaning of the Commerce Clause. Its meaning was first enunciated 140 years ago by the great Chief Justice John Marshall in *Gibbons v. Ogden* ....

In short, the determinative test of the exercise of power by the Congress under the Commerce Clause is simply whether the activity sought to be regulated is "commerce which concerns more States than one" and has a real and substantial relation to the national interest. Let us now turn to this facet of the problem....

It is said that the operation of the motel here is of a purely local character. But, assuming this to be true, "[i]f it is interstate commerce that feels the pinch, it does not matter how local the operation which applies the squeeze." *United States v. Women's Sportswear Mfrs. Assn.*, 336 U.S. 460, 464 (1949)....

Thus the power of Congress to promote interstate commerce also includes the power to regulate the local incidents thereof, including local activities in both the states of origin and destination, which might have a substantial and harmful effect upon that commerce. One need only examine the evidence which we have discussed above to see that Congress may—as it has—prohibit racial discrimination by motels serving travelers, however "local" their operations may appear.

Nor does the Act deprive appellant of liberty or property under the Fifth Amendment. The commerce power invoked here by the Congress is a specific and plenary one authorized by the Constitution itself. The only questions are: (1) whether Congress had a rational basis for finding that racial discrimination by motels affected commerce, and (2) if it had such a basis, whether the means it selected to eliminate that evil are reasonable and appropriate. If they are, appellant has no "right" to select its guests as it sees fit, free from governmental regulation.

There is nothing novel about such legislation. Thirty-two States now have it on their books either by statute or executive order and many cities provide such regulation. Some of these Acts go back fourscore years. It has been repeatedly held by this Court that such laws do not violate the Due Process Clause of the Fourteenth Amendment....

As we have pointed out, 32 states now have such provisions and no case has been cited to us where the attack on a state statute has been successful, either in federal or state courts....

It is doubtful if in the long run appellant will suffer economic loss as a result of the Act. Experience is to the contrary where discrimination is completely obliterated as to all public accommodations. But whether this be true or not is of no consequence, since this Court has specifically held that the fact that a "member of the class which is regulated may suffer economic losses not shared by others ... has never been a barrier" to such legislation.... Likewise, in a long line of cases, this Court has rejected the claim that the prohibition of racial discrimination in public accommodations interferes with personal liberty.... Neither do we find any merit in the claim that the Act is a taking of property without just compensation. The cases are to the contrary.... We find no merit in the remainder of appellant's contentions, including that of "involuntary servitude." As we have seen, 32 States prohibit racial discrimination in public accommodations. These laws but codify the common-law innkeeper rule which long predated the Thirteenth Amendment. It is difficult to believe that the Amendment was intended to abrogate this principle....

We therefore conclude that the action of the Congress in the adoption of the Act as applied here to a motel which concededly serves interstate travelers is within the power granted it by the Commerce Clause of the Constitution, as interpreted by this Court for 140 years. It may be argued that

Congress could have pursued other methods to eliminate the obstructions it found in interstate commerce caused by racial discrimination. But this is a matter of policy that rests entirely with the Congress, not with the courts. How obstructions in commerce may be removed—what means are to be employed—is within the sound and exclusive discretion of the Congress. It is subject only to one caveat—that the means chosen by it must be reasonably adapted to the end permitted by the Constitution. We cannot say that its choice here was not so adapted. The Constitution requires no more.

Affirmed.

CHAPTER 27

The Equal Rights Amendment

A. Representative Shirley Chisholm, Address to the United States House of Representatives, May 21, 1969
B. Ruth Bader Ginsburg, "The Need for the Equal Rights Amendment," September 1973
C. Opposition to the Equal Rights Amendment, Florida, November 10, 1975
D. Dialogue with Phyllis Schlafly on the Equal Rights Amendment, November 1978
E. Reaction to the Defeat of the Equal Rights Amendment in the Florida Senate, 1982

As the United States struggled with the issue of civil rights, another issue of rights began to gain attention: equal rights or equal opportunities for women. As with African American civil rights, the movement for women's rights had been part of American politics since the Revolution. It too gained momentum following the Civil War; one accomplishment was the Nineteenth Amendment (1920), which gave women the right to vote. (Several states had granted them that right earlier.) Advocates for women's rights also proposed an amendment guaranteeing equality of rights for women. First introduced in Congress in 1923, the amendment was introduced every year thereafter and passed and submitted to the states finally in 1972, with a deadline for ratification of March 22, 1979. The amendment read:

Section 1. Equality of rights under the law shall not be denied or abridged by the United States or by any State on account of sex.

Section 2. The Congress shall have the power to enforce, by appropriate legislation, the provisions of this article.

Section 3. This amendment shall take effect two years after the date of ratification.

Thirty-five of the necessary 38 states ratified the amendment before opposition to it (Document C), led largely by Phyllis Schlafly (Document D), stalled the process. Under pressure from women's groups like the National Organization for Women, Congress extended the ratification deadline, but the amendment never passed. The Florida House of Representatives passed the amendment several times but the Senate did not, rejecting it by a vote of 16 for, 22 against a week before the extension deadline (see Document E).

Study Questions

A. In what ways does Shirley Chisholm compare the issues of equal rights for women and African Americans? Why does she think passage of the Equal Rights Amendment is necessary? Does Ruth Bader Ginsburg's discussion of the "horribles" ascribed to the ERA by its opponents address all of Phyllis Schafly's objections?

B. Compare the discussion of women's rights in these documents with the discussions of rights for freed slaves, African Americans, and workingmen in Chapters 16, 18, and 26. How are they alike? Are they dissimilar in any ways?

C. Consider the arguments presented here in light of the discussion of citizenship in Volume 1, Chapter 6; how have attitudes from the earlier time period remained in force? How have they changed?

A. Representative Shirley Chisholm, Address to The United States House of Representatives, May 21, 1969[1]

Mr. Speaker, when a young woman graduates from college and starts looking for a job, she is likely to have a frustrating and even demeaning experience ahead of her. If she walks into an office for an interview, the first question she will be asked is, "Do you type?"

There is a calculated system of prejudice that lies unspoken behind that question. Why is it acceptable for women to be secretaries, librarians, and teachers, but totally unacceptable for them to be managers, administrators, doctors, lawyers, and Members of Congress?

The unspoken assumption is that women are different. They do not have

---

[1] *Congressional Record*, May 21, 1969, Extensions of Remarks E4165-6. Available from Duke University Digital Repository. https://goo.gl/STMGed. Chisholm (1924–2005), the first black woman elected to Congress, represented her district in New York City from 1969 to 1983.

executive ability, orderly minds, stability, leadership skills, and they are too emotional.

It has been observed before, that society for a long time discriminated against another minority, the blacks, on the same basis—that they were different and inferior. The happy little homemaker and the contented "old darkey" on the plantation were both produced by prejudice.

As a black person, I am no stranger to race prejudice. But the truth is that in the political world I have been far oftener discriminated against because I am a woman than because I am black.

Prejudice against blacks is becoming unacceptable although it will take years to eliminate it. But it is doomed because, slowly, white America is beginning to admit that it exists. Prejudice against women is still acceptable. There is very little understanding yet of the immorality involved in double pay scales and the classification of most of the better jobs as "for men only."

More than half of the population of the United States is female. But women occupy only 2 percent of the managerial positions. They have not even reached the level of tokenism yet. No women sit on the AFL-CIO council[2] or Supreme Court. There have been only two women who have held Cabinet rank, and at present there are none. Only two women now hold ambassadorial rank in the diplomatic corps. In Congress, we are down to one Senator and 10 Representatives.

Considering that there are about 3½ million more women in the United States than men, this situation is outrageous.

It is true that part of the problem has been that women have not been aggressive in demanding their rights. This was also true of the black population for many years. They submitted to oppression and even cooperated with it. Women have done the same thing. But now there is an awareness of this situation particularly among the younger segment of the population.

As in the field of equal rights for blacks, Spanish-Americans, the Indians, and other groups, laws will not change such deep-seated problems overnight. But they can be used to provide protection for those who are most abused, and to begin the process of evolutionary change by compelling the insensitive majority to reexamine its unconscious attitudes.

It is for this reason that I wish to introduce today a proposal that has been before every Congress for the last forty years and that sooner or later must become part of the basic law of the land—the equal rights amendment.

------

[2] The American Federation of Labor and Congress of Industrial Organizations, a federation off 55 national and international labor unions.

Let me note and try to refute two of the commonest arguments that are offered against this amendment. One is that women are already protected under the law and do not need legislation. Existing laws are not adequate to secure equal rights for women. Sufficient proof of this is the concentration of women in lower paying, menial, unrewarding jobs and their incredible scarcity in the upper level jobs. If women are already equal, why is it such an event whenever one happens to be elected to Congress?

It is obvious that discrimination exists. Women do not have the opportunities that men do. And women that do not conform to the system, who try to break with the accepted patterns, are stigmatized as "odd" and "unfeminine." The fact is that a woman who aspires to be chairman of the board, or a Member of the House, does so for exactly the same reasons as any man. Basically, these are that she thinks she can do the job and she wants to try.

A second argument often heard against the equal rights amendment is that it would eliminate legislation that many States and the Federal Government have enacted giving special protection to women and that it would throw the marriage and divorce laws into chaos.

As for the marriage laws, they are due for a sweeping reform, and an excellent beginning would be to wipe the existing ones off the books. Regarding special protection for working women, I cannot understand why it should be needed. Women need no protection that men do not need. What we need are laws to protect working people, to guarantee them fair pay, safe working conditions, protection against sickness and layoffs, and provision for dignified, comfortable retirement. Men and women need these things equally. That one sex needs protection more than the other is a male supremacist myth as ridiculous and unworthy of respect as the white supremacist myths that society is trying to cure itself of at this time.

B. Ruth Bader Ginsburg, The Need for the Equal Rights Amendment, September 1973[3]

The notion that men and women stand as equals before the law was not the original understanding, nor was it the understanding of the Congress that framed the Civil War amendments. . . .

---

[3] Ruth Bader Ginsburg, "The Need for the Equal Rights Amendment," *American Bar Association Journal*, 59 (September, 1973), 1013–1019. We have omitted the article's footnotes and subheadings. Ruth Bader Ginsburg was the first tenured female law professor at the Columbia School of Law. She became an Associate Justice of the

Mid-nineteenth century feminists, many of them diligent workers in the cause of abolition, looked to Congress after the Civil War for an express guarantee of equal rights for men and women.[4] But the text of the Four-teenth Amendment appalled the proponents of a sex equality guarantee. Their concern centered on the abortive second section of the amendment, which placed in the Constitution for the first time, the word "male." Three-fold use of the word "male," always in conjunction with the term "citizen," caused concern that the grand phrases of the first section of the Fourteenth Amendment—due process and equal protection of the laws—would have, at best, qualified application to women.

After close to a century's effort, the suffrage amendment was ratified, according to female citizens the right to vote. The most vigorous proponents of that amendment saw it as a beginning, not as a terminal point. Three years after the ratification of the Nineteenth Amendment, the National Women's Party succeeded in putting before Congress the equal rights amendment that has been reintroduced in every Congress since 1923. . . .

Persons unacquainted with the history of the amendment deplore its gen-erality and the absence of investigation concerning its impact. The models of the due process and equal protection clauses should suffice to indicate that the wording of the amendment is a thoroughly responsible way of embody-ing fundamental principle in the Constitution. Before the amendment was proposed, the National Women's Party, with the aid of a staff of lawyers and expert consultants, tabulated state and federal legislation and court decisions relating to the status of women. Advisory councils were formed, composed of different economic and professional groups of women—industrial work-ers, homemakers, teachers and students, federal employees. Each council conducted studies of the desirability of equal rights and responsibilities for men and women. Reading debates on the amendment in the law journals of the 1920s is enlightening. The objections still voiced in 1973 were solidly answered then.

Opponents of the amendment suggest the pursuit of alternate routes:

---

[4] Ginsburg refers to the attempts made by some women's rights advocates to argue that insofar as women were citizens of the United States, the language of the Four-teenth and Fifteenth Amendments ought to be understood as guaranteeing them (among other equal rights) the right to vote. This argument was rejected by the Supreme Court in *Minor v. Happersett*, 88 U.S. (21 Wall.) 162 (1875), which ruled that voting was not a citizenship right.

particularized statutes through the regular legislative process in Congress and in the states, and test case litigation under the Fourteenth Amendment. Only those who have failed to learn the lessons of the past can accept that counsel....

...A recent government computer search, the solicitor general told the Supreme Court this term, revealed that 876 sections in the United States Code contain sex-based references. Similar searches in some of the states have turned up hundreds of state statutes in need of revision.

Will major legislative revision occur without the impetus of the equal rights amendment? Probably not if past experience is an accurate barometer....

A preview of the kind of revision that can be expected under the stimulus of the amendment has been provided by legislative analyses in some of the states. These analyses should reassure those who fear intolerable change in the wake of the amendment. They propose extension of desirable protection to both sexes; for example, state minimum wage laws would be extended to men; in no case do they propose depriving either sex of a genuine benefit now enjoyed.

As a sample of laws destined for the scrap heap if the amendment is ratified, consider these: Arizona law stipulates that the governor, secretary of state, and treasurer must be male. In Ohio only men may serve as arbitrators in county court proceedings. In Wisconsin barbers are licensed to cut men's hair and women's hair, but cosmeticians may attend to women only. Georgia law, still faithful to Blackstone, provides:

> The husband is head of the family and the wife is subject to him; her legal civil existence is merged in the hus-band's, except so far as the law recognizes her separate-ly, either for her own protection, or for her benefit, or for the preservation of public order.

Another embarrassment from the same state reads: "Any charge or intimation against a white female of having sexual intercourse with a person of color is slanderous without proof of special damages." Legislative inertia keeps laws of this kind on the books. Prof. Thomas Emerson summarized the situation this way: "It is not a weakness but a strength of the amendment that it will force prompt consideration of changes that are long overdue."...

In the 1971 term, a new direction was signaled when the Supreme Court responded affirmatively to two complaints of unconstitutional sex discrimination. In *Reed v. Reed*, 404 U.S. 71 (1971), the Court... relied on the due process clause to hold that an unwed father who wished to retain custody of his children had to be given a hearing of the kind that would be accorded to any mother or any married father. The opinions in both cases were laconic; they provided an uncertain basis for predicting the Court's future course.

On May 14, 1973, in *Frontiero v. Richardson*, 411 U.S. 677, the Court moved forward more swiftly than many had anticipated; in effect, it served notice that sex discrimination by law would no longer escape rigorous constitutional review....

... If the equal rights amendment is adopted, the hard task of revision will be undertaken in earnest; absent ratification, comprehensive revision may continue to be regarded as "premature and unnecessary."

Reasoned appraisal of the amendment requires consideration of the realities of life for an increasing population of women in the latter half of the twentieth century.... [O]ver the last fifty years the percentage of working women in the population has approximately doubled, and the projection is that this trend will accelerate....

With the disappearance of home-centered economic activity, and the possibility now open to women to determine whether and when to bear children, perceptive persons of both sexes recognize that there is no justification for confining women to a role of their own.

Some aspects of the traditional arrangement disfavor men, and some exact a toll from both sexes. Women who have paid serious attention to laws that appear to disfavor men agree with the position stated by Sarah Grimke, noted abolitionist and advocate of equal rights for men and women. She said in 1837: "I ask no favors for my sex. All I ask of our brethren is that they take their feet off our necks." Favors rarely come without an accompanying detriment. Too often men of the law fail to grasp this basic point.

A number of "horribles" have been raised in opposition to the amendment. Four of them dominate the literature of amendment opponents.

First horrible. Women will lose the benefit of protective labor laws. Today, challenges to these laws rarely emanate from male employers who wish to overwork women. Since the passage of Title VII,[5] they have come overwhelmingly from blue-collar working women to overcome what they regard as a system that protects them against higher paying jobs and promotions. In the vast majority of Title VII employment discriminations cases,

---

[5] a clause of the 1964 Civil Rights Act that bars discrimination in employment based on race, color, religion, sex or national origin

courts have understood these challenges. Legislatures are beginning to abandon disingenuous protection for women and to extend genuine protection to all workers. Models are ample. In Norway, for example, where opposition to "special protection for women only" came predominantly from women's organizations, a 1956 workers protective act assures safe and healthy conditions for employees of both sexes. Moreover, extension rather than invalidation of laws that benefit only one sex is a route recently traveled by the Supreme Court. In *Frontiers v. Richardson*, fringe benefits for married male members of the military were extended to married female members. The National Women's Party put it this way decades ago in 1926: protective legislation that is desirable

> Should be enacted for all workers.... Legislation that in-cludes women but exempts men ... limits the woman worker's scope of activity ... by barring her from econ-omic opportunity. Moreover, restrictive conditions [*for women but not for men*] fortifies the harmful assump-tions that labor for pay is primarily the prerogative of the male.

Second horrible. Wives will lose the right to support. Only if our legislatures or courts act capriciously, spitefully, without regard for the public welfare, and in flagrant disregard of the intent of the Amendment's proponents. In a growing number of states the equal rights amendment will occasion no change whatever in current support law. In these states, and under the amendment in all states, either husband or wife can be awarded support depending on the couple's circumstances. Who pays in any particular family will depend upon the division of responsibilities within that family unit. If one spouse is the breadwinner and the other performs uncompensated services at home, the breadwinning spouse will be required to support the spouse who works at home.

Underlying the amendment is the premise that a person who works at home should do so because she, or he, wants to, not because of an unarticulated belief that there is no choice. The essential point, sadly ignored by the amendment's detractors, is this: the equal rights amendment does not force anyone happy as a housewife to relinquish that role. On the contrary, it enhances that role by making it plain that it was chosen, not thrust on her without regard to preference.

Third horrible. Women will be forced to serve in the military. Only if men are, and assignments would be made on the basis of the individual capacity rather than sex. With the draft terminated, it is high time for consideration of the other side of that coin. Women who wish to enlist must meet considerably higher standards than men; women in service are denied fringe benefits granted men and do not receive equal vocational training opportunities. The reason for higher standards for women was given by an Air Force colonel in a deposition taken in December, 1972. He explained: "We have had and we continue to have roughly twice as many women apply[ing] as we are able to ... take.... We don't have an excess of men over what we can take."

Young women's groups uniformly testified during congressional hearings on the amendment that they did not wish exemption from responsibility for service. Conspicuous among these groups was the 200,000 member Intercollegiate Association of Women Students, a group appropriately characterized as "middle American."

In 1948, long before women and the military became an emotion-charged issue in connection with the equal rights amendment, Gen. Dwight D. Eisenhower observed:

> Like most old soldiers I was violently against women sol-diers. I thought a tremendous number of difficulties would occur, not only of an administrative nature ... but others of a more personal type that would get us into trouble. None of that occurred.... In the disciplinary field, they were ... a model for the Army. More than this their influence throughout the whole command was good. I am convinced that in another war they have got to be drafted just like the men.

Final horrible. Rest rooms in public places could not be sex separated. Emphatically not so, according to the amendment's proponents in Congress, who were amused at the focus on the "potty problem." Apart from referring to the constitutional regard for personal privacy, they expressed curiosity about the quarter from which objections to current arrangements would come. Did the people who voiced concern suppose that men would want to use women's rest rooms or that women would want to use men's? In any event, the clever solution devised by the airlines suggests one way out of the problem.

Some people have expressed fear of a "flood of litigation" in the wake of the equal rights amendment. But the dramatic increase in sex discrimination litigation under the Fifth and Fourteenth Amendments in the 1970s is indicative that, if anything, ratification of the amendment will stem the tide. The amendment will impel the comprehensive legislative revision that neither Congress nor the states have undertaken to date. The absence of long overdue statutory revision is generating cases by the hundreds across the country. Legislatures remain quiescent despite the mounting judicial challenges, challenges given further impetus by the Supreme Court's decision in *Frontiero v. Richardson*. Ratification of the amendment, however, would plainly mark as irresponsible any legislature that did not undertake the necessary repairs during the two-year period between ratification and effective date.

To date, three fifths of the states have ratified the amendment; these thirty states represent a clear majority of the country's population. One state, Nebraska, has attempted to withdraw its ratification. But New Jersey and Ohio took the same action with respect to the Fourteenth Amendment, and New York ratified and then withdrew its ratification of the Fifteenth Amendment. Congress at that time evidently concluded that ratification, once accomplished, could not be undone. New Jersey and Ohio counted to constitute the requisite three fourths for promulgation of the Fourteenth Amendment. New York was counted among the states that ratified the Fifteenth Amendment.

The equal rights amendment, in sum, would dedicate the nation to a new view of the rights and responsibilities of men and women. It firmly rejects sharp legislative lines between the sexes as constitutionally tolerable. Instead, it looks toward a legal system in which each person will be judged on the basis of individual merit and not on the basis of an unalterable trait of birth that bears no necessary relationship to need or ability. As the Federal Legislation Committee of the Association of the Bar of the City of New York explained:

> [T]he Amendment would eliminate patent discrim-ination, including all laws which prohibit or discourage women from making full use of their political and economic capabilities on the strength of notions about the proper "role" for women in society. Any special exemptions or other favorable treatment required by some women because of their physical stature or family roles could be preserved by statutes which utilize those factors—rather than sex—as the basis for distinction.

C. Opposition to the Equal Rights Amendment, Florida, November 10, 1975

See photo on page H.

D. Dialogue with Phyllis Schlafly on the Equal Rights Amendment, November 1978[6]

GW: Why are you against the ERA?

PS: Because of its effect on the family. It will drive the wife out of the home, and it will take away the legal rights of wives and mothers.

My major objections can be stated in three parts. First it is a fraud. It doesn't do anything for women. It doesn't give them any rights, opportunities, or benefits that they don't have now. Most of the real objectives have been covered by existing legislation—The Equal Employment Opportunity Act of 1974.

Second, Section One of the ERA is designed to convert us into a unisex society. It would prevent us from making any distinction between men and woman. So the next time we have a war, women would have to be drafted and put in combat just like men. You couldn't have laws that say a husband must support his wife. You couldn't give any preferential treatment to wives, mothers, and widows. You wouldn't be able to make a reasonable, common sense separation of treatment such as in single sex schools, fraternities, or athletics; or in other areas such as prison regulations and insurance regulations.

ERA also makes it impossible to have any laws against homosexuals. They would have to be treated with the same rights as husbands and wives because you couldn't discriminate on the basis of sex.

Third, ERA would shift most of the remaining powers of the states to Washington, including power over marriage, divorce, child custody, prison regulations, insurance rates, homosexual laws—any type of legislation that has traditionally distinguished between men and women.

GW: Do you see any good things in the ERA?

PS: Nothing, because I see it as anti-family. If it is anti-family, nothing can be good about it. It is the vehicle for achievement for certain radical, political, and social goals....

---

[6] "Dialogue with Phyllis Schlafly," *Moody Monthly* (November, 1978), 44–49, 125. "GW" are the initials of the editor of the *Moody Monthly*, which between 1900 and 2003 was a nationally circulated publication of the Moody Bible Institute in Chicago. Phyllis Schlafly (1924–2016), who earned a law degree in 1978, was an author, political activist, and founder of the self-described "grassroots conservative" Eagle Forum. Copyright 1978 Moody Publishers.

GW: Why are you against women's liberation?

PS: I used to think I was against it because there was more bad than is good about it. But after working with these people, I know there is nothing good about it. Women's lib is anti-family, and once you realize that, nothing is good about it. Women's lib is a major cause of divorce. What it does to a woman is much like a disease. It is particularly contagious among women in their forties, especially after the children go off to school. Libbers tell these women, "You poor creature. You've wasted your life. You don't have an identity of your own. Go and seek your own self-fulfillment under your own name."

Women in that age group are walking out on marriage in tremendous numbers. These breakups don't have the typical causes—adultery, alcohol, and money.

Besides the bitter women who are ripe for anyone to tell them how mistreated they've been . . . are the young college educated women and college girls. They've had some women's study courses and have been told that the worst career in the world is homemaking.

Women's lib is basically a negative approach towards life. They tell women, "The cards are stacked against you. If you get married, life is nothing but a bunch of dirty diapers and dishes because your husband will treat you like a servant." After they flatten them with this negativism, they say, "Seek self-fulfillment over every other value."

There's no percentage in marrying a girl who isn't willing to take care of her children. If they want to set their values that way, nobody's stopping them. But it isn't compatible with a happy marriage and motherhood.

GW: In their literature, the radical feminists say they want to do away with family, love, marriage, heterosex[*uality*], and religion. Can they accomplish that with the ERA?

PS: Yes. It is the vehicle to achieve all their goals. If the wife's support is taken away—as I believe ERA will do, she will need to get a job. When that happens, you take away the child's right to have his mother in the house. The next step is what the Ohio task force on the ERA proposes: child care centers for all children. This puts children in an institution. Legalized abortion is a main goal of the women's movement because they look upon women's susceptibility to pregnancy as a grave injustice.

In seeking their total independence from men, women want to make homosexuals entitled to the same dignity and respect husbands and wives have. ERA is the vehicle that would enable them to achieve this; ERA says you can't deny or abridge any right on account of sex. So how can you deny a marriage license under ERA to two men or two women? Can they do it? They get their people in the government and work for it with our money.

GW: How have the radical feminists done this?

PS: They started with nothing. But they have worked hard. They now have so much tax money that they are a very powerful force. They are working in the offices of the federal government.

I am on the Illinois Commission on the Status of Women. A few months ago a woman who is paid by the federal government to work on the enforcement of Title IX spoke to us.... Her job is to change people's attitudes because not enough girls are taking shop and not enough boys are taking cooking, needlework or whatever. So now we don't have the right to our own attitudes.

... The feminists are making our laws. They are taking over our educational system and the media and they are going to get all the male jobs, too. This is their goal....

GW: What are your other problems with feminists?

PS: They are in league with pornographers. Two of the biggest and best known adult men's magazines give them money. They are a powerful anti-family force. You don't see any pictures of families with children in these magazines....

I consider pornography the ultimate degradation of women. It's an anti-family movement.

GW: You say the feminists want to change male and female roles, but what about the women who are happy in their role and don't want to work outside the home?

PS: They can get to her. I have friends whose husbands have been told they won't get a promotion for ten years because all the promotions are going to women to bring up their quotas. Then she will find it hard to live on one income.

Another plan feminists have is to change Social Security so that the husband has to pay a tax on the assumed earnings of his wife. This would cost an additional $1,000 a year in federal tax for the privilege of having the wife in the home....

GW: What is the link between feminist and ERA forces and the lesbian groups?

PS: The National Women's Conference in Houston is where they joined together.[7] Prior to Houston, women's lib had not been able to define their relationship. But there, they were all in the same conference, on the same commission, with identifiable names and goals, and they passed their resolutions. They got the whole group to close ranks on everything, including the privileges for homosexuals to teach and have child custody and so forth.

They got all the libbers who prior to that time had not been pro-lesbian to join ranks. Betty Friedan is a good example. For the first time, she said that they had to work together. The National Organization for Women (NOW) has always been for the lesbian....

E. Reaction to the Defeat of the Equal Rights Amendment in the Florida Senate, 1982

See illustration on page H.

---

[7] The National Women's Conference was a federally-funded event held in 1977 in conjunction with the United Nation's "Year of the Woman."

CHAPTER 28

Political Economy at the End of the 20th Century

A. Address to the Nation on the Economy, President Ronald Reagan, February 5, 1981

B. The President's Address to a Joint Session of Congress, President Bill Clinton, February 17, 1993

R onald Reagan won election as president in 1980 promising to restore American self-confidence undermined by a decade of low economic growth, inflation, the Iranian hostage crisis (November 4, 1979–January 20, 1981), and the apparent success of the Soviet Union in extending its influence in Africa, the Middle East and Central Asia. (The Soviet Union invaded and occupied Afghanistan in December 1979.) Central to Reagan's plans was reviving the American economy. After a deep recession early in Reagan's first term, economic growth remained strong for the rest of the 1980s. The Berlin Wall fell in November 1989; Germans united their country by October 1990; and a year later, the Soviet Union collapsed. A few months before German reunification, the U.S. economy entered a recession that lasted until March 1991, although its effects, including unemployment, lingered on. (Unemployment reached a height of 7.5% in 1992, in part because of layoffs in defense industries as the Cold War ended.) The economic downturn, and a sense that a new era had begun with the end of the Cold War that required new leadership, helped Bill Clinton win election as President in November 1992. Clinton's unofficial campaign slogan was: "It's the economy, stupid." Like Reagan twelve years before him, Clinton made restoring the economy a central part of his plans. The economic recovery was underway before Clinton took office. The economy continued to grow strongly throughout the decade until another brief recession occurred in 2001. Economists debate the effect of both Reagan's and Clinton's policies on the economic growth America enjoyed during their presidencies.

Study Questions

A. Both President Ronald Reagan and President Bill Clinton spoke of opportunity. What did they mean by this term? Why was it important? What policies did they propose to create opportunity? Reagan proposed tax cuts and Clinton tax increases. Why did they make these different proposals? Clinton used the term "invest" or "investment" 29 times in his speech. Reagan hardly mentioned it. What is an investment? What did Clinton mean by investment? Why was it important to him? How did Reagan and Clinton differ on the role of government in the economy?

B. Compare the speeches of Reagan and Clinton with the documents in Chapter 21, "Boom to Bust," especially the documents A, C, D, and E. How do the ideas and proposals of Clinton and Reagan compare to those of Hoover and Roosevelt?

C. Consider the issues raised by the texts here in light of the discussion of politics and economics presented in Volume 1, Chapters 2 and 10; how do the claims and preferences of Reagan and Clinton relate to these earlier understandings of politics and economics and what Americans owe to one another and to their government?

A. "Address to the Nation on the Economy," President Ronald Reagan, February 5, 1981[1]

Good evening.

I'm speaking to you tonight to give you a report on the state of our Nation's economy. I regret to say that we're in the worst economic mess since the Great Depression.

A few days ago I was presented with a report I'd asked for, a comprehensive audit, if you will, of our economic condition. You won't like it. I didn't like it. But we have to face the truth and then go to work to turn things around. And make no mistake about it, we can turn them around.

I'm not going to subject you to the jumble of charts, figures, and economic jargon of that audit, but rather will try to explain where we are, how we got there, and how we can get back. First, however, let me just give a few "attention getters" from the audit.

The federal budget is out of control, and we face runaway deficits of almost $80 billion for this budget year that ends September 30th. That deficit is larger

---

[1] Ronald Reagan, "Address to the Nation on the Economy," February 5, 1981. President Reagan's Public Speeches and Statements, Reagan Presidential Library. https://goo.gl/Wt6UVR.

than the entire Federal budget in 1957, and so is the almost $80 billion we will pay in interest this year on the national debt.

Twenty years ago, in 1960, our federal government payroll was less than $13 billion. Today it is 75 billion. During these twenty years our population has only increased by 23.3 percent. The federal budget has gone up 528 percent.

Now, we've just had two years of back-to-back double-digit inflation—13.3 percent in 1979, 12.4 percent last year. The last time this happened was in World War I.

In 1960 mortgage interest rates averaged about 6 percent. They're 2½ times as high now, 15.4 percent.

The percentage of your earnings the federal Government took in taxes in 1960 has almost doubled.

And finally there are 7 million Americans caught up in the personal indignity and human tragedy of unemployment. If they stood in a line, allowing three feet for each person, the line would reach from the coast of Maine to California.

Well, so much for the audit itself. Let me try to put this in personal terms. Here is a dollar such as you earned, spent, or saved in 1960. And here is a quarter, a dime, and a penny—36 cents. That's what this 1960 dollar is worth today. And if the present world inflation rate should continue 3 more years, that dollar of 1960 will be worth a quarter. What initiative[2] is there to save? And if we don't save we're short of the investment capital needed for business and industry expansion. Workers in Japan and West Germany save several times the percentage of their income that Americans do.

What's happened to that American dream of owning a home? Only ten years ago a family could buy a home, and the monthly payment averaged little more than a quarter—27 cents out of each dollar earned. Today, it takes 42 cents out of every dollar of income. So, fewer than 1 out of 11 families can afford to buy their first new home.

Regulations adopted by government with the best of intentions have added $666 to the cost of an automobile. It is estimated that altogether regulations of every kind, on shopkeepers, farmers, and major industries, add $100 billion or more to the cost of the goods and services we buy. And then another 20 billion is spent by government handling the paperwork created by those regulations.

I'm sure you're getting the idea that the audit presented to me found

[2] "Initiative" is the word in the source document, but it may be an error for "incentive."

government policies of the last few decades responsible for our economic troubles. We forgot or just overlooked the fact that government—any government—has a built-in tendency to grow. Now, we all had a hand in looking to government for benefits as if government had some source of revenue other than our earnings. Many if not most of the things we thought of or that government offered to us seemed attractive.

In the years following the Second World War it was easy, for a while at least, to overlook the price tag. Our income more than doubled in the 25 years after the war. We increased our take-home pay in those 25 years by more than we had amassed in all the preceding 150 years put together. Yes, there was some inflation, 1 or 1½ percent a year. That didn't bother us. But if we look back at those golden years, we recall that even then voices had been raised, warning that inflation, like radioactivity, was cumulative and that once started it could get out of control.

Some government programs seemed so worthwhile that borrowing to fund them didn't bother us. By 1960 our national debt stood at $284 billion. Congress in 1971 decided to put a ceiling of 400 billion on our ability to borrow. Today the debt is 934 billion. So-called temporary increases or extensions in the debt ceiling have been allowed 21 times in these 10 years, and now I've been forced to ask for another increase in the debt ceiling or the government will be unable to function past the middle of February—and I've only been here 16 days. Before we reach the day when we can reduce the debt ceiling, we may in spite of our best efforts see a national debt in excess of a trillion dollars. Now, this is a figure that's literally beyond our comprehension.

We know now that inflation results from all that deficit spending. Government has only two ways of getting money other than raising taxes. It can go into the money market and borrow, competing with its own citizens and driving up interest rates, which it has done, or it can print money, and it's done that. Both methods are inflationary.

We're victims of language. The very word "inflation" leads us to think of it as just high prices. Then, of course, we resent the person who puts on the price tags, forgetting that he or she is also a victim of inflation. Inflation is not just high prices; it's a reduction in the value of our money. When the money supply is increased but the goods and services available for buying are not, we have too much money chasing too few goods. Wars are usually accompanied by inflation. Everyone is working or fighting, but production is of weapons and munitions, not things we can buy and use.

Now, one way out would be to raise taxes so that government need not borrow or print money. But in all these years of government growth, we've reached, indeed surpassed, the limit of our people's tolerance or ability to bear an increase in the tax burden. Prior to World War II, taxes were such that on the average we only had to work just a little over 1 month each year to pay our total federal, state, and local tax bill. Today we have to work 4 months to pay that bill.

Some say shift the tax burden to business and industry, but business doesn't pay taxes. Oh, don't get the wrong idea. Business is being taxed, so much so that we're being priced out of the world market. But business must pass its costs of operations—and that includes taxes—on to the customer in the price of the product. Only people pay taxes, all the taxes. Government just uses business in a kind of sneaky way to help collect the taxes. They're hidden in the price; we aren't aware of how much tax we actually pay.

Today this once great industrial giant of ours has the lowest rate of gain in productivity of virtually all the industrial nations with whom we must compete in the world market. We can't even hold our own market here in America against foreign automobiles, steel, and a number of other products. Japanese production of automobiles is almost twice as great per worker as it is in America. Japanese steelworkers outproduce their American counterparts by about 25 percent.

Now, this isn't because they're better workers. I'll match the American working man or woman against anyone in the world. But we have to give them the tools and equipment that workers in the other industrial nations have.

We invented the assembly line and mass production, but punitive tax policies and excessive and unnecessary regulations plus government borrowing have stifled our ability to update plant and equipment. When capital investment is made, it's too often for some unproductive alterations demanded by government to meet various of its regulations. Excessive taxation of individuals has robbed us of incentive and made overtime unprofitable.

We once produced about 40 percent of the world's steel. We now produce 19 percent. We were once the greatest producer of automobiles, producing more than all the rest of the world combined. That is no longer true, and in addition, the "Big Three," the major auto companies in our land,[3] have sustained tremendous losses in the past year and have been forced to lay off thousands of workers.

All of you who are working know that even with cost-of-living pay raises,

---

[3] GM, Ford, and Chrysler

you can't keep up with inflation. In our progressive tax system, as you increase the number of dollars you earn, you find yourself moved up into higher tax brackets, paying a higher tax rate just for trying to hold your own. The result? Your standard of living is going down.

Over the past decades we've talked of curtailing government spending so that we can then lower the tax burden. Sometimes we've even taken a run at doing that. But there were always those who told us that taxes couldn't be cut until spending was reduced. Well, you know, we can lecture our children about extravagance until we run out of voice and breath. Or we can cure their extravagance by simply reducing their allowance.

It's time to recognize that we've come to a turning point. We're threatened with an economic calamity of tremendous proportions, and the old business-as-usual treatment can't save us. Together, we must chart a different course.

We must increase productivity. That means making it possible for industry to modernize and make use of the technology which we ourselves invented. That means putting Americans back to work. And that means above all bringing government spending back within government revenues, which is the only way, together with increased productivity, that we can reduce and, yes, eliminate inflation.

In the past we've tried to fight inflation one year and then, with unemployment increased, turn the next year to fighting unemployment with more deficit spending as a pump primer. So, again, up goes inflation. It hasn't worked. We don't have to choose between inflation and unemployment—they go hand in hand. It's time to try something different, and that's what we're going to do....

On February 18th, I will present in detail an economic program to Congress embodying the features I've just stated. It will propose budget cuts in virtually every department of government. It is my belief that these actual budget cuts will only be part of the savings. As our Cabinet Secretaries take charge of their departments, they will search out areas of waste, extravagance, and costly overhead which could yield additional and substantial reductions.

Now, at the same time we're doing this, we must go forward with a tax relief package. I shall ask for a 10-percent reduction across the board in personal income tax rates for each of the next 3 years. Proposals will also be submitted for accelerated depreciation allowances for business to provide necessary capital so as to create jobs.

Now, here again, in saying this, I know that language, as I said earlier, can get in the way of a clear understanding of what our program is intended to do. Budget cuts can sound as if we're going to reduce total government spending to a lower level than was spent the year before. Well, this is not the case. The budgets will increase as our population increases, and each year we'll see spending increases to match that growth. Government revenues will increase as the economy grows, but the burden will be lighter for each individual, because the economic base will have been expanded by reason of the reduced rates....

Our spending cuts will not be at the expense of the truly needy. We will, however, seek to eliminate benefits to those who are not really qualified by reason of need....

Our basic system is sound. We can, with compassion, continue to meet our responsibility to those who, through no fault of their own, need our help. We can meet fully the other legitimate responsibilities of government. We cannot continue any longer our wasteful ways at the expense of the workers of this land or of our children.

Since 1960 our government has spent $5.1 trillion. Our debt has grown by 648 billion. Prices have exploded by 178 percent. How much better off are we for all that? Well, we all know we're very much worse off. When we measure how harshly these years of inflation, lower productivity, and uncontrolled government growth have affected our lives, we know we must act and act now. We must not be timid. We will restore the freedom of all men and women to excel and to create. We will unleash the energy and genius of the American people, traits which have never failed us....

We can create the incentives which take advantage of the genius of our economic system—a system, as Walter Lippmann observed more than 40 years ago, which for the first time in history gave men "a way of producing wealth in which the good fortune of others multiplied their own."

Our aim is to increase our national wealth so all will have more, not just redistribute what we already have which is just a sharing of scarcity. We can begin to reward hard work and risk-taking, by forcing this Government to live within its means....

And to you, my fellow citizens, let us join in a new determination to rebuild the foundation of our society, to work together, to act responsibly. Let us do so with the most profound respect for that which must be preserved as well as with sensitive understanding and compassion for those who must be protected.

We can leave our children with an unrepayable massive debt and a shattered economy, or we can leave them liberty in a land where every individual has the opportunity to be whatever God intended us to be. All it takes is a little common sense and recognition of our own ability. Together we can forge a new beginning for America.

Thank you, and good night.

B. The President's Address to a Joint Session of Congress, President Bill Clinton, February 17, 1993[4]

... When Presidents speak to the Congress and the nation from this podium, typically they comment on the full range and challenges and opportunities that face the United States. But this is not an ordinary time, and for all the many tasks that require our attention, I believe tonight one calls on us to focus, to unite and to act, and that is our economy. For more than anything else, our task tonight as Americans is to make our economy thrive again. Let me begin by saying that it has been too long—at least three decades—since a President has come and challenged Americans to join him on a great national journey, not merely to consume the bounty of today but to invest for a much greater one tomorrow. ...

We have always been a people of youthful energy and daring spirit. And at this historic moment, as Communism has fallen, as freedom is spreading around the world, as a global economy is taking shape before our eyes, Americans have called for change—and now it is up to those of us in this room to deliver for them.

Our nation needs a new direction. Tonight, I present to you a comprehensive plan to set our nation on that new course.

I believe we will find our new direction in the basic old values that brought us here over the last two centuries: a commitment to opportunity, to individual responsibility, to community, to work, to family and to faith. We must now break the old habits of both political parties and say that there can be no more something for nothing, and admit frankly that we are all in this together.

The conditions which brought us as a nation to this point are well known. Two decades of low productivity growth and stagnant wages; persistent unemployment and underemployment; years of huge government deficits and declining investment in our future; exploding health care costs and lack

---

[4] https://goo.gl/S98Zon. This is a video of President Clinton's speech produced by White House TV and made available by the Clinton Presidential Library. The speech is also available online by Gerhard Peters and John T. Woolley, *The American Presidency Project*. https://goo.gl/p9n42R.

of coverage for millions of Americans; legions of poor children; education and job training opportunities inadequate to the demands of this tough global economy. For too long we drifted without a strong sense of purpose or responsibility or community, and our political system so often has seemed paralyzed by special interest groups, by partisan bickering and by the sheer complexity of our problems.

I believe we can do better, because we remain the greatest nation on earth, the world's strongest economy, the world's only military superpower. If we have the vision, the will and the heart to make the changes we must, we can still enter the 21st century with possibilities our parents could not even have imagined, and enter it having secured the American dream for ourselves and for future generations.

I well remember twelve years ago President Reagan stood at this very podium and told you and the American people that if our national debt were stacked in thousand dollar bills, the stack would reach 67 miles into space. Well, today, that stack would reach 267 miles. . . .

The plan I offer you has four fundamental components:

First, it shifts our emphasis in public and private spending from consumption to investment[,] initially by jump-starting the economy in the short term and investing in our people, their jobs and their incomes over the long run.

Second, it changes the rhetoric of the past into the actions of the present, by honoring work and families in every part of our public decision-making.

Third, it substantially reduces the federal deficit, honestly and credibly, by using in the beginning the most conservative estimates of government revenues, not as the Executive Branch has done so often in the past, using the most optimistic ones.

And finally, it seeks to earn the trust of the American people by paying for these plans first with cuts in government waste and efficiency, second with cuts, not gimmicks, in government spending, and by fairness, for a change, in the way additional burdens are borne.

Tonight, I want to talk with you about what government can do, because I believe government must do more. But let me say first that the real engine of economic growth in this country is the private sector. And second that each of us must be an engine of growth and change. The truth is that as government creates more opportunity in this new and different time, we must also demand more responsibility in turn.

Our immediate priority must be to create jobs. . . . Some people say well we're in a recovery and we don't have to do that. Well, we all hope we're in a

recovery. But we're sure not creating new jobs. And there's no recovery worth
its salt that doesn't put the American people back to work.

To create jobs and guarantee a strong recovery, I call on Congress to enact
an immediate package of jobs investments over $30 billion to put people to
work now to create a half a million jobs: jobs to rebuild our highways and air-
ports, to renovate housing, to bring new life to rural communities and spread
hope and opportunity among our nation's youth. Especially I want to emphasize after the events of last year in Los Angeles and the countless stories of
despair in our cities and in our poor rural communities, this proposal will
create almost 700,000 new summer jobs for displaced unemployed young
people alone this summer. And tonight I invite America's business leaders to
join us in this effort so that together we can provide over one million summer
jobs in cities and poor rural areas for our young people.

Second, our plan looks beyond today's business cycle, because our aspirations extend into the next century. The heart of this plan deals with the
long term. It is an investment program designed to increase public and private investment in areas critical to our economic future. And it has a deficit
reduction program that will increase the savings available for the private
sector to invest, will lower interest rates, will decrease the percentage of the
Federal budget claimed by interest payments, and decrease the risk of financial market disruptions that could adversely affect our economy.

Over the long run, all this will bring us a higher rate of economic growth,
improved productivity, more high-quality jobs and an improved economic
competitive position in the world.

In order to accomplish both increased investment and deficit reduction—
something no American Government has ever been called upon to do at the
same time before, spending must be cut and taxes must be raised. Spending
cuts I recommend were carefully thought through in a way to minimize any
adverse economic impact, to capture the peace dividend for investment purposes, and to switch the balance in the budget from consumption to more
investment. The tax increases and the spending cuts were both designed to
assure that the cost of this historic program to face and deal with our problems will be borne by those who could readily afford it the most.

Our plan is designed, furthermore, and perhaps in some ways most
important, to improve the health of American business through lower interest rates, more incentives to invest and better-trained workers.

Because small business has created such a high percentage of all the jobs
in our nation over the last 10 or 15 years, our plan includes the boldest targeted

incentives for small business in history. We propose a permanent investment tax credit for the smallest firms in this country with revenues of under $5 million. That's about 90 percent of the firms in America, employing about 40 percent of the work force but creating a big majority of the net new jobs for more than a decade. And we propose new rewards for entrepreneurs who take new risks. We propose to give small business access to all the new technologies of our time, and we propose to attack this credit crunch which has denied small business the credit they need to flourish and prosper.

With a new network of community development banks, and one billion dollars to make the dream of enterprise zones real, we propose to bring new hope and new jobs to storefronts and factories from South Boston to South Texas to South-Central Los Angeles.

This plan invests in our roads, our bridges, our transit systems; in high-speed railways and high-tech information systems; and it provides the most ambitious environmental cleanup in partnership with state and local government of our time to put people to work and to preserve the environment for our future.

Standing as we are on the edge of the new century, we know that economic growth depends as never before on opening up new markets overseas and expanding the volume of world trade. And so we will insist on fair trade rules in international markets as a part of a national economic strategy to expand trade, including the successful completion of the latest round of world trade talks and the successful completion of a North American Free Trade Agreement with appropriate safeguards for our workers and for the environment....

... The world is changing so fast that we must have aggressive targeted attempts to create the high-wage jobs of the future; that's what all our competitors are doing. We must give special attention to those critical industries that are going to explode in the 21st century but that are in trouble in America today, like aerospace. We must provide special assistance to areas and to workers displaced by cuts in defense budget and by other unavoidable economic dislocations....

But all of our efforts to strengthen the economy will fail—let me say this again—I feel so strongly about this. All of our efforts to strengthen the economy will fail unless we also take, this year, not next year, not five years from now, but this year, bold steps to reform our health care system....

The combination of the rising costs of care and the lack of care and the fear of losing care are endangering the security and the very lives of millions of our people, and they are weakening our economy every day. Reducing health-care costs can liberate literally hundreds of billions of dollars for new investment in growth and jobs. Bringing health costs in line with inflation would do more for the private sector in this country than any tax cut we could give and any spending program we could promote. Reforming health care over the long run is critically essential to reducing not only our deficit but to expanding investment in America....

Perhaps the most fundamental change the new direction I propose offers is its focus on the future and its investment which I seek in our children. Each day we delay really making a commitment to our children carries a dear cost. Half of the 2-year-olds in this country today don't receive the immunizations they need against deadly diseases. Our plan will provide them for every eligible child and we know now that we will save $10 later for every $1 we spend by eliminating preventable childhood diseases—that's a good investment no matter how you measure it.

I recommend that the Women, Infants and Children's nutrition program be expanded so that every expectant mother who needs the help gets it. We all know that Head Start, a program that prepares children for school, is a success story. We all know that it saves money, but today it just reaches barely over a third of all the eligible children. Under this plan, every eligible child will be able to get a head start.

This is not just the right thing to do; it is the smart thing to do. For every dollar we invest today we'll save three tomorrow....

We have to recognize that all of our high school graduates need some further education in order to be competitive in this global economy. So we have to establish a partnership between businesses and education and the government, for apprenticeship programs in every state in this country to give our people the skills they need. Lifelong learning must benefit not just young high school graduates but workers, too, throughout their career. The average 18-year-old today will change jobs seven times in a lifetime.

We have done a lot in this country on worker training in the last few years, but the system is too fractured. We must develop a unified, simplified, sensible, streamlined worker-training program so that workers receive the training they need regardless of why they lost their jobs or whether they simply need to learn something new to keep them. We have got to do better on this.

Finally, I propose a program that got a great response from the American people all across this country last year, a program of national service to make college loans available to all Americans; and to challenge them at the same time to give something back to their country—as teachers or police officers or community service workers. To give them the option to pay the loans back, but at tax time so they can't beat the bill, but to encourage them instead to pay it back by making their country stronger and making their country better and giving us the benefit of their talents.

A generation ago, when President Kennedy proposed and the United States Congress embraced the Peace Corps, it defined the character of a whole generation of Americans committed to serving people around the world. In this national service program we will provide more than twice as many slots for people before they go to college to be in national service than ever served in the Peace Corps....

If we believe in jobs and we believe in learning, we must believe in rewarding work. If we believe in restoring the values that make America special, we must believe that there is dignity in all work and there must be dignity for all workers.

For those who care for our sick and tend our children who do our most difficult and tiring jobs, the new direction I propose will make this solemn simple commitment. By expanding the refundable earned income tax credit we will make history, we will reward the work of millions of working poor Americans by realizing the principle that if you work 40 hours a week and you've got a child in the house, you will no longer be in poverty.

Later this year we will offer a plan to end welfare as we know it. I have worked on this issue for the better part of a decade and I know from personal conversations with many people, that no one wants to change the welfare system as badly as those who are trapped in it. I want to offer the people on welfare the education, the training, the child care, the health care they need to get back on their feet, but say after two years they must get back to work, too, in private business if possible, in public service if necessary. We have to end welfare as a way of life and make it a path to independence and dignity.

Our next great goal should be to strengthen our families. I compliment the Congress for passing the Family and Medical Leave Act as a good first step, but it is time to do more. This plan will give this country the toughest child-support enforcement system it has ever had. It is time to demand that people take responsibility for the children they bring in this world....

Next, to revolutionize government we have to insure that we live within our means, and that should start at the top and with the White House. In the last few days I have announced a cut in the White House staff of 25 percent, saving approximately $10 million. I have ordered administrative cuts in budgets of agencies and departments; I have cut the federal bureaucracy—or will over the next four years—by approximately 100,000 positions, for a combined savings of $9 billion.

It is time for government to demonstrate, in the condition we're in, that we can be as frugal as any household in America, and that's why I also want to congratulate the Congress. I noticed the announcement of the leadership today that Congress is taking similar steps to cut its costs. I think that is important; I think it will send a very clear signal to the American people.

But if we really want to cut spending we're going to have to do more and some of it will be difficult. Tonight I call for an across-the-board freeze in federal government salaries for one year. And thereafter during this four-year period I recommend that salaries rise at one point lower than the cost-of-living allowance normally involved in federal pay increases.

Next, I recommend that we make 150 specific budget cuts, as you know, and that all those who say we should cut more, be as specific as I have been.

Finally let me say to my friends on both sides of the aisle, it is not enough simply to cut government—we have to rethink the whole way it works....

So I want to bring a new spirit of innovation into every government department....

In the aftermath of all the difficulties with the savings and loans, we must use federal bank regulators to protect the security and safety of our financial institutions—but they should not be used to continue the credit crunch, to stop people from making sensible loans.

I'd like for us to not only have welfare reform, but to re-examine the whole focus of all of our programs that help people to shift them from entitlement programs to empowerment programs. In the end, we want people not to need us anymore. I think that's important.

But in the end, we have to get back to the deficit.... [T]his plan does—it tackles the budget deficit seriously and over the long term. It puts in place one of the biggest deficit reductions and one of the biggest changes in federal priorities, from consumption to investment, in the history of this country at the same time[:] over the next four years....

... We have to cut the deficit because the more we spend paying off the debt, the less tax dollars we have to invest in jobs and education and the future of this country.

And the more money we take out of the pool of available savings, the harder it is for people in the private sector to borrow money at affordable interest rates for a college loan for their children, for a home mortgage, or to start a new business. That's why we've got to reduce the debt, because it is crowding out other activities that we ought to be engaged in and that the American people ought to be engaged in.

We cut the deficit so that our children will be able to buy a home, so that our companies can invest in the future and in retraining their workers, so that our government can make the kinds of investments we need to be a stronger and smarter and safer nation.

If we don't act now, you and I might not even recognize this Government 10 years from now....

We'll still be the world's largest debtor and when members of Congress come here, they'll be devoting over 20 cents on the dollar to interest payments, more than half of the budget to health care and to other entitlements. And you will come here and deliberate and argue over six or seven cents on the dollar, no matter what America's problems are. We will not be able to have the independence we need to chart the future that we must and we'll be terribly dependent on foreign funds for a large portion of our investment.

This budget plan by contrast will, by 1997, cut $140 billion in that year alone from the deficit, a real spending cut, a real revenue increase, a real deficit reduction, using the independent numbers of the Congressional Budget Office....

I know this economic plan is ambitious but I honestly believe it is necessary for the continued greatness of the United States. And I think it is paid for fairly, first by cutting Government, then by asking the most of those who benefited the most in the past and by asking more Americans to contribute today so that all of us can prosper tomorrow. For the wealthiest, those earning more than $180,000 per year, I ask you all who are listening tonight to support a raise in the top rate for federal income taxes from 31 to 36 percent.

We recommend a 10 percent surtax on incomes over $250,000 a year and we recommend closing some loopholes that let some people get away without paying any tax at all.

For businesses with taxable incomes in excess of $10 million, we recommend a rate raise in the corporate tax rate, also [to] 36 percent, as well as a cut in the deduction for business entertainment expenses. Our plan seeks to attack tax subsidies that actually reward companies more for shutting their operations down here and moving them overseas, than for staying here and reinvesting in America....

... We will seek to ensure that through effective tax enforcement, foreign corporations who do make money in America simply pay the same taxes that American companies make on the same income.

To middle-class Americans who have paid a great deal for the last 12 years and from whom I ask a contribution tonight, I will say again as I did on Monday night: You're not going alone anymore, you're certainly not going first and you're not going to pay more for less as you have too often in the past.

I want to emphasize the facts about this plan: 98.8 percent of America's families will have no increase in their income tax rates. Only 1.2 percent at the top.

Let me be clear: There will also be no new cuts in benefits for Medicare. As we move toward the fourth year with the explosion in health-care costs, as I said, projected to account for 50 percent of the growth in the deficit between now and the year 2000, there must be planned cuts in payments to providers—the doctors, the hospitals, the labs—as a way of controlling health-care costs. But I see these only as a stopgap until we can reform the entire health-care system. If you'll help me do that, we can be fair to the providers and to the consumers of health care.. . .

Secondly, the only change we are making in Social Security is one that has already been publicized: the plan does ask older Americans with higher incomes, who do not rely solely on Social Security to get by, to contribute more. This plan will not affect the 80 percent of Social Security recipients who do not pay taxes on Social Security now. Those who do not pay tax on Social Security now will not be affected by this plan.

Our plan does include a broad-base tax on energy.. . .

Taken together, these measures will cost an American family with an income of about $40,000 a year less than $17 a month. It will cost American families with incomes under $30,000 nothing, because of other programs we propose, principally those raising the earned income tax credit.

Because of our publicly stated determination to reduce the deficit, if we do these things we will see the continuation of what's happened just since the election. Just since the election, since the Secretary of the Treasury, the director of the Office of Management and Budget and others who have begun to speak out publicly in favor of a tough deficit reduction plan, interest rates have continued to fall long-term.

That means that for the middle class who will pay something more each month, if they have any credit needs or demands, their increased energy costs will be more than offset by lower interest costs for mortgages, con- sumer loans, credit cards. This can be a wise investment for them and their country now.. . .

Now I ask all of you to consider this: whatever you think of the tax pro- gram, whatever you think of the spending cuts—consider the cost of not changing. Remember the numbers that you all know.

If we just keep on doing what we're doing, by the end of the decade we'll have a $650 billion a year deficit. If we just keep on doing what we're doing, by the end of the decade 20 percent of our national income will go to health care every year—twice as much as any other country on the face of the globe. If we just keep on doing what we're doing, over 20 cents on the dollar will have to go to service the debt.

Unless we have the courage now to start building our future and stop borrowing from it, we're condemning ourselves to years of stagnation interrupted by occasional recession, to slow growth in jobs, to no more growth in income, to more debt, to more disappointment. Worse, unless we change, unless we increase investment and reduce the debt to raise productivity so that we can generate both jobs and incomes, we will be condemning our children and our children's children to a lesser life than we enjoy.

Once Americans looked forward to doubling their living standards every 25 years. At present productivity rates it will take a hundred years to double living standards, until our grandchildren's grandchildren are born. I say that is too long to wait....

My fellow Americans, the test of this plan cannot be "what is in it for me." It has got to be "what is in it for us."...

There's so much good, so much possibility, so much excitement in this country now that if we act boldly and honestly, as leaders should, our legacy will be one of prosperity and progress. This must be America's new direction. Let us summon the courage to seize it.

Thank you. God bless America.

CHAPTER 29

America and the World

A. President George W. Bush, Inaugural Address, January 20, 2005
B. President Barack Obama, Address at Cairo University, June 4, 2009
C. Senator Rand Paul, "Containment and Radical Islam," February 6, 2013

The end of the Cold War (1947–1991; Chapters 24 and 25) ushered in a new era in international relations and raised the question of how the United States should deal with the post-Cold War world. Like his immediate predecessors, President George W. Bush argued that the United States should promote democracy for America's sake and for the benefit of the world. This included a global struggle against the people and ideas that sponsored the attacks on the United States on September 11, 2001. No less committed to protecting the United States and promoting democracy, President Obama sought a different approach to Islam and less commitment overseas. Senator Paul dissented from the consensus that he argued included both Bush and Obama. Denying he was an isolationist, Paul argued for greater restraint politically, militarily, and financially than he felt recent administrations of either party had shown.

Study Questions

A. Do Obama and Bush represent a consensus? If so, in what ways do they agree? How do they differ? Does Paul succeed in outlining a foreign policy that is more restrained than the policy of either Bush or Obama but is not isolationist?

B. Compare the speeches of Presidents George W. Bush and Barack Obama to those of Senator Albert Beveridge and Henry Van Dyke in Chapter 20. In what ways are the attitudes and ideas in these speeches similar or different? How does each of these men understand the role of human agency and the power of ideology in moving "history" forward?

C. Consider the issues raised by the texts here in light of the views of America's place in the world expressed by those who colonized America and those who participated in the American Revolution (see Volume 1, Chapters 1-6). How do the arguments of Bush, Obama, and Paul compare with those made about war with Mexico (Volume 1, Chapter 13)?

A. President George W. Bush, Second Inaugural Address, January 20, 2005[1]

... At this second gathering, our duties are defined not by the words I use but by the history we have seen together. For a half a century, America defended our own freedom by standing watch on distant borders. After the shipwreck of communism came years of relative quiet, years of repose, years of sabbatical, and then there came a day of fire.

We have seen our vulnerability, and we have seen its deepest source. For as long as whole regions of the world simmer in resentment and tyranny, prone to ideologies that feed hatred and excuse murder, violence will gather and multiply in destructive power and cross the most defended borders and raise a mortal threat. There is only one force of history that can break the reign of hatred and resentment and expose the pretensions of tyrants and reward the hopes of the decent and tolerant, and that is the force of human freedom.

We are led, by events and common sense, to one conclusion: The survival of liberty in our land increasingly depends on the success of liberty in other lands. The best hope for peace in our world is the expansion of freedom in all the world.

America's vital interests and our deepest beliefs are now one. From the day of our founding, we have proclaimed that every man and woman on this Earth has rights and dignity and matchless value, because they bear the image of the Maker of heaven and Earth. Across the generations, we have proclaimed the imperative of self-government, because no one is fit to be a master and no one deserves to be a slave. Advancing these ideals is the mission that created our Nation. It is the honorable achievement of our fathers. Now, it is the urgent requirement of our Nation's security and the calling of our time.

So it is the policy of the United States to seek and support the growth of democratic movements and institutions in every nation and culture, with the ultimate goal of ending tyranny in our world. This is not primarily the

---

[1] "President Sworn In to Second Term," Presidential Records, George W. Bush Presidential Library. https://goo.gl/q2L5Qr

task of arms, though we will defend ourselves and our friends by force of arms when necessary. Freedom, by its nature, must be chosen and defended by citizens and sustained by the rule of law and the protection of minorities. And when the soul of a nation finally speaks, the institutions that arise may reflect customs and traditions very different from our own. America will not impose our own style of government on the unwilling. Our goal instead is to help others find their own voice, attain their own freedom, and make their own way.

The great objective of ending tyranny is the concentrated work of generations. The difficulty of the task is no excuse for avoiding it. America's influence is not unlimited, but fortunately for the oppressed, America's influence is considerable and we will use it confidently in freedom's cause.

My most solemn duty is to protect this nation and its people from further attacks and emerging threats. Some have unwisely chosen to test America's resolve and have found it firm. We will persistently clarify the choice before every ruler and every nation, the moral choice between oppression, which is always wrong, and freedom, which is eternally right. . . .

Some, I know, have questioned the global appeal of liberty, though this time in history, four decades defined by the swiftest advance of freedom ever seen, is an odd time for doubt. Americans, of all people, should never be surprised by the power of our ideals. Eventually, the call of freedom comes to every mind and every soul. We do not accept the existence of permanent tyranny because we do not accept the possibility of permanent slavery. Liberty will come to those who love it. . . .

B. President Barack Obama, Address at Cairo University, June 4, 2009[2]

. . . I've come here to Cairo to seek a new beginning between the United States and Muslims around the world, one based on mutual interest and mutual respect and one based upon the truth that America and Islam are not exclusive and need not be in competition. Instead, they overlap and share common principles—principles of justice and progress, tolerance and the dignity of all human beings. . . .

. . . [H]uman history has often been a record of nations and tribes and, yes, religions subjugating one another in pursuit of their own interests. Yet

[2] "Remarks by the President On a New Beginning," Archived White House Website, Obama Presidential Library. https://goo.gl/YXTuJU and https://goo.gl/fZQGRp

in this new age, such attitudes are self-defeating. Given our interdependence, any world order that elevates one nation or group of people over another will inevitably fail....

... [L]et me speak as clearly and as plainly as I can about some specific issues that I believe we must finally confront together.

The first issue that we have to confront is violent extremism in all of its forms. In Ankara, I made clear that America is not, and never will be, at war with Islam. We will, however, relentlessly confront violent extremists who pose a grave threat to our security, because we reject the same thing that people of all faiths reject: the killing of innocent men, women, and children. And it is my first duty as President to protect the American people....

[The President next discussed Palestine, and nuclear proliferation.]

The fourth issue that I will address is democracy.... No system of government can or should be imposed by one nation on any other.

That does not lessen my commitment, however, to governments that reflect the will of the people. Each nation gives life to this principle in its own way, grounded in the traditions of its own people. America does not presume to know what is best for everyone, just as we would not presume to pick the outcome of a peaceful election. But I do have an unyielding belief that all people yearn for certain things: the ability to speak your mind and have a say in how you are governed, confidence in the rule of law and the equal administration of justice, government that is transparent and doesn't steal from the people, the freedom to live as you choose. These are not just American ideas, they are human rights. And that is why we will support them everywhere.

Now, there is no straight line to realize this promise, but this much is clear: Governments that protect these rights are ultimately more stable, successful, and secure. Suppressing ideas never succeeds in making them go away. America respects the right of all peaceful and law-abiding voices to be heard around the world, even if we disagree with them. And we will welcome all elected, peaceful governments, provided they govern with respect for all their people.

This last point is important, because there are some who advocate for democracy only when they're out of power. Once in power, they are ruthless in suppressing the rights of others. So no matter where it takes hold, government of the people and by the people sets a single standard for all who would hold power. You must maintain your power through consent, not coercion; you must respect the rights of minorities and participate with a spirit of tolerance and compromise; you must place the interests of your people and the legitimate workings of the political process above your party. Without these ingredients, elections alone do not make true democracy.

The fifth issue that we must address together is religious freedom. Islam has a proud tradition of tolerance. We see it in the history of Andalusia and Cordoba³ during the Inquisition. I saw it firsthand as a child in Indonesia, where devout Christians worshiped freely in an overwhelmingly Muslim country. That is the spirit we need today. People in every country should be free to choose and live their faith based upon the persuasion of the mind and the heart and the soul. This tolerance is essential for religion to thrive, but it's being challenged in many different ways....

The sixth issue that I want to address is women's rights. I know—[applause]—I know, and you can tell from this audience, that there is a healthy debate about this issue. I reject the view of some in the West that a woman who chooses to cover her hair is somehow less equal, but I do believe that a woman who is denied an education is denied equality. And it is no coincidence that countries where women are well educated are far more likely to be prosperous....

I am convinced that our daughters can contribute just as much to society as our sons. Our common prosperity will be advanced by allowing all humanity, men and women, to reach their full potential. I do not believe that women must make the same choices as men in order to be equal, and I respect those women who choose to live their lives in traditional roles. But it should be their choice. And that is why the United States will partner with any Muslim-majority country to support expanded literacy for girls and to help young women pursue employment through microfinancing that helps people live their dreams.

Finally, I want to discuss economic development and opportunity. I know that for many, the face of globalization is contradictory. The Internet and television can bring knowledge and information, but also offensive sexuality and mindless violence into the home. Trade can bring new wealth and opportunities, but also huge disruptions and change in communities. In all nations, including America, this change can bring fear. Fear that because of modernity, we lose control over our economic choices, our politics, and, most importantly, our identities, those things we most cherish about our communities, our families, our traditions, and our faith.

³ Cordoba was the seat of government for the Muslim rulers in Al-Andalús (the area in present-day Southern Spain known as Andalusia). During the 9th and 10th centuries, it was known as a center of learning where Jews and Christians were tolerated.

But I also know that human progress cannot be denied. There need not be contradictions between development and tradition. Countries like Japan and South Korea grew their economies enormously while maintaining distinct cultures. The same is true for the astonishing progress within Muslim-majority countries from Kuala Lumpur to Dubai. In ancient times and in our times, Muslim communities have been at the forefront of innovation and education....

I know there are many, Muslim and non-Muslim, who question whether we can forge this new beginning. Some are eager to stoke the flames of division and to stand in the way of progress. Some suggest that it isn't worth the effort, that we are fated to disagree and civilizations are doomed to clash. Many more are simply skeptical that real change can occur. There's so much fear, so much mistrust that has built up over the years. But if we choose to be bound by the past, we will never move forward. And I want to particularly say this to young people of every faith in every country: You, more than anyone, have the ability to reimagine the world, to remake this world....

...It's easier to start wars than to end them. It's easier to blame others than to look inward. It's easier to see what is different about someone than to find the things we share. But we should choose the right path, not just the easy path. There's one rule that lies at the heart of every religion, that we do unto others as we would have them do unto us. This truth transcends nations and peoples, a belief that isn't new, that isn't black or white or brown, that isn't Christian or Muslim or Jew. It's a belief that pulsed in the cradle of civilization and that still beats in the hearts of billions around the world. It's a faith in other people, and it's what brought me here today. We have the power to make the world we seek, but only if we have the courage to make a new beginning, keeping in mind what has been written.

The Holy Koran tells us: "O mankind! We have created you male and a female, and we have made you into nations and tribes so that you may know one another."[4] The Talmud tells us: "The whole of the Torah is for the purpose of promoting peace."[5] The Holy Bible tells us: "Blessed are the peacemakers, for they shall be called sons of God."[6] The people of the world can

---

[4] Koran 49:13. The use of the article "a" before "female" seems to be a translation error. Compare the various translations offered in *The Quranic Arabic Corpus*, an online annotated linguistic resource, https://goo.gl/Lzs16g.
[5] The Talmud is the collective body of rabbinic commentaries on the Torah, the first five books of the Bible.
[6] Matthew 5:9.

live together in peace. We know that is God's vision. Now that must be our work here on Earth.

Thank you, and may God's peace be upon you.

C. Senator Rand Paul (R-KY), Containment and Radical Islam, February 6, 2013[7]

I got the idea for this speech when I read a book about George Kennan.[8]... The topic of the speech is containment and radical Islam.

Foreign policy is uniquely an arena where we should base decisions on the landscape of the world as it is, not as we wish it to be. I see the world as it is. I am a realist, not a neoconservative, nor an isolationist.[9]

When candidate John McCain[10] argued in 2007 that we should remain in Iraq for 100 years, I blanched and I wondered what the unintended consequences of prolonged occupation would be. But McCain's call for a hundred year occupation does capture some truth: that the West is in for a long, irregular confrontation not with terrorism, which is simply a tactic, but with Radical Islam.

As many are quick to note, the war is not with Islam but with a radical element of Islam—the problem is that this element is no small minority but a vibrant, often mainstream, vocal and numerous minority. Whole countries, such as Saudi Arabia, Pakistan and Afghanistan, where we presided over a constitution written by "moderates," adhere to at least certain radical concepts, such as the death penalty for blasphemy, conversion, or apostasy. A survey in Britain after the subway bombings showed 20% of the Muslim population in Britain approved of the violence.

Some libertarians[11] argue that western occupation and intervention fans

---

[7] The text is from a speech delivered by Senator Paul at the Heritage Foundation. The audio is available at https://goo.gl/eCsHJo.

[8] George Kennan (1904–2005) was an American diplomat and the author of the containment policy. See Chapter 24.

[9] Neo-conservatives are those, often former liberals, who have come to mistrust certain liberal policy preferences. In foreign policy, neo-conservatives tend to believe that the United States must be active in the world and promote democracy for the sake of both the United States and the world. Isolationists are those who believe that the United can and should, for its own sake, limit its involvement in the world.

[10] Senator John McCain (AZ-R) was the Republican candidate for President in 2008.

[11] those who make individual freedom a priority and therefore wish to limit the power of government

AMERICA AND THE WORLD

the flames of radical Islam—I agree. But I don't agree that absent western occupation that radical Islam "goes quietly into that good night."[12] I don't agree with [*President Franklin D. Roosevelt's Vice-President*] Henry Wallace that the Soviets (or Radical Islam in today's case) can be discouraged by "the glad hand and the winning smile."[13]

Americans need to understand that Islam has a long and perseverant memory. As Bernard Lewis writes, "the general level of historical knowledge in American society is abysmally low. The Muslim peoples, like everyone else in the world, are shaped by their history, but unlike some others, they are keenly aware of it."

Radical Islam is no fleeting fad but a relentless force. Though at times stateless, radical Islam is also supported by radicalized nations such as Iran. Though often militarily weak, radical Islam makes up for its lack of conventional armies with unlimited zeal.

For Americans to grasp the mindset of radical Islam we need to understand that they are still hopping mad about the massacre at Karbala some thirteen hundred years ago.[14] Meanwhile, many Americans seem to be more concerned with who is winning *Dancing with the Stars*. Over 50 percent of Americans still believe Iraq attacked us on 9/11.

Until we understand the world around us, until we understand at least a modicum of what animates our enemies, we cannot defend ourselves and we cannot contain our enemies.

To understand how we will contain radical Islam, we need to understand the longest, most dangerous war in our history, the Cold War. In February 1946, George Kennan sent a five thousand word telegram heard round the world. The Long Telegram gained him instant and near universal fame, as it called for containment of the Soviet Union....

I think all of us have the duty to ask where are the Kennans of our generation? When foreign policy has become so monolithic, so lacking in debate that Republicans and Democrats routinely pass foreign policy statements

---

[12] Rand quotes from a poem by Dylan Thomas, "Do Not Go Gentle into that Good Night."
[13] Kennan attributed these words to Wallace.
[14] The battle of Karbala (680 CE) was part of the succession struggle that followed the death of Mohammed. Mohammed's grandson, Husayn, was killed in the battle, in which the forces of Yazid I triumphed. Shia and Sunni Muslims continue to hold different interpretations of the significance of Husayn's death.

without debate and without votes, where are the calls for moderation, the calls for restraint?

Anyone who questions the bipartisan consensus is immediately castigated, rebuked and their patriotism challenged....

Containment, though, should be discussed as an option with regard to a larger threat, the more generalized threat from radical Islam. Radical Islam, like communism, is an ideology with far reach and will require a firm and patient opposition....

... [T]he concept of containment succinctly described a strategy... "a path between the appeasement that had failed to prevent WWII and the alternative of a third world war."

What the United States needs now is a policy that finds a middle path. A policy that is not rash or reckless. A foreign policy that is reluctant, restrained by Constitutional checks and balances, but does not appease. A foreign policy that recognizes the danger of radical Islam but also the inherent weaknesses of radical Islam. A foreign policy that recognizes the danger of bombing countries on [the assumption of] what they might someday do. A foreign policy that requires, as Kennan put it, "a long term, patient but firm and vigilant containment of... expansive tendencies." A policy that understands the "distinction between vital and peripheral interests."

No one believes that Kennan was an isolationist but Kennan did advise that non-interference in the internal affairs of another country was, after all, a long-standing principle of American diplomacy that should be excepted only when "there is a sufficiently powerful national interest" and when "we have the means to conduct such intervention successfully and can afford the cost."

In Kennan's famous X article[15] he argues that containment meant the "application of counter-force at a series of constantly shifting geographical and political points, corresponding to the shifts and maneuvers of Soviet policy." He later clarified, though, that did not necessarily mean that the application of counter-force had to mean a military response. He argued that containment was not a strategy to counter "entirely by military means." "But containment was not diplomacy [alone] either."

Like communism, radical Islam is an ideology with worldwide reach. Containing radical Islam requires a worldwide strategy like containment.

---

[15] Kennan adapted his telegram for publication in Foreign Affairs, where it appeared in 1947 as "The Sources of Soviet Conduct." The author of the article was given as Mr. X.

It requires counterforce at a series of constantly shifting worldwide points. But counterforce does not necessarily mean large-scale land wars with hundreds of thousands of troops, nor does it always mean a military action at all.

Kennan objected to the Truman Doctrine's[16] "implied obligation to act wherever Soviet aggression or intimidation occurred, without regard to whether American interests were at stake or the means existed with which to defend them." He was also concerned that the Truman doctrine was "a blank check to give economic and military aid to any area in the world."

Likewise, today's "Truman" caucus wants boots on the ground and weapons in the hands of freedom fighters everywhere, including Syrian rebels. Perhaps we might want to ask the opinion of the one million Syrian Christians, many of whom fled Iraq after our Shiite allies were installed. Perhaps, we might want to ask: Will the Syrian rebels respect the rights of Christians, women, and other ethnic minorities?

In the 1980s, the war caucus in Congress armed bin Laden and the *mujaheddin* in their fight with the Soviet Union.[17] In fact, it was the official position of the State Department to support radical jihad against the Soviets. We all know how well that worked out.

Out of the Arab Spring[18] new nations have emerged. While discussion of Iran dominates foreign affairs, I think more time should be allotted to whether we should continue to send aid and weapons to countries that are hostile to Israel and to the United States. I, for one, believe it is unwise to be sending more M1 tanks and F-16 fighters to Egypt.

Kennan argued that "integrating force with foreign policy did not mean 'blustering, threatening, waving clubs at people and telling them if they don't do this or that we are going to drop a bomb on them.'" But it did mean maintaining "a preponderance of strength."

Kennan wrote, "The strength of the Kremlin lies in the fact that it knows how to wait. But the strength of the Russian people lies in the fact that they know how to wait longer." Radical Islam's only real strength is just such an endless patience. They know we eventually will leave. They simply wait for

---

[16] See Chapter 24.

[17] *Mujaheddin* was a word applied to those in Afghanistan who fought against the Soviet occupation of the country (1979–1989). It derives from the Arabic word *jihad*, which means struggle and typically implies war or conflict. There is no evidence that arms or support went to bin Laden or his organization al Qaeda.

[18] A term used to denote protests calling for democratic reform in Arab countries that began in late 2010 and ran through the following spring.

AMERICA AND THE WORLD

us to leave. We cannot afford endless occupation, but this does not mean that by leaving we cannot and will not still contain radical Islam....

Strategic ambiguity is still of value. The world knows we possess an enormous ability of nuclear retaliation. Over 60 years of not using our nuclear weapons shows wise restraint. But for our enemies to be uncertain what provocation may awaken an overwhelming response, nuclear or conventional, is an uncertainty that still helps to keep the peace.

I recognize that foreign policy is complicated. It is inherently less black and white to most people than domestic policy. I think there is room for a foreign policy that strikes a balance.

If for example, we imagine a foreign policy that is everything to everyone, that is everywhere all the time, that would be one polar extreme. Likewise if we imagine a foreign policy that is nowhere any of the time and is completely disengaged from the challenges and dangers to our security that really do exist in the world—well, that would be the other polar extreme.

There are times, such as existed in Afghanistan with the bin Laden terrorist camps, that do require intervention. Maybe, we could be somewhere, some of the time and do so while respecting our Constitution and the legal powers of Congress and the Presidency....

I'd argue that a more restrained foreign policy is the true conservative foreign policy, as it includes two basic tenets of true conservatism: respect for the Constitution and fiscal discipline.

I am convinced that what we need is a foreign policy that works within these two constraints, a foreign policy that works within the confines of the Constitution and the realities of our fiscal crisis. Today in Congress there is no such nuance, no such moderation of dollars or executive power....

[James] Madison wrote, "The Constitution supposes what history demonstrates, that the executive is the branch most prone to war and most interested in it, therefore the Constitution has with studied care vested that power in the legislature."[19] We have forgotten this.

Since the Korean War, Congress has ignored its responsibility to restrain the President. Congress has abdicated its role in declaring war.

What would a foreign policy look like that tried to strike a balance? First, it would have less soldiers stationed overseas and less bases. Instead of large, limitless land wars in multiple theaters, we would—when necessary—target our enemy and strike with lethal force.

---

[19] This is a paraphrase of a passage in a letter that Madison wrote to Thomas Jefferson, April 2, 1798.

We would not presume that we build nations nor would we presume that we have the resources to build nations. Many of the countries formed after WWI are collections of tribal regions that have never been governed by a central government and may, in fact, be ungovernable.

When we must intervene with force, we should attempt to intervene in cooperation with the host government. Intervention against the will of another nation is war, such as in Afghanistan or Libya, and it should require a declaration of war by Congress. Such constitutional obstacles purposefully make it more difficult to go to war. That was the Founders' intention: To make war less likely.

We did not declare war or authorize force to begin war with Libya. This is a dangerous precedent. In our foreign policy, Congress has become not even a rubber stamp but an irrelevancy. With Libya, the president sought permission from the UN ... from NATO ... from the Arab League—everyone *but* the US Congress! And how did Congress react? Congress let him get away with it.

The looming debt crisis will force us to reassess our role in the world....

It is time for all Americans, and especially conservatives, to become as critical and reflective when examining foreign policy as we are with domestic policy. Should our military be defending this nation or constantly building other nations? What constitutes our actual "national defense" and what parts of our foreign policy are more like an irrational offense? It is the soldier's job to do his duty—but it is the citizen's job to question their government— particularly when it comes to putting our soldiers in harm's way.

And of course, the question we are forced to ask today is, can we afford this?

I hope such questions begin to be asked and we see some sort of return to a constitutional foreign policy. I hope this occurs before the debt crisis occurs and not amidst a crisis. To that end, I will fight to have a voice for those who wish to see a saner, more-balanced approach to foreign policy.

Declaration of Independence

In CONGRESS, July 4, 1776

The unanimous Declaration of the thirteen united States of America, When in the Course of human events, it becomes necessary for one people to dissolve the political bands which have connected them with another, and to assume among the powers of the earth, the separate and equal station to which the Laws of Nature and of Nature's God entitle them, a decent respect to the opinions of mankind requires that they should declare the causes which impel them to the separation.

We hold these truths to be self-evident, that all men are created equal, that they are endowed by their Creator with certain unalienable Rights, that among these are Life, Liberty and the pursuit of Happiness.—That to secure these rights, Governments are instituted among Men, deriving their just powers from the consent of the governed,—that whenever any Form of Government becomes destructive of these ends, it is the Right of the People to alter or to abolish it, and to institute new Government, laying its foundation on such principles and organizing its powers in such form, as to them shall seem most likely to effect their Safety and Happiness. Prudence, indeed, will dictate that Governments long established should not be changed for light and transient causes; and accordingly all experience hath shewn, that mankind are more disposed to suffer, while evils are sufferable, than to right themselves by abolishing the forms to which they are accustomed. But when a long train of abuses and usurpations, pursuing invariably the same Object evinces a design to reduce them under absolute Despotism, it is their right, it is their duty, to throw off such Government, and to provide new Guards for their future security.—Such has been the patient sufferance of these Colonies; and such is now the necessity which constrains them to alter their former Systems of Government. The history of the present King of Great Britain is a history of repeated injuries and usurpations, all having in direct object the establishment of an absolute Tyranny over these States. To prove this, let Facts be submitted to a candid world.

He has refused his Assent to Laws, the most wholesome and necessary for the public good.

He has forbidden his Governors to pass Laws of immediate and pressing importance, unless suspended in their operation till his Assent should be obtained; and when so suspended, he has utterly neglected to attend to them.

He has refused to pass other Laws for the accommodation of large districts of people, unless those people would relinquish the right of Representation in the Legislature, a right inestimable to them and formidable to tyrants only.

He has called together legislative bodies at places unusual, uncomfortable, and distant from the depository of their public Records, for the sole purpose of fatiguing them into compliance with his measures.

He has dissolved Representative Houses repeatedly, for opposing with manly firmness his invasions on the rights of the people.

He has refused for a long time, after such dissolutions, to cause others to be elected; whereby the Legislative powers, incapable of Annihilation, have returned to the People at large for their exercise; the State remaining in the mean time exposed to all the dangers of invasion from without, and convulsions within.

He has endeavoured to prevent the population of these States; for that purpose obstructing the Laws for Naturalization of Foreigners; refusing to pass others to encourage their migrations hither, and raising the conditions of new Appropriations of Lands.

He has obstructed the Administration of Justice, by refusing his Assent to Laws for establishing Judiciary powers.

He has made Judges dependent on his Will alone, for the tenure of their offices, and the amount and payment of their salaries.

He has erected a multitude of New Offices, and sent hither swarms of Officers to harrass our people, and eat out their substance.

He has kept among us, in times of peace, Standing Armies without the Consent of our legislatures.

He has affected to render the Military independent of and superior to the Civil power.

He has combined with others to subject us to a jurisdiction foreign to our constitution, and unacknowledged by our laws; giving his Assent to their Acts of pretended Legislation:

For Quartering large bodies of armed troops among us:

For protecting them, by a mock Trial, from punishment for any Murders which they should commit on the Inhabitants of these States:

For cutting off our Trade with all parts of the world:

For imposing Taxes on us without our Consent:

For depriving us in many cases, of the benefits of Trial by Jury:

For transporting us beyond Seas to be tried for pretended offences:

For abolishing the free System of English Laws in a neighbouring Province, establishing therein an Arbitrary government, and enlarging its Boundaries so as to render it at once an example and fit instrument for introducing the same absolute rule into these Colonies:

For taking away our Charters, abolishing our most valuable Laws, and altering fundamentally the Forms of our Governments:

For suspending our own Legislatures, and declaring themselves invested with power to legislate for us in all cases whatsoever.

He has abdicated Government here, by declaring us out of his Protection and waging War against us.

He has plundered our seas, ravaged our Coasts, burnt our towns, and destroyed the lives of our people.

He is at this time transporting large Armies of foreign Mercenaries to compleat the works of death, desolation and tyranny, already begun with circumstances of Cruelty & perfidy scarcely paralleled in the most barbarous ages, and totally unworthy the Head of a civilized nation.

He has constrained our fellow Citizens taken Captive on the high Seas to bear Arms against their Country, to become the executioners of their friends and Brethren, or to fall themselves by their Hands.

He has excited domestic insurrections amongst us, and has endeavoured to bring on the inhabitants of our frontiers, the merciless Indian Savages, whose known rule of warfare, is an undistinguished destruction of all ages, sexes and conditions.

In every stage of these Oppressions We have Petitioned for Redress in the most humble terms: Our repeated Petitions have been answered only by repeated injury. A Prince whose character is thus marked by every act which may define a Tyrant, is unfit to be the ruler of a free people.

Nor have We been wanting in attentions to our British brethren. We have warned them from time to time of attempts by their legislature to extend an unwarrantable jurisdiction over us. We have reminded them of the circumstances of our emigration and settlement here. We have appealed to their native justice and magnanimity, and we have conjured them by the ties of our common kindred to disavow these usurpations, which, would inevitably interrupt our connections and correspondence. They too have been deaf to the voice of justice and of consanguinity. We must, therefore, acquiesce in the necessity, which denounces our Separation, and hold them, as we hold the rest of mankind, Enemies in War, in Peace Friends.

We, THEREFORE, the Representatives of the UNITED STATES OF AMERICA, in General Congress, Assembled, appealing to the Supreme Judge of the world for the rectitude of our intentions, do, in the Name, and by Authority of the good People of these Colonies, solemnly publish and declare, That these United Colonies are, and of Right ought to be FREE AND INDEPENDENT STATES; that they are Absolved from all Allegiance to the British Crown, and that all political connection between them and the State of Great Britain, is and ought to be totally dissolved; and that as Free and Independent States, they have full Power to levy War, conclude Peace, contract Alliances, establish Commerce, and to do all other Acts and Things which Independent States may of right do. And for the support of this Declaration, with a firm reliance on the protection of divine Providence, we mutually pledge to each other our Lives, our Fortunes and our sacred Honor.

[Georgia:]
Button Gwinnett
Lyman Hall
George Walton

[North Carolina:]
William Hooper
Joseph Hewes
John Penn

[South Carolina:]
Edward Rutledge
Thomas Heyward, Jr.
Thomas Lynch, Jr.
Arthur Middleton

[Maryland:]
Samuel Chase
William Paca
Thomas Stone
Charles Carroll of Carrollton

[Virginia:]
George Wythe
Richard Henry Lee
Thomas Jefferson

Benjamin Harrison
Thomas Nelson, Jr.
Francis Lightfoot Lee
Carter Braxton

[Pennsylvania:]
Robert Morris
Benjamin Rush
Benjamin Franklin
John Morton
George Clymer
James Smith
George Taylor
James Wilson
George Ross

[Delaware:]
Caesar Rodney
George Read
Thomas McKean

[New York:]
William Floyd
Philip Livingston
Francis Lewis
Lewis Morris

[New Jersey:]
Richard Stockton
John Witherspoon
Francis Hopkinson
John Hart
Abraham Clark

[New Hampshire:]
Josiah Bartlett
William Whipple
Matthew Thornton

[Massachusetts:]
John Hancock
Samuel Adams

John Adams
Robert Treat Paine
Elbridge Gerry

[Rhode Island:]
Stephen Hopkins
William Ellery

[Connecticut:]
Roger Sherman
Samuel Huntington
William Williams
Oliver Wolcott

Constitution of the United States of America

September 17, 1787

[Editors' note: Bracketed sections in the text of the Constitution have been superceded or modified by Constitutional amendments.]

W e the People of the United States, in Order to form a more perfect Union, establish Justice, insure domestic Tranquility, provide for the common defence, promote the general Welfare, and secure the Blessings of Liberty to ourselves and our Posterity, do ordain and establish this Constitution for the United States of America.

Article I

Section 1. All legislative Powers herein granted shall be vested in a Congress of the United States, which shall consist of a Senate and House of Representatives.

Section 2. The House of Representatives shall be composed of Members chosen every second Year by the People of the several States, and the Electors in each State shall have the Qualifications requisite for Electors of the most numerous Branch of the State Legislature.

No Person shall be a Representative who shall not have attained to the Age of twenty five Years, and been seven Years a Citizen of the United States, and who shall not, when elected, be an Inhabitant of that State in which he shall be chosen.

[Representatives and direct Taxes shall be apportioned among the several States which may be included within this Union, according to their respective Numbers, which shall be determined by adding to the whole Number of free Persons, including those bound to Service for a Term of Years, and excluding Indians not taxed, three fifths of all other Persons.][1] The actual Enumeration shall be made within three Years after the first

---

[1] modified by Section 2 of the Fourteenth Amendment

Meeting of the Congress of the United States, and within every subsequent Term of ten Years, in such Manner as they shall by Law direct. The Number of Representatives shall not exceed one for every thirty Thousand, but each State shall have at Least one Representative; and until such enumeration shall be made, the State of New Hampshire shall be entitled to chuse three, Massachusetts eight, Rhode-Island and Providence Plantations one, Connecticut five, New-York six, New Jersey four, Pennsylvania eight, Delaware one, Maryland six, Virginia ten, North Carolina five, South Carolina five, and Georgia three.

When vacancies happen in the Representation from any State, the Executive Authority thereof shall issue Writs of Election to fill such Vacancies.

The House of Representatives shall chuse their Speaker and other Officers; and shall have the sole Power of Impeachment.

Section 3. The Senate of the United States shall be composed of two Senators from each State, [*chosen by the Legislature thereof,*][2] for six Years; and each Senator shall have one Vote.

Immediately after they shall be assembled in Consequence of the first Election, they shall be divided as equally as may be into three Classes. The Seats of the Senators of the first Class shall be vacated at the Expiration of the second Year, of the second Class at the Expiration of the fourth Year, and of the third Class at the Expiration of the sixth Year, so that one third may be chosen every second Year; [*and if Vacancies happen by Resignation, or otherwise, during the Recess of the Legislature of any State, the Executive thereof may make temporary Appointments until the next Meeting of the Legislature, which shall then fill such Vacancies.*][3]

No Person shall be a Senator who shall not have attained to the Age of thirty Years, and been nine Years a Citizen of the United States, and who shall not, when elected, be an Inhabitant of that State for which he shall be chosen.

The Vice President of the United States shall be President of the Senate, but shall have no Vote, unless they be equally divided.

The Senate shall chuse their other Officers, and also a President pro tempore, in the Absence of the Vice President, or when he shall exercise the Office of President of the United States.

The Senate shall have the sole Power to try all Impeachments. When sitting for that Purpose, they shall be on Oath or Affirmation. When the

[2] superseded by the Seventeenth Amendment
[3] modified by the Seventeenth Amendment

President of the United States is tried, the Chief Justice shall preside: And no Person shall be convicted without the Concurrence of two thirds of the Members present.

Judgment in Cases of Impeachment shall not extend further than to removal from Office, and disqualification to hold and enjoy any Office of honor, Trust or Profit under the United States: but the Party convicted shall nevertheless be liable and subject to Indictment, Trial, Judgment and Punishment, according to Law.

Section 4. The Times, Places and Manner of holding Elections for Senators and Representatives, shall be prescribed in each State by the Legislature thereof; but the Congress may at any time by Law make or alter such Regulations, except as to the Places of chusing Senators.

The Congress shall assemble at least once in every Year, and such Meeting shall be [on the first Monday in December,][4] unless they shall by Law appoint a different Day.

Section 5. Each House shall be the Judge of the Elections, Returns and Qualifications of its own Members, and a Majority of each shall constitute a Quorum to do Business; but a smaller Number may adjourn from day to day, and may be authorized to compel the Attendance of absent Members, in such Manner, and under such Penalties as each House may provide.

Each House may determine the Rules of its Proceedings, punish its Members for disorderly Behaviour, and, with the Concurrence of two thirds, expel a Member.

Each House shall keep a Journal of its Proceedings, and from time to time publish the same, excepting such Parts as may in their Judgment require Secrecy; and the Yeas and Nays of the Members of either House on any question shall, at the Desire of one fifth of those Present, be entered on the Journal.

Neither House, during the Session of Congress, shall, without the Consent of the other, adjourn for more than three days, nor to any other Place than that in which the two Houses shall be sitting.

Section 6. The Senators and Representatives shall receive a Compensation for their Services, to be ascertained by Law, and paid out of the Treasury of the United States. They shall in all Cases, except Treason, Felony and

---

[4] modified by Section 2 of the Twentieth Amendment

Breach of the Peace, be privileged from Arrest during their Attendance at the Session of their respective Houses, and in going to and returning from the same; and for any Speech or Debate in either House, they shall not be questioned in any other Place.

No Senator or Representative shall, during the Time for which he was elected, be appointed to any civil Office under the Authority of the United States, which shall have been created, or the Emoluments whereof shall have been encreased during such time; and no Person holding any Office under the United States, shall be a Member of either House during his Continuance in Office.

Section 7. All Bills for raising Revenue shall originate in the House of Representatives; but the Senate may propose or concur with Amendments as on other Bills.

Every Bill which shall have passed the House of Representatives and the Senate, shall, before it become a Law, be presented to the President of the United States; If he approve he shall sign it, but if not he shall return it, with his Objections to that House in which it shall have originated, who shall enter the Objections at large on their Journal, and proceed to reconsider it. If after such Reconsideration two thirds of that House shall agree to pass the Bill, it shall be sent, together with the Objections, to the other House, by which it shall likewise be reconsidered, and if approved by two thirds of that House, it shall become a Law. But in all such Cases the Votes of both Houses shall be determined by yeas and Nays, and the Names of the Persons voting for and against the Bill shall be entered on the Journal of each House respectively. If any Bill shall not be returned by the President within ten Days (Sundays excepted) after it shall have been presented to him, the Same shall be a Law, in like Manner as if he had signed it, unless the Congress by their Adjournment prevent its Return, in which Case it shall not be a Law.

Every Order, Resolution, or Vote to which the Concurrence of the Senate and House of Representatives may be necessary (except on a question of Adjournment) shall be presented to the President of the United States; and before the Same shall take Effect, shall be approved by him, or being disapproved by him, shall be repassed by two thirds of the Senate and House of Representatives, according to the Rules and Limitations prescribed in the Case of a Bill.

Section 8. The Congress shall have Power To lay and collect Taxes, Duties, Imposts and Excises, to pay the Debts and provide for the common Defence and general Welfare of the United States; but all Duties, Imposts and Excises shall be uniform throughout the United States;

To borrow Money on the credit of the United States;

To regulate Commerce with foreign Nations, and among the several States, and with the Indian Tribes;

To establish an uniform Rule of Naturalization, and uniform Laws on the subject of Bankruptcies throughout the United States;

To coin Money, regulate the Value thereof, and of foreign Coin, and fix the Standard of Weights and Measures;

To provide for the Punishment of counterfeiting the Securities and current Coin of the United States;

To establish Post Offices and post Roads;

To promote the Progress of Science and useful Arts, by securing for limited Times to Authors and Inventors the exclusive Right to their respective Writings and Discoveries;

To constitute Tribunals inferior to the supreme Court;

To define and punish Piracies and Felonies committed on the high Seas, and Offenses against the Law of Nations;

To declare War, grant Letters of Marque and Reprisal, and make Rules concerning Captures on Land and Water;

To raise and support Armies, but no Appropriation of Money to that Use shall be for a longer Term than two Years;

To provide and maintain a Navy;

To make Rules for the Government and Regulation of the land and naval Forces;

To provide for calling forth the Militia to execute the Laws of the Union, suppress Insurrections and repel Invasions;

To provide for organizing, arming, and disciplining, the Militia, and for governing such Part of them as may be employed in the Service of the United States, reserving to the States respectively, the Appointment of the Officers, and the Authority of training the Militia according to the discipline prescribed by Congress;

To exercise exclusive Legislation in all Cases whatsoever, over such District (not exceeding ten Miles square) as may, by Cession of particular States, and the Acceptance of Congress, become the Seat of the Government of the United States, and to exercise like Authority over all Places purchased by the Consent of the Legislature of the State in which the Same shall be, for the Erection of Forts, Magazines, Arsenals, dock-Yards, and other needful Buildings;—And

To make all Laws which shall be necessary and proper for carrying into Execution the foregoing Powers, and all other Powers vested by this Constitution in the Government of the United States, or in any Department or Officer thereof.

Section 9. The Migration or Importation of such Persons as any of the States now existing shall think proper to admit, shall not be prohibited by the Congress prior to the Year one thousand eight hundred and eight, but a Tax or duty may be imposed on such Importation, not exceeding ten dollars for each Person.

The Privilege of the Writ of Habeas Corpus shall not be suspended, unless when in Cases of Rebellion or Invasion the public Safety may require it.

No Bill of Attainder or ex post facto Law shall be passed.

No Capitation, or other direct, Tax shall be laid, unless in Proportion to the Census or Enumeration herein before directed to be taken.[5]

No Tax or Duty shall be laid on Articles exported from any State.

No Preference shall be given by any Regulation of Commerce or Revenue to the Ports of one State over those of another: nor shall Vessels bound to, or from, one State, be obliged to enter, clear, or pay Duties in another.

No Money shall be drawn from the Treasury, but in Consequence of Appropriations made by Law; and a regular Statement and Account of the Receipts and Expenditures of all public Money shall be published from time to time.

No Title of Nobility shall be granted by the United States: And no Person holding any Office of Profit or Trust under them, shall, without the Consent of the Congress, accept of any present, Emolument, Office, or Title, of any kind whatever, from any King, Prince, or foreign State.

Section 10. No State shall enter into any Treaty, Alliance, or Confederation; grant Letters of Marque and Reprisal; coin Money; emit Bills of Credit; make any Thing but gold and silver Coin a Tender in Payment of Debts; pass any Bill of Attainder, ex post facto Law, or Law impairing the Obligation of Contracts, or grant any Title of Nobility.

No State shall, without the Consent of the Congress, lay any Imposts or Duties on Imports or Exports, except what may be absolutely necessary for executing it's inspection Laws: and the net Produce of all Duties and Imposts, laid by any State on Imports or Exports, shall be for the Use of the Treasury

---

[5] modified by the Sixteenth Amendment

of the United States; and all such Laws shall be subject to the Revision and Controul of the Congress.

No State shall, without the Consent of Congress, lay any Duty of Tonnage, keep Troops, or Ships of War in time of Peace, enter into any Agreement or Compact with another State, or with a foreign Power, or engage in War, unless actually invaded, or in such imminent Danger as will not admit of delay.

Article II

Section 1. The executive Power shall be vested in a President of the United States of America. He shall hold his Office during the Term of four Years, and, together with the Vice President, chosen for the same Term, be elected, as follows:

Each State shall appoint, in such Manner as the Legislature thereof may direct, a Number of Electors, equal to the whole Number of Senators and Representatives to which the State may be entitled in the Congress: but no Senator or Representative, or Person holding an Office of Trust or Profit under the United States, shall be appointed an Elector.

[The Electors shall meet in their respective States, and vote by Ballot for two Persons, of whom one at least shall not be an Inhabitant of the same State with themselves. And they shall make a List of all the Persons voted for, and of the Number of Votes for each; which List they shall sign and certify, and transmit sealed to the Seat of the Government of the United States, directed to the President of the Senate. The President of the Senate shall, in the Presence of the Senate and House of Representatives, open all the Certificates, and the Votes shall then be counted. The Person having the greatest Number of Votes shall be the President, if such Number be a Majority of the whole Number of Electors appointed; and if there be more than one who have such Majority, and have an equal Number of Votes, then the House of Representatives shall immediately chuse by Ballot one of them for President; and if no Person have a Majority, then from the five highest on the List the said House shall in like Manner chuse the President. But in chusing the President, the Votes shall be taken by States, the Representation from each State having one Vote; A quorum for this purpose shall consist of a Member or Members from two thirds of the States, and a Majority of all the States shall be necessary to a Choice. In every Case, after the Choice of the President, the Person having the greatest Number of Votes of the Electors shall be the Vice President. But if there should remain two or more who have equal Votes, the Senate shall chuse from them by Ballot the Vice President.][6]

The Congress may determine the Time of chusing the Electors, and the Day on which they shall give their Votes; which Day shall be the same throughout the United States.

No Persons except a natural born Citizen, or a Citizen of the United States, at the time of the Adoption of this Constitution, shall be eligible to the Office of President; neither shall any Person be eligible to that Office who shall not have attained to the Age of thirty five Years, and been fourteen Years a Resident within the United States.

[In Case of the Removal of the President from Office, or of his Death, Resignation, or Inability to discharge the Powers and Duties of the said Office, the Same shall devolve on the Vice President, and the Congress may by Law provide for the Case of Removal, Death, Resignation or Inability, both of the President and Vice President, declaring what Officer shall then act as President, and such Officer shall act accordingly, until the Disability be removed, or a President shall be elected.][7]

The President shall, at stated Times, receive for his Services, a Compensation, which shall neither be increased nor diminished during the Period for which he shall have been elected, and he shall not receive within that Period any other Emolument from the United States, or any of them.

Before he enter on the Execution of his Office, he shall take the following Oath or Affirmation:—"I do solemnly swear (or affirm) that I will faithfully execute the Office of President of the United States, and will to the best of my Ability, preserve, protect and defend the Constitution of the United States."

Section 2. The President shall be Commander in Chief of the Army and Navy of the United States, and of the Militia of the several States, when called into the actual Service of the United States; he may require the Opinion, in writing, of the principal Officer in each of the executive Departments, upon any Subject relating to the Duties of their respective Offices, and he shall have Power to grant Reprieves and Pardons for Offences against the United States, except in Cases of Impeachment.

He shall have Power, by and with the Advice and Consent of the Senate, to make Treaties, provided two thirds of the Senators present concur; and he

---

[6] modifed by the Twelfth Amendment
[7] modified by the Twenty-Fifth Amendment

shall nominate, and by and with the Advice and Consent of the Senate, shall appoint Ambassadors, other public Ministers and Consuls, Judges of the supreme Court, and all other Officers of the United States, whose Appointments are not herein otherwise provided for, and which shall be established by Law: but the Congress may by Law vest the Appointment of such inferior Officers, as they think proper, in the President alone, in the Courts of Law, or in the Heads of Departments.

The President shall have Power to fill up all Vacancies that may happen during the Recess of the Senate, by granting Commissions which shall expire at the End of their next Session.

Section 3. He shall from time to time give to the Congress Information of the State of the Union, and recommend to their Consideration such Measures as he shall judge necessary and expedient; he may, on extraordinary Occasions, convene both Houses, or either of them, and in Case of Disagreement between them, with Respect to the Time of Adjournment, he may adjourn them to such Time as he shall think proper; he shall receive Ambassadors and other public Ministers; he shall take Care that the Laws be faithfully executed, and shall Commission all the Officers of the United States.

Section 4. The President, Vice President and all civil Officers of the United States, shall be removed from Office on Impeachment for, and Conviction of, Treason, Bribery, or other high Crimes and Misdemeanors.

Article III

Section 1. The judicial Power of the United States, shall be vested in one supreme Court, and in such inferior Courts as the Congress may from time to time ordain and establish. The Judges, both of the supreme and inferior Courts, shall hold their Offices during good Behaviour, and shall, at stated Times, receive for their Services, a Compensation, which shall not be diminished during their Continuance in Office.

Section 2. The judicial Power shall extend to all Cases, in Law and Equity, arising under this Constitution, the Laws of the United States, and Treaties made, or which shall be made, under their Authority;—to all Cases affecting Ambassadors, other public Ministers and Consuls;—to all Cases of admiralty and maritime Jurisdiction;—to Controversies to which the United States

CONSTITUTION OF THE UNITED STATES OF AMERICA

shall be a Party;—to Controversies between two or more States;—[*between a State and Citizens of another State;—*][8] between Citizens of different States;—between Citizens of the same State claiming Lands under Grants of different States, [*and between a State, or the Citizens thereof, and foreign States, Citizens or Subjects.*][9]

In all Cases affecting Ambassadors, other public Ministers and Consuls, and those in which a State shall be Party, the supreme Court shall have original Jurisdiction. In all the other Cases before mentioned, the supreme Court shall have appellate Jurisdiction, both as to Law and Fact, with such Exceptions, and under such Regulations as the Congress shall make.

The Trial of all Crimes, except in Cases of Impeachment, shall be by Jury; and such Trial shall be held in the State where the said Crimes shall have been committed; but when not committed within any State, the Trial shall be at such Place or Places as the Congress may by Law have directed.

Section 3. Treason against the United States, shall consist only in levying War against them, or in adhering to their Enemies, giving them Aid and Comfort. No Person shall be convicted of Treason unless on the Testimony of two Witnesses to the same overt Act, or on Confession in open Court.

The Congress shall have Power to declare the Punishment of Treason, but no Attainder of Treason shall work Corruption of Blood, or Forfeiture except during the Life of the Person attained.

Article IV

Section 1. Full Faith and Credit shall be given in each State to the public Acts, Records, and judicial Proceedings of every other State. And the Congress may by general Laws prescribe the Manner in which such Acts, Records and Proceedings shall be proved, and the Effect thereof.

Section 2. The Citizens of each State shall be entitled to all Privileges and Immunities of Citizens in the several States.

A Person charged in any State with Treason, Felony, or other Crime, who shall flee from Justice, and be found in another State, shall on Demand of

---

[8] superseded by the Eleventh Amendment
[9] superseded by the Eleventh Amendment

the executive Authority of the State from which he fled, be delivered up, to
be removed to the State having Jurisdiction of the Crime.

[No Person held to Service or Labour in one State, under the Laws
thereof, escaping into another, shall, in Consequence of any Law or Regulation therein, be discharged from such Service or Labour, but shall be delivered up on Claim of the Party to whom such Service or Labour may be due.][10]

Section 3. New States may be admitted by the Congress into this Union;
but no new State shall be formed or erected within the Jurisdiction of any
other State; nor any State be formed by the Junction of two or more States,
or Parts of States, without the Consent of the Legislatures of the States concerned as well as of the Congress.

The Congress shall have Power to dispose of and make all needful Rules
and Regulations respecting the Territory or other Property belonging to the
United States; and nothing in this Constitution shall be so construed as to
Prejudice any Claims of the United States, or of any particular State.

Section 4. The United States shall guarantee to every State in this Union
a Republican Form of Government, and shall protect each of them against
Invasion; and on Application of the Legislature, or of the Executive (when
the Legislature cannot be convened) against domestic Violence.

Article V

The Congress, whenever two thirds of both Houses shall deem it necessary,
shall propose Amendments to this Constitution, or, on the Application of
the Legislatures of two thirds of the several States, shall call a Convention for
proposing Amendments, which, in either Case, shall be valid to all Intents
and Purposes, as Part of this Constitution, when ratified by the Legislatures
of three fourths of the several States, or by Conventions in three fourths
thereof, as the one or the other Mode of Ratification may be proposed by
the Congress; Provided that no Amendment which may be made prior to
the Year One thousand eight hundred and eight shall in any Manner affect
the first and fourth Clauses in the Ninth Section of the first Article; and that
no State, without its Consent, shall be deprived of its equal Suffrage in the
Senate.

---

[10] superseded by the Thirteenth Amendment

Article VI

All Debts contracted and Engagements entered into, before the Adoption of this Constitution, shall be as valid against the United States under this Constitution, as under the Confederation.

This Constitution, and the Laws of the United States which shall be made in Pursuance thereof; and all Treaties made, or which shall be made, under the Authority of the United States, shall be the supreme Law of the Land; and the Judges in every State shall be bound thereby, any Thing in the Constitution or Laws of any State to the Contrary notwithstanding.

The Senators and Representatives before mentioned, and the Members of the several State Legislatures, and all executive and judicial Officers, both of the United States and of the several States, shall be bound by Oath or Affirmation, to support this Constitution; but no religious Test shall ever be required as a Qualification to any Office or public Trust under the United States.

Article VII

The Ratification of the Conventions of nine States, shall be sufficient for the Establishment of this Constitution between the States so ratifying the Same.

Done in Convention by the Unanimous Consent of the States present the Seventeenth Day of September in the Year of our Lord one thousand seven hundred and Eighty seven and of the Independence of the United States of America the Twelfth In Witness whereof We have hereunto subscribed our Names,

Go. Washington—
Presidt. and deputy from Virginia

New Hampshire
John Langdon
Nicholas Gilman

Massachusetts
Nathaniel Gorham
Rufus King

Connecticut
Wm. Saml. Johnson
Roger Sherman

New York
Alexander Hamilton

New Jersey
Wil: Livingston
David Brearley
Wm. Paterson
Jona: Dayton

Pennsylvania
B Franklin

Thomas Mifflin
Robt. Morris
Geo. Clymer
Thos. FitzSimons
Jared Ingersoll
James Wilson
Gouv Morris

Delaware
Geo: Read
Gunning Bedford jun
John Dickinson
Richard Bassett
Jaco: Broom

Maryland
James McHenry
Dan of St Thos. Jenifer
Danl. Carroll

Virginia
John Blair—
James Madison Jr.

North Carolina
Wm. Blount
Richd. Dobbs Spaight
Hu Williamson

South Carolina
J. Rutledge
Charles Cotesworth Pinckney
Charles Pinckney
Pierce Butler

Georgia
William Few
Abr Baldwin

Attest William Jackson Secretary

AMENDMENTS TO THE CONSTITUTION OF THE UNITED STATES OF AMERICA

Amendment I

Ratified December 15, 1791

Congress shall make no law respecting an establishment of religion, or prohibiting the free exercise thereof; or abridging the freedom of speech, or of the press; or the right of the people peaceably to assemble, and to petition the Government for a redress of grievances.

Amendment II

Ratified December 15, 1791

A well regulated Militia, being necessary to the security of a free State, the right of the people to keep and bear Arms, shall not be infringed.

Amendment III

Ratified December 15, 1791

No Soldier shall, in time of peace be quartered in any house, without the consent of the Owner, nor in time of war, but in a manner to be prescribed by law.

Amendment IV

Ratified December 15, 1791

The right of the people to be secure in their persons, houses, papers, and effects, against unreasonable searches and seizures, shall not be violated, and no Warrants shall issue, but upon probable cause, supported by Oath or affirmation, and particularly describing the place to be searched, and the persons or things to be seized.

Amendment V

Ratified December 15, 1791

No person shall be held to answer for a capital, or otherwise infamous crime, unless on a presentment or indictment of a Grand Jury, except in cases arising in the land or naval forces, or in the Militia, when in actual service in time of War or public danger; nor shall any person be subject for the same offence to be twice put in jeopardy of life or limb, nor shall be compelled in any criminal case to be a witness against himself, nor be deprived of life, liberty, or property, without due process of law; nor shall private property be taken for public use, without just compensation.

Amendment VI

Ratified December 15, 1791

In all criminal prosecutions, the accused shall enjoy the right to a speedy and public trial, by an impartial jury of the State and district wherein the crime shall have been committed, which district shall have been previously ascertained by law, and to be informed of the nature and cause of the accusation; to be confronted with the witnesses against him; to have compulsory process for obtaining witnesses in his favor, and to have the assistance of counsel for his defence.

Amendment VII

Ratified December 15, 1791

In Suits at common law, where the value in controversy shall exceed twenty dollars, the right of trial by jury shall be preserved, and no fact tried by a jury, shall be otherwise reexamined in any Court of the United States, than according to the rules of the common law.

Amendment VIII

Ratified December 15, 1791

Excessive bail shall not be required, nor excessive fines imposed, nor cruel and unusual punishments inflicted.

Amendment IX

Ratified December 15, 1791

The enumeration in the Constitution, of certain rights, shall not be construed to deny or disparage others retained by the people.

Amendment X

Ratified December 15, 1791

The powers not delegated to the United States by the Constitution, nor prohibited by it to the States, are reserved to the States respectively, or to the people.